A Perfect Babel of Confusion

Religion in America Series

Harry S. Stout

GENERAL EDITOR

A Perfect Babel of Confusion: Dutch Religion
and English Culture in the Middle Colonies

RANDALL BALMER

RANDALL BALMER

A Perfect Babel
of Confusion

Dutch Religion and English Culture
in the Middle Colonies

OXFORD
UNIVERSITY PRESS

OXFORD

UNIVERSITY PRESS

Oxford   New York
Auckland   Bangkok   Buenos Aires   Cape Town   Chennai
Dar es Salaam   Delhi   Hong Kong   Istanbul   Karachi   Kolkata
Kuala Lumpur   Madrid   Melbourne   Mexico City   Mumbai   Nairobi
São Paulo   Shanghai   Singapore   Taipei   Tokyo   Toronto
and an associated company in Berlin

Copyright © 1989 by Randall Balmer

Published by Oxford University Press, Inc.
198 Madison Avenue, New York, New York 10016

www.oup.com

First issued as an Oxford University Press paperback, 2002

Oxford is a registered trademark of Oxford University Press

Library of Congress Cataloging-in-Publication Data
Balmer, Randall Herbert.
A perfect babel of confusion : Dutch religion and English Culture
in the middle colonies / Randall H. Balmer.
p. cm. —(Religion in America series)
Bibliography: p.   Includes index.
ISBN 0-19-505873-9; ISBN 0-19-515265-4 (Pbk.)
1. Reformed church—New York (State)—History.   2. Reformed Church—
New Jersey—History.   3. Dutch Americans—New York (State)—Religion.
4. Dutch Americans—New Jersey—Religion.   5. New York (State)—Religious life and customs.
6. New Jersey—Religious life and customs.   7. New York (State)—
Ethnic relations.   8. New Jersey—Ethnic relations.
I.Title.   II. Series: Religion in America series (Oxford University Press)
BX9496.N7B35 1989   88-25241
285.7'747—dc19   CIP

2 4 6 8 9 7 5 3 1
Printed in the United States of America
on acid-free paper

for Kathryn

PREFACE

From the earliest days of European settlement, the Middle Atlantic colonies of North America foreshadowed the religious and ethnic diversity that later became the region's hallmark. Nearly a century after Giovanni da Verrazano, an Italian navigator in the service of France, discovered the inlet into New York Harbor, Henry Hudson, an Englishman under contract to the Dutch East India Company, nosed the *Half Moon* through the same Narrows and struggled north on the river that now bears his name. The first group of settlers to disembark at Manhattan were Walloons, French-speaking Belgians, followed shortly by a modest influx of Netherlanders, Germans, and French. English Puritans bracketed Dutch settlement to the north and east in New England and on Long Island, while Swedes and Finns became the early denizens on the Delaware River to the south. Black slaves began arriving in the 1620s, and a considerable number of Sephardic Jews came in 1654 and 1655.

The region's religious configuration bespoke even more diversity. Early reports filtering back to Amsterdam told of Huguenots, Mennonites, Brownists, Presbyterians, Quakers, Catholics, even "many atheists and various other servants of Baal." The Jews proposed to erect a synagogue, French Jesuits from Canada mounted several missionary sorties among the Indians, and the spiritual guidance of the Scandinavians on the Delaware lay in the hands of a certain Lutheran preacher "more inclined to look into the wine can than into the Bible."[1]

If all this seemed a perilous environment in which to raise the standard of Reformed Calvinism, the ministers (dominies) assigned to the task never flagged in their zeal. Shortly after his arrival in 1628, Dominie Jonas Michaëlius assembled fifty of the faithful for the administration of Holy Communion. While acknowledging that "one cannot observe strictly all the usual formalities in making a beginning under such circumstances," Michaëlius and his successors managed to establish an outpost of Dutch Calvinism in New Netherland under the watchful eye of the Classis of Amsterdam.[2] Soon (with the assistance of pledges exacted during the revelry of a besotted wedding feast) a chapel was constructed, and over the course of half a century the Dutch Reformed Church survived a perpetual shortage of clergy, various inept governors, and the colony's rampant pluralism.

But the one thing Dutch Calvinism could not withstand was the incursion of English culture and Anglican religion. The English Conquest of 1664 triggered a long, steady decline in the fortunes of Dutch culture in general and the Dutch Reformed Church in particular. By the turn of the century the church had suffered a disabling schism along social and economic lines, which prompted an exodus of farmers and artisans to New Jersey. Within a short time the Jersey Dutch became enamored of pietism as defined by clergy alienated from the religious establishment in New York and Amsterdam. New York's rapid Anglicization thereafter placed the orthodox Dutch on the defensive, struggling valiantly to reestablish Dutch schools and maintain their ethnic distinctiveness. They resisted the Great Awakening but by the mid-eighteenth century finally succumbed to the colony's dominant English culture.

This study examines the clash of Dutch and English cultures and charts the religious effects of that confrontation. No institution reflected the vicissitudes of Anglicization with greater clarity than the Dutch Reformed Church over the course of a century. The awkward posturings of the Dutch clergy mirrored the difficulties facing the Dutch as a conquered people. Moreover, the displacement of the Dutch by the English affected not only cultural institutions but also the religious beliefs and spiritual expressions of colonial Hollanders. Leisler's Rebellion in 1689, an insurrection of lower-class Dutch who had grown restive under English rule, provided the first real indication of fissures within the Dutch community itself. The restoration of English government in 1691, followed closely by the execution of the rebellion's leaders, prompted many Dutch to flee the cauldron of discontent in New York City and Long Island for the Hudson Valley and northern New Jersey. This migration, in turn, laid the groundwork for the arrival of Dutch pietism and, eventually, the Great Awakening in the Middle Colonies.

The eighteenth century saw the emergence of two disparate Dutch cultures, both irrevocably changed by the presence of the English. In New York City and on parts of Long Island the Dutch came under the influence of an English culture shaped, in large measure, by the Church of England. The Anglican Society for the Propagation of the Gospel exerted an enormous influence over the colony through its schools and its unabashed efforts to proselytize members of the Dutch Reformed Church. With varying degrees of zealotry, successive Anglican governors sought to favor the Church of England and advance the designs of Anglicanism in the colony. In New Jersey, however, the Dutch drifted toward an evangelical pietism that transcended ethnic boundaries and thereby assimilated to a culture defined by New Light Presbyterians and other evangelicals. Whereas the Church of England guided the course of Dutch assimilation in New York, the Dutch in New Jersey plunged headlong into a kind of pancthnic revivalism, which characterized the Great Awakening in the Middle Colonies. Denominational barriers eroded and language barriers receded in the waves of revival, and, thus assimilated, the Jersey Dutch prepared to enter the larger political arena of the late eighteenth century.

In addition to showing that the Dutch were among the first to evince signs of revivalism, this study illustrates the power of political events and social forces in shaping theological beliefs and religious behavior. The predilection to pietism among Jersey Dutch grew quite decidedly out of the alienation of ordinary Hollanders from both the English and from those among their compatriots who had assimilated to English ways. But the reverse is also true: religious affiliations among the Dutch in the Middle Colonies provide a clue to political alignments during the Revolutionary era as well as to postures toward the dominant culture. The revivalistic Dutch, centered in New Jersey and the Hudson Valley, by and large identified with the patriot cause, whereas the orthodox Dutch who had Anglicized by the mid-eighteenth century supported the loyalists.

Histories, according to the old maxim, arc written by victors, and so it is with colonial Dutch religion. A succession of nineteenth-century Reformed church historians exulted in the triumph of an indigenous Reformed church that had assimilated to the dominant culture and fairly throbbed with pietistic vitality.[3] These same historians characterized opponents of revivalism as stodgy traditionalists bent on thwarting the march of progress. Such a slant is understandable and perhaps even defensible, but it fails to account for the complex social, political, and economic factors that lay behind that triumph. More recent analyses have failed to recognize the profound differences between the Dutch cultures of New York and New Jersey, differences that emerge only when the two are juxtaposed.

This study attempts to view Dutch religion and culture within a broader context, one that considers the entire range of ethnic conflict between the earliest settlers of a given colony and an overwhelming foreign entity, a power that conquered the founders and then proceeded to recast their political, legal, economic, and religious customs and institutions. The English succeeded first in dividing the Dutch, largely along economic lines, and then drove them away from their hereditary culture. Admitting the peculiarities of the Dutch experience in New York and New Jersey, English cultural aggression against the Dutch fits into a larger pattern common to other ethnic groups—the French, for example, or the Germans, Irish, or Scandinavians—as by the latter half of the eighteenth century various ethnic distinctions were swept before the juggernaut of Anglo-American culture, language, and institutions.[4]

I have accrued a large number of scholarly debts in the course of this project. Douglas Greenberg provided advice and suggestions at an early stage. Patricia Bonomi directed me to the rich resources in the records of the Society for the Propagation of the Gospel. Eugene Sheridan provided a careful reading of the manuscript at various stages, as did Albert Raboteau, Edwin Gaustad, Gregg Roeber, Mark Noll, Ned Landsman, and Philip Morgan. James Tanis, Frelinghuysen's biographer, shared his considerable knowledge of Dutch pietism. Horton Davies, Joyce Goodfriend, and Henry Bowden also read various sections and offered useful criticisms. The mistakes that remain should be attributed to my own obduracy rather than their lack of vigilance.

The generosity of the Holland Society of New York allowed me to forsake a promising career in summer house-painting in favor of such recondite pursuits as Anglicization and Dutch migration patterns. Frederick Bogert and especially Howard Hageman of the Society offered timely encouragement and suggestions, as did Charles Gehring of the New Netherland Project at the New York State Library. The New Jersey Historical Commission supplied a grant-in-aid and then graciously rewarded the completion of this manuscript with the Governor Alfred E. Driscoll Prize, which included a generous subvention for publication. I am grateful also to the New York State Historical Association for deeming this study worthy of their Manuscript Award. After an unhappy experience elsewhere, my faith in the editorial process has been more than adequately restored by the consummate professionalism of Cynthia Read and her colleagues at Oxford University Press.

I have considered at length how to thank John Murrin and John F. Wilson, the guiding forces behind this project, but I have found no formula equal to the task. For students of colonial history, John Murrin's ability to synthesize large quantities of information and render nimble, eloquent interpretations is the stuff of legends. I am always tempted to say of him that he has *forgotten* more about colonial America than most of us will ever know—except that I am not yet convinced he has forgotten anything. It is a measure of his continuing influence that I still vacillate at times between being inspired by his genius and wishing I had chosen another vocation. John Wilson's gentle and unprepossessing demeanor belies his wisdom and his quiet, steady direction. Quite unaccountably, he trusted me with this project and allowed me to navigate freely in these uncharted waters. I can only hope that I have vindicated his trust.

My wife, Kathryn, provided unflagging encouragement and good cheer, without which I can all too easily imagine where this project might now stand. She deserves a far gentler fate than marriage to a historian, but she has accepted that lot with her customary grace and dignity.

New York   R. B.
July 2, 1988

CONTENTS

A Perfect Babel of Confusion

1

Confusion and Scattering:
Anglo-Dutch Wars
and the Demise of Reformed Hegemony

After a long and stormy voyage, Jonas Michaëlius stepped onto the soil of New Netherland in the spring of 1628 to embark on a mission for the Dutch West India Company. Michaëlius, already seasoned as a pioneer churchman for the Dutch colony in Brazil, set about to convene a Reformed church in this new outpost of the Netherlands commercial empire. "Our coming here was agreeable to all," he wrote, "and I hope, by the grace of the Lord, that my service will not be unfruitful." Dominie Michaëlius proceeded to carve out a small constituency from among the colony's settlers. "At the first administration of the Lord's Supper which was observed, not without great joy and comfort to many, we had fully fifty communicants—Walloons and Dutch," he reported in a letter to Amsterdam, although he conceded that "one cannot observe strictly all the usual formalities in making a beginning under such circumstances." Amid such a tentative configuration the Dutch Reformed Church began its long and colorful history in North America, and even the colony itself started to exhibit some signs of permanence. "We are busy now in building a fort of good quarry stone, which is to be found not far from here in abundance," Michaëlius wrote. "May the Lord only build and watch over our walls."[1]

Quarry stone, however, even if fortified by the mortar of divine sanction, provided an inadequate defense against the English. On July 27, 1664, Captain Richard Nicolls and four English frigates sailed

3

through the Narrows, moored at Brooklyn, and demanded the sub-mission of the Dutch. Some months earlier, King Charles II of En-gland had granted a patent to his brother, the duke of York, for vast tracts of land in North America. Because much of the territory com-prised what the Dutch called New Netherland, the duke was obliged to vindicate his claim forcibly. Nicolls insisted that England's title to the land was "unquestionable" and urged the Dutch to surrender promptly and thereby prevent "the effusion of Christian Blood."[2]

Initially disposed to resist the English, Pieter Stuyvesant, director-general of the province for the West India Company, was dissuaded by those who recognized the vulnerability of Dutch defenses and who trusted Nicolls to keep his pledge that the Dutch would enjoy the same rights as the English. Early on the morning of August 27, 1664, representatives of both sides met at Stuyvesant's farm and signed the Articles of Capitulation. The English lost little time securing their victory and soon demanded oaths of allegiance. Within a month, the English had subdued the Dutch at New Orange and renamed it Al-bany and then completed the rout of New Netherland with similar success in the Delaware Valley.[3]

Although Article VIII of the Articles of Capitulation ensured that the Dutch "here shall enjoy the liberty of their consciences in Divine Worship and church discipline," the English Conquest of 1664 sig-naled a long decline in the fortunes of the Dutch Reformed Church in New York.[4] Heretofore Dutch Calvinism had enjoyed a privileged status as the established religion in New Netherland. On September 15, not yet a month after the Conquest, Dominie Samuel Drisius solemnly wrote to the Classis of Amsterdam: "I cannot refrain from informing you of our present situation, namely, that we have been brought under the government of the King of England." Noting the guarantees of Article VIII, Drisius pledged that the dominies would stay with their flocks under these new arrangements, "that they may not scatter and run wild."[5]

The English Conquest ended a period of growth and stability both in New Netherland as a whole and among the colony's Dutch churches, which numbered thirteen at the conclusion of the New Netherland period (see Table 1.1). Just three months before the English invasion, Dominie Henricus Selyns had reported to the Classis a "considerable increase of members" in the Brooklyn churches. Selyns exulted in the "quietness and harmony" among his congregations and noted: "The English are quiet, the savages peaceful; our lamentations have been

TABLE 1.1.   Dutch Reformed Churches in 1664

	Date Founded	1664 Minister
New York (New Amsterdam)	1628	Megapolensis/Drisius
Albany (Fort Orange)	1642	Schaats
New Castle (New Amstel)	1654	(vacant)
Flatlands (Amersfoort)	1654	Selyns
Bushwick	1654	Selyns
Gravesend	1654	Selyns
Flatbush (Midwout)	1654	Selyns
Kingston (Esopus)	1659	Blom
Bergen, N.J.*	1660	Megapolensis
Brooklyn	1660	Selyns
Harlem*	1660	Megapolensis
Stuyvesant's Chapel*	1660	Selyns
Schenectady*	1662	Schaats

*Indicates mission or "out-station" of another church.

turned into songs of praise, and the monthly day of fasting into a day of thanksgiving."[6] Succeeding reports would not be quite so sanguine. Writing four years later, another minister chronicled the Dutch decline in the colony. "The Lord begins to deal in judgment with his people," he wrote. Conquered by the English, afflicted with an epidemic of dysentery, and threatened by Indians, "it appears as if God were punishing this land for its sins." To add to their woes, "a terrible comet in the west" portended even further judgment.[7]

I

In the years following the Conquest, a considerable controversy arose regarding the surrender of the colony to the English, revealing an undercurrent of division and resentment among the Dutch. As Stuyvesant had contemplated his response to English demands and word of the colony's predicament leaked among the settlers, some vented their anger against "those devilish traders who have so long salted us."[8] Many New Netherlanders viewed the surrender itself as a betrayal of Dutch interests. Wealthy Dutch merchants and the clergy, they believed, had abandoned the colony's defense all too willingly. Determined at first to mount a resistance, Stuyvesant had ripped up a letter containing English ultimatums, whereupon "three of the principal Burghers" demanded to see the document. Stuyvesant, "fearing that mutiny might break out," reassembled the torn letter. Shortly thereafter, at the behest of Dominie Johannes Megapolensis, ninety-three of New Amsterdam's most prominent men petitioned Stuyvesant to accede to the English without a struggle.[9]

An inquiry conducted by the West India Company some time later chided Stuyvesant and the clergy for surrendering to the English so readily. Stuyvesant refuted the charges, claiming that a shortage of munitions and provisions coupled with popular unwillingness to engage the English had forced him to capitulate. At one juncture, as English frigates passed the fort, Stuyvesant was ready to order an attack, but Dominies Johannes and Samuel Megapolensis "led him away and prevailed on him to retire."[10] The ministers and the merchants, Stuyvesant said, evinced a reluctance to resist the English for fear of jeopardizing their own interests. Many of their houses, situated next to the fort, would likely suffer damage in any exchange of volleys. The West India Company rebuked the Dutch officials for their comportment and charged that "the Company was served by men who preferred to save their own property, which they had gained in the Company's employ, than to observe their oath and honor." The Amsterdam mercantilists eventually exonerated Stuyvesant, who, they said, "would have easily enough resolved upon the pulling down of the aforesaid buildings, were it not that Councillors and Clergymen were desirous of saving their houses lying next to the fort." The company denied that the fort was indefensible, as magistrates and clergy had claimed, and praised those among the colonists who "did not suffer themselves to be moved by the flattering tongues of Preachers and others who were troubled about their private property, without regarding the interest of the State and Company."[11]

The entire Dutch community felt the repercussions of this controversy, and as the years passed some of the signatories to the Articles of Capitulation continued to feel defensive about their role in the surrender. On August 27, 1668, four years to the day after the Articles were signed, prominent Dutchmen swore an affidavit confirming the loyalty of Dominie Johannes Megapolensis to the West India Company and swore another as late as 1676, twelve years after the English Conquest.[12] The magistrates' capitulation perturbed the West India Company because the surrender cut quite significantly into their own economic interests.[13] The English invasion had been a thinly veiled attempt to gain control of the Atlantic trade that Dutch merchants had found so profitable.[14] When Nicolls had commissioned his subordinates to secure the Conquest in the Delaware Valley, he noted that "the Dutch had seated themselves" there and "drawne a great trade thither."[15] More important, the controversy over the surrender—the ready acquiescence of clergy and traders to the English—suggests an alliance between wealthy Dutch merchants and the Dutch Reformed ministers. As in the Dutch Republic, the merchant class in New Netherland occupied the highest social stratum, and the clergy, all of whom added their signatures to the 1664 Oath of Allegiance to England, quickly became identified in popular consciousness with the wealthy merchants and magistrates.[16]

In a broader historical sense, there was nothing novel about this association. Martin Luther had relied on the patronage and protection of the elector of Saxony in order to carry out his reforms, and he believed fervently in the duty and utility of government to restrain evil. With the cooperation of the magistrates, John Calvin had recast Geneva's social and political institutions according to his understanding of biblical precepts, and in turn he advocated submission to constituted rulers. Other Reformers—Ulrich Zwingli in Zurich, Martin Bucer in Strasbourg—depended on the indulgence of civil magistrates. And even in the Netherlands, politics and religion were hopelessly entwined, as witness the political repercussions of the Calvinist-Arminian controversy early in the seventeenth century.

But if the Dutch Calvinist clergy submitted to their new English overlords out of theological conviction, economic considerations also figured into their allegiances. A compelling reason for clerical cooperation within the ruling elite was that many of the dominies throughout the colonial period were affluent themselves or at least aspired to wealth. In 1638, Everardus Bogardus, minister of the church in New Amsterdam from 1633 to 1647, had married a widow whose considerable estate included a sixty-two acre plot on Manhattan, which became known as the dominie's *bouwerie*.[17] Another clergyman, whose father in the Netherlands "through God's blessing is enriched with real and personal estate," left behind "silver, gold, jewels" and real property when he died in 1716.[18] The estate of a minister on Long Island included two "Turkey worked" carpets, several gold pieces and rings, a "Moorish tobacco pipe topped with silver," and an assortment of "silver plate, rings and jewells to be put up in 4 bundles" and distributed among four children.[19]

Several clergymen owned property on both sides of the Atlantic.

One left to his wife "all estate either within the province of Holland or elsewhere," and another dominie owned three houses in Holland in addition to a house and lot on Manhattan. An Albany minister (thought to have owned the first watch in the colony), left an estate valued at more than four thousand guilders.[20] A later clergyman from Albany held joint title to a tract of land stretching seventy miles long and twelve miles wide.[21] In at least one case the indebtedness of communicants to the minister may have aroused disaffection among the Dutch; when Dominie Selyns married the widow of Cornelius Steenwyck, one of the colony's wealthiest Dutch traders, he counted among his inheritances "a very extensive list of small debts due from a large number of persons."[22] Selyns's own will later apportioned five thousand guilders to friends on both sides of the Atlantic, before leaving the major share of his estate to his wife.[23] Gualtherus Du Bois, Selyns's successor in New York, was descended from a Rotterdam merchant family of considerable means and political influence.[24]

This is not to suggest that all of the colony's Dutch ministers were affluent; indeed, some ministerial candidates sought ordination as a means of elevating their social status. Yet even in instances where a certain clergyman could not claim affluence in his own right, his social connections and alliances placed him unmistakably in the upper echelons of the Dutch community. Cornelius Van Ruyven, for example, whose 1674 tax assessment ranked him as the sixth wealthiest resident in the city, argued on behalf of Dominies Johannes and Samuel Megapolensis for arrears in salary.[25] When Dominie Wilhelmus Lupardus and his wife christened their daughter on January 9, 1698, they summoned Captain Joseph Hegemen and Gerardus Beekman, two prominent laymen, as witnesses.[26] Intermarriage between clerical and mercantile families occurred frequently. As already noted, Dominie Selyns married into the Steenwyck fortune; the widow of an Albany minister married Robert Livingston; another widow married Nicholas De Meyer; and Dominie Samuel Drisius's two daughters both married into wealth.[27] Though perhaps not universal, the alliance between dominie and trader almost certainly caught the attention of less prosperous colonists.

But this alliance enjoyed the cooperation of still another entity: the English themselves. Dutch merchants, eager to protect their pecuniary interests, sidled up to the English in hopes of winning commercial advantages, and the Dutch Reformed ministers, for economic as well as religious reasons, also aligned themselves with the English. Those in fact least affected by the English takeover were the wealthy Dutch, who, through the administrations of Governors Richard Nicolls, Francis Lovelace, and Edmund Andros, continued to operate their commercial empire. Indeed, some evidence suggests that the merchants welcomed the opportunity to sever their connection with the parsimonious West India Company and pursue mercantile profit with the cooperation of benign English governors.[28] These Anglicizers—people of Dutch descent who freely acquiesced to the English, as indicated by a willingness to Anglicize their names, socialize and perhaps intermarry with the English, and generally cooperate with English officials—reaped economic benefits from their assimilation.[29] Just four months after the Dutch surrender, for example, Cornelius Steenwyck, one of twelve signatories to the Articles of Capitulation, won commercial trading privileges from the English governor. Frederick Philipse readily Anglicized his name (formerly Fredryck Flypsen) and signed the Oath of Allegiance in 1664, gestures that allowed him to continue building his trading empire and to become, by 1674, the colony's wealthiest man and a member of the Governor's Council.[30]

Some Dutch merchant families, such as the Van Rensselaers near Albany, exercised their political connections at Whitehall in order to win trading concessions from the colony's new rulers.[31] This cozy relationship between Dutch merchants and English magistrates continued, with some interruptions, into the early 1680s, when mercantile interests in London, clamoring for their share of the market, forced the recall of Governor Andros and broke up the trading monopoly.[32]

Though perhaps to a lesser degree, the dominies also profited from this alliance, as illustrated in the *Duke of York* episode. In 1670, a coterie of English and Dutch merchants (including New York's governor, Francis Lovelace) arranged to import a shipment of goods from the Netherlands to New York, a speculative venture made all the more hazardous by Anglo-Dutch hostilities then brewing in Europe. When the *Duke of York* arrived safely in the colony, the agent responsible for selling the goods (at ten-percent commission) and sending furs back to the Netherlands was one Aegidius Luyck, Dutch schoolmaster and assistant minister of New York's Dutch Reformed church.[33] Despite legal sanctions against such trade, the venture succeeded, bringing considerable profit to all concerned.[34] Luyck, who by 1674 ranked among the colony's wealthiest men, was not alone in his quest for profit from the sea lanes. In another instance, Dominie Rudolphus Varick of Long Island owned one-sixth interest in a sloop called *Flying Fish*.[35] Whether the Dutch clergy in the years immediately following the

English Conquest acted from principle, from self-interest, or from a combination of the two, many of their congregants felt betrayed by the dominies' complicity in the surrender. The dominies' political posture, moreover, and their own pursuit of wealth served to undermine the financial interests of lower-class Dutch, who in the years just prior to the Conquest had begun to share in the colony's commercial success. Economically, New Netherland had a checkered past. Ever since Henry Hudson's voyage, mercantilists back in the Netherlands had devised various strategies for settling the new region and extracting profits. A succession of schemes—joint-stock companies, monopolies, even the feudalism of patroonships—had largely failed, however, and only when the Amsterdam merchants relaxed their grip in 1639 and allowed private initiative did the colony begin to show any signs of permanence. Thus freed from monopolistic restraints and energized by the arrival of small, young families, New Netherland, with its population of approximately nine thousand, had looked almost salubrious in its waning years.

But the Dutch in New Netherland had built their economy almost exclusively around trade with the Caribbean, the Netherlands, and the Indians, so that the plight of the lower classes in particular depended on the commercial policies of the merchants and the magistrates. Many among the lower classes served as apprentices, hoping thereby to learn an economically sustaining skill, one that might also offer the possibility of social advancement. Unlike the settlers in New England and the planters on the Chesapeake, moreover, the Dutch of New Netherland had largely shied away from agriculture as a means of livelihood and therefore could not—or, at least, did not—sustain themselves from the land; to a considerable degree, their rather precarious fate lay in the hands of the ruling elite, and they could ill afford to ignore the political vicissitudes in the colony.[36]

The immigration to New Netherland, furthermore, had consisted primarily of those with modest means, the vast majority of them farmers, soldiers, and craftsmen from economically distressed regions—people who had not shared in the storied prosperity and affluence of seventeenth-century Holland, people for whom the New World represented a ticket to fortune or, at least, respectability.[37] And indeed many, such as Pieter Claessen Wyckoff and Frederick Philipse, had found that promise amply fulfilled. More than one mercantilist in New Netherland had emerged from humble beginnings, and a far greater number nurtured similar hopes.[38] The sudden incursion of the English, then, placed Dutch commonfolk one remove farther from the avenues of economic advancement and therefore represented a setback for their aspirations. Their resentments flared in proportion to their sense of exclusion from the corridors of power and the paths of upward mobility.

The tripartite cooperation of Dutch merchants, English magistrates, and Dutch clergy dominated the colony's economic and political life in the early years of English rule. Dutch artisans and small traders, however, were excluded from this collusion of interests, and a protracted series of salary disputes between Dutch clergy and their communicants provided the most visible manifestation of the resentment this association engendered. As ministers became alienated from the people and identified with the English, their congregants grew increasingly unwilling to take on the financial burdens of providing for their support. Johannes Megapolensis, whose loyalties had come under suspicion immediately after the surrender to the English, complained to the Classis that a minister's salary "is limited and comes in slow."[39] Dependent now on voluntary contributions from their congregants rather than support from the West India Company, the dominies were vulnerable to popular opprobrium because "now the salary is made by collections from house to house, in the congregation." This system, one minister complained, invited expressions of disgruntlement from church members. He wrote: "you may imagine the slights and murmurings occasioned thereby concerning the ministry and the ministers."[40]

At least one dominie recognized that diminished clerical salaries bore some relation to the English Conquest and the consequent economic stringency visited on communicants. Gideon Schaats of Albany reported to the Classis of Amsterdam that "the people are mostly needy themselves by the failure of trade."[41] When Dominie Hermanus Blom prepared to return to Holland in 1668, the Ordinary Court at Kingston pledged to help him "collect as much of his back salary as it will be possible to obtain in these hard times."[42] So serious had the salary crisis become that the courts intervened on the dominies' behalf. Three years after the Conquest, the Court of New York called on twenty-six wealthy Dutch churchmen to supplement the minister's salary because several subscribers had "departed from this Place and others disinable to pay towards the same, whom the Last Yeare had Subscribed."[43] The mayor and aldermen, "with the advise of the Hon. Governor," commanded "all the inhabitants of this City, who are in arrears to the said salary, promptly to pay their dues on this warning." The court at Kingston made similar provisions for Hermanus Blom.[44] In 1670, Governor Francis Lovelace, at the request of the deacons of the Dutch church in New York, issued an order guaranteeing "in the behalfe of myselfe & Successors the Gouernors of theise his Royall Highnesse Territories" that any minister the Classis of Amsterdam would send over for the New York church would "receive a Competent Salary or Allowance for his Exercising the Ministeriall function." This salary was to be "raised or Levyed annually uppon the Inhabitants of the Citty."[45] The next year, Lovelace issued an order which again empowered the officers of New York's Dutch church "to make a Rate or Tax amongst ye Inhabitants" for the "Maintenance of their Minister."[46] Other cases also found their way to the magistrates. On May 16, 1671, the Court of New York ordered that arrears in salary payments to Dominies Drisius and Megapolensis be paid within fourteen days, and the same court shortly thereafter made provisions to pay ministers out of public funds, which again entailed the raising of taxes.[47] Despite these measures, however, Dominie Schaats thought the situation so severe that he feared a "general exodus" by the clergy from the colony.[48]

The intervention of English officials on behalf of the Dutch clergy, however, cemented their alliance. The ministers, Calvinists all, believed that only extraordinary circumstances justified resistance to the temporal authorities; the authorities reciprocated. Although the dominies doubtless welcomed the magistrates' action on their behalf, it established a precedent for political meddling in ecclesiastical affairs. Not long thereafter, Governor Lovelace ordered an assessment to pay for a Dutch parsonage in Brooklyn and alloted five hundred guilders to repair the roof of the New York church.[49] Some years later, the Ordinary Court at Albany agreed to renovate the Dutch minister's house out of public funds.[50] The dominies became increasingly dependent on the imprimatur of English rule to maintain their authority, not to mention their livings. Succeeding English governors, less benign than Lovelace, would manipulate this dependence for their own political ends or shrewdly withdraw that support in order to advance the Church of England in the colony.

English magisterial intervention in salary disputes also exacerbated the divisions among the Dutch and enlarged the distance between Dutch clergy and their congregants. Responding to what they viewed as the clerical betrayal of Dutch interests in the peaceable surrender to the English, Dutch communicants had resisted assuming the support of those they regarded as English sympathizers. Magisterial enforcement of clerical dues only fueled their resentments. By seeking recourse from English rulers, the dominies strengthened their identification with the alien English and aggravated the nascent tensions within the Dutch community.

The plight of Dominie Johannes Megapolensis, who ran afoul of the West India Company for his counsel to surrender to the English, illustrates these tensions. Megapolensis complained that the "West India Company unjustly withholds two thousand florins, justly owing me for salary," and noted that his congregants did not seem willing to provide adequate compensation. "On Sundays we have many hearers," he wrote. "People crowd into the church, and apparently like the sermon; but most of the listeners are not inclined to contribute to the support and salary of the preacher." Megapolensis and the other clergy had no qualms about seeking redress from the English magistrates. "We have several times spoken to our Governor, but he answers, that if the Dutch will have divine service their own way, then let them also take care of and support their own preachers, and thus nothing is done for our salary." Already, as Megapolensis's letter indicates, English favor proved erratic and unreliable, and this, together with an alienated lay majority, did not augur well for Dutch religion in New York. Megapolensis predicted that when the present clergy passed on, there would be "great confusion and scattering among our people at this place."[51]

Despite occasional interventions by English magistrates, salary complaints soon became a fixture of clerical life in New York. Like his father, Dominie Samuel Megapolensis complained about his paltry earnings and said that "even this small amount is irregularly paid, not at the appointed time, but little by little, and that in the uncurrent money of this country." The English takeover, he said, heightened the tensions: "Under this English government the case is thus: when the labor ceases, the salary also ceases."[52] Like Schaats and Blom before him, the younger Megapolensis requested a recall to Holland.

II

The Dutch Reconquest of New Netherland relieved some of the tensions within the Dutch community. With Charles II's attention riveted on European affairs, Dutch frigates arrived off Staten Island on

July 30, 1673; John Manning, commander of the fort, secretly allowed their safe passage. They moored their ships, "landed their men, and entered the garrison, without giving or receiving a shot."[53] The conquering Dutch speedily assembled a Council of War, seized English properties as war reparations, and summoned the magistrates and constables of New Netherland towns, who promptly swore allegiance to the prince of Orange and the Netherlands States-General. The Dutch banished Governor Lovelace from the colony and replaced him with Captain Anthony Colve, who proclaimed a monthly day of humiliation and thanksgiving to acknowledge God's manifold blessings, "amongst which is to be Esteemed beyond all others the free & pure worshipp of God."[54]

The Council of War approached its task of restoring Dutch rule to the colony with energy and considerable aplomb. Shortly after the Reconquest, the council ordered the various towns "to send hither immediately their Deputies together with their Constables' staves and English flags, when they would, as circumstances permit, be furnished Prince's flags instead of those of the English." The Dutch undertook an ambitious program for restoring and augmenting the colony's defenses and established an intricate canon of punishments, including capital punishment, for dereliction of guard duty at the fort (briefly renamed Fort Willem Hendrick). At one point, the council even interdicted the exchange of letters with the inhabitants of New England "and other enemies of this state" and forbade the colonists to lodge guests overnight "unless they have previously given due communication thereof to their officer or Magistrate before sunset."[55]

The new Dutch rulers also regulated the inns and taverns and issued a strict set of laws governing public behavior on the Sabbath, an indication that popular dissatisfaction with the dominies had already affected attendance at Dutch worship. The council established fines for any person "found on Sunday in a club or gaming hall" and provided that "if any children be caught on the street playing, racing and shouting, previous to the termination of the last preaching, the officers of the law may take their hat or upper garment, which shall not be restored to the parents, until they have paid a fine of two guilders." The magistrates issued a list of activities forbidden on the Sabbath between sunrise and sundown, including drunkenness, fishing, boat racing, "running with carts or wagons," picking strawberries, dancing, card playing, and "rolling nine pins."[56]

In the brief interval of Dutch rule from 1673 to 1674, moreover, the magistrates sought to restore the government of the colony to followers of the Reformed faith, while at the same time strengthening the bond among clergy, magistrates, and the upper echelons of the Dutch community. Systematically, the council summoned representatives of various towns and instructed them to nominate "a double number of the best qualified, the honestest, most intelligent and wealthiest inhabitants, exclusively of the Reformed Christian religion or at least well affected thereunto." Those finally chosen as magistrates from this list of nominees took an oath promising to "defend the upright and true Christian religion agreeably to the Word of God and the order of the Synod of Dordrecht taught in the Netherland church."[57] Regardless of its political ramifications, this oath, required of magistrates throughout the colony from Albany to New Jersey to the Delaware, effectively underscored the identification of Dutch religion and clergy with the upper tiers of the Dutch community.[58]

Despite the Hollanders' ambitious program to reestablish military defenses and to buttress the fort, however, the Treaty of Westminster, concluded February 9, 1674, peacefully restored New York to the English. Dutch rule in the colony drew finally to a close. The brief interlude of Dutch control, however, had rekindled nationalistic sentiments among Dutch artisans and farmers, so the colony's peaceful cession to England stirred resentments yet again and elicited promises to "slay the English Doggs."[59] The Dutch elite, however, were more pliable. After a brief, perfunctory resistance to Edmund Andros, the new governor, they submitted once again to English rule, and Andros rewarded their cooperation by seeking from Whitehall permission for New York merchants to trade directly with the Netherlands.[60]

Indeed, the Dutch merchants who had accommodated to English rule and had won trading privileges from the English greeted the cessation of Dutch rule with an almost palpable sense of relief, for they recognized the economic benefits of fealty to England. Fully half (thirty-one of sixty-two) of New York City's wealthiest men in 1674 had signed the Oath of Allegiance to England ten years earlier. They had flourished under the English. They translated an uncertain political situation to their pecuniary advantage.[61] They reestablished their allegiance to England in 1674 with ease and without apparent reservations. Indeed, these Dutchmen issued a Thanksgiving Proclamation of their own on June 30, 1674, after the colony reverted to England;

they observed not only "the continuance of the pure religion" occasioned by the peaceful transfer of power but also the "renewal of a previous union and alliance with the crown of England."[62]

III

After the restoration of English rule, however, Nicholas Van Rensselaer would convince the Dutch clergy that the alliance with England was not always benign. Born in 1647, a younger son of the first patroon of Rensselaerswyck, Van Rensselaer drifted in and out of schools and apprenticeships before opting for the ministry and then embarking on a quixotic trip to Brussels. There he made a lasting impression on the exiled Charles II by predicting the monarch's restoration to the English throne. "We fear that he is half crazy," Richard Van Rensselaer wrote to his brother Jeremias in New York. "From what he says and does we notice that he is a good deal of a Quaker, for he claims that he has the spirit of truth, that in his dreams he sees many visions."[63]

Others apparently imbibed similar doubts about young Van Rensselaer's stability, for he had spent time in confinement at Delft, Holland, under pretext of insanity. But despite his peculiarities, his clever prophecies—for what had he to lose by making such a prediction?—had ingratiated him to the English court after Charles's restoration in 1660. Just prior to the first Anglo-Dutch war, Charles appointed Van Rensselaer chaplain to the Dutch ambassador and licensed him to preach to the Dutch congregation at Westminster. Soon thereafter, the bishop of Salisbury ordained him a deacon in the Church of England and appointed him lecturer at St. Margaret's, Lothbury. Van Rensselaer matriculated at Leiden University in 1670, and on April 4, 1672, he appeared before the Classis of Amsterdam as a candidate for foreign service and was admitted as an "expectant" after preaching a sermon.[64]

Van Rensselaer's reasons for migrating to the New World remain somewhat enigmatic, although he fled considerable indebtedness in London and the Netherlands, and he sought to lay claim to Rensselaerswyck, near Albany.[65] Van Rensselaer had apparently used his years in England to curry favor with friends in high places, because when he arrived in New York in October 1674, he came by authority not of the Classis of Amsterdam but of James, Duke of York, who wrote to Governor Andros on July 23, 1674:

Nichalaus Van Renseslaer [*sic*] having made his humble request unto
me, that I would recommend him to be Minister to one of the Dutch
churches in New York or New Albany when a vacancy shall happen;
whereunto I have consented. I do hereby desire you to signify the
same unto the Parishoners at that [place] wherein I shall look upon
their compliance as a mark of their respect and good inclinations
towards me.

Upon Van Rensselaer's arrival in New York, Andros assigned him to
the Dutch church in Albany as colleague of Dominie Gideon Schaats,
who was aged and infirm.[66]

No one in the New World questioned Van Rensselaer's education;
at his death his estate included "about 200 bookes, quarto and octavo, the most of them in Strainge Languages."[67] Instead, the dominies contested the propriety of his appointment at Albany. The magisterial placement of clergy, after all, was something common among
the hierarchical Anglicans, perhaps, but surely not among Dutch
Calvinists. Clearly this action represented a threat to the integrity of
the Dutch Reformed Church. Van Rensselaer, never fully ordained
by the Classis of Amsterdam but holding his licensure from the Anglican bishop of Salisbury, was foisted upon the Dutch without their
consent. But challenging Van Rensselaer's legality also meant challenging the authority of the recently restored English government in
the colony. Such insubordination could not be undertaken lightly or
hastily.

Although the clergy had disliked the arrangement from the outset—
Dominie Schaats, Van Rensselaer's colleague, had complained about
the intruder's "disorderly preaching"—Dominie Wilhelmus Van Nieuwenhuysen of New York City finally took up the case against Van
Rensselaer in the fall of 1675, when he sent his church elders to Albany
to prevent Van Rensselaer from conducting baptismal services.[68] Van
Rensselaer promptly complained to the governor, who ordered an
investigation into the matter. Called before the Governor's Council on
September 25, 1675, to account for his actions, Van Nieuwenhuysen
disputed the legality of Van Rensselaer's appointment because, although ordained a deacon in England, the latter lacked certification
from the Classis of Amsterdam and therefore could not legitimately
administer the sacraments.[69] The meeting proved inconclusive, with
Van Nieuwenhuysen given the space of "two, three or four dayes to
sett in writing what his opinion or judgement is in this case" and to
show "whether the Ordination of ye Church of England be not suffi-

cient qualification for a minister comporting himselfe accordingly, to be admitted, officiate & administer ye Sacraments, according to ye Constitucons of ye reformed Churches of Holland." Van Rensselaer, on the other hand, presented his papers to the council, which included his Anglican ordination, Charles II's approval to preach to the Dutch at Westminster, a certificate from a church in London attesting to his tenure there, and the duke of York's recommendation to Andros.[70]

When Van Nieuwenhuysen reappeared before the council on July 30, he did not presume to question Van Rensselaer's calling as a minister, but he objected to Van Rensselaer's placement in a Dutch church without the approbation of the Classis of Amsterdam or consultation with the colonial dominies. He proceeded carefully: "It is my opinion that the ordination of the Church of England is a sufficient qualification for the institution of a minister, lawfully called by the laying on of hands, and for the sending of him, as such, in the dominions of his Majesty, wherever it shall please their Honors." Nevertheless, he continued, "such a minister would not be permitted to administer the sacraments, as a minister of the Dutch Church, which has its own rights to be governed according to the customs of the Netherlands Reformed Church, without having previously solemnly promised, as is usual in the admission of ministers in the Netherlands, to conduct himself in his services, conformably to their Confession, Catechism and Mode of Government." Van Nieuwenhuysen felt certain that the Anglicans would not allow such an irregularity if the situation were reversed. The New York consistory subsequently outlined the conditions under which an Anglican minister might be acknowledged in a Dutch church, namely a promise "to conduct himself in his service according to the Constitution of the Reformed Church of Holland," whereupon Van Rensselaer swore allegiance to the Dutch Reformed Church on October 2, 1675.[71]

But more troubles lay ahead. Dominie Schaats's continued qualms about Van Rensselaer's orthodoxy prompted a letter to the New York consistory in August 1676. In response, two New York City merchants, Jacob Leisler and Jacob Milborne, attended one of Van Rensselaer's sermons and pronounced the minister "not orthodox but heterodox in his preaching." Van Rensselaer soon faced charges of heresy in the Albany court, but, as he had with Van Nieuwenhuysen, he promptly filed suit against Leisler and Milborne, accusing them of uttering "passionate words, blasphemies and slander" against him. Not satisfied with the Albany court's handling of the matter, Van

Rensselaer decided "to appeal and seek redress from the right honorable governor."[72]

Andros required the defendants to post security. Leisler refused, and Milborne, unable to raise the bond, surrendered to the Albany sheriff.[73] Haled before the council and ministers of New York City, Leisler appeared without counsel; Stephanus Van Cortlandt, one of the colony's wealthiest Dutch merchants, represented Van Rensselaer.[74] The council referred the case back to Albany, where the Extraordinary Court resolved "unanimously and by a plurality of Votes, that Parties shall both forgive & forget as it becomes Preachers of the Reformed Religion to do."[75]

Through the offices of Albany church elders, the case was resolved speedily and even with some degree of amity, but a dispute over responsibility for court costs persisted, resulting in Van Rensselaer's confinement to his home by the Albany authorities.[76] Governor Andros again intervened, ordering Van Rensselaer's release so that the council could hear the case. The council and ministers in New York decided for Van Rensselaer and ruled that Leisler and Milborne must pay court costs for the entire proceeding, both in New York and in Albany. The council ordered that "Dominie Renslaer [*sic*] bee freed from bearing any part thereof."[77]

IV

Although he was later "deposed by the Governor on account of his bad and offensive life," Van Rensselaer's appearance in the New World triggered a succession of difficulties for the Dutch Reformed Church, and the handling of the case caused further troubles in the years ahead.[78] The entire episode, moreover, underscored the dominies' inability to counter English intrusions into their ecclesiastical affairs. A man of questionable orthodoxy and even more dubious motives, Van Rensselaer had forced himself upon the Dutch church through the political authority of the English monarch, the duke of York, and Governor Andros. The governor's reluctance to countermand the duke's instructions placed the Dutch ministers in the uncomfortable position of challenging the newly restored secular authorities in a matter that they preferred to settle independently of English mediation altogether.

Here the earlier civil guarantees of Dutch clerical salaries seemed less palatable, for by taking their grievances to the foreign magistrates the dominies had established a precedent for English intervention into Dutch ecclesiastical affairs. Surely Van Nieuwenhuysen and other dominies sensed the delicacy of the Van Rensselaer affair. How could the same ministers who had run to the English to protect their livelihoods turn around later and protest the appointment of an Anglican minister to a Dutch church? And how, furthermore, could the Dutch dominies expect that the matter would be adjudicated other than in an English court, according to the alien standards of English justice?[79]

The Van Rensselaer affair portended vexing problems for the Dutch Reformed Church in the years ahead, because here, as early as 1675, the differences between Dutch and English understandings of church and state came into bold relief. Calvinists, popular misconceptions about "theocracy" notwithstanding, held to the two-kingdoms scheme of ecclesiastical and political government, a formulation especially conspicuous back in the Netherlands of the early seventeenth century.[80] The Cambridge Platform, for example, formulated by the New England Puritans in 1648, staked out clear boundaries. "As it is unlawful for church-officers to meddle with the sword of the Magistrate," these Calvinists wrote, "so it is unlawful for the Magistrate to meddle with the work proper to church officers." Though certainly not antithetical, the two spheres were distinct entities, each with its own organization, governance, and jurisdiction.[81]

Dutch Calvinists had brought this notion with them to the New World. Writing in 1628, Dominie Jonas Michaëlius, the first clergyman in New Netherland, conceded that although "political and ecclesiastical persons can greatly assist each other, nevertheless the matters and offices belonging together must not be mixed but kept separate, in order to prevent all confusion and disorder."[82] Indeed, quite often throughout the New Netherland period the clergy and the West India Company directors-general found themselves at odds; the most notorious such conflict occurred between Dominie Everardus Bogardus and Director-General Willem Kieft, who battled each other so fiercely that they sailed together back to Holland for arbitration only to be shipwrecked and perish off the coast of Wales.[83]

This adversarial relationship of church and state was foreign to Restoration Englishmen, however. Building on the writings of Thomas Erastus, a sixteenth-century political theorist, Anglicans believed that the church should be subject to the powers of the state. Richard

Hooker, apologist for the Church of England, wrote that "there is not any restraint or limitation of matter for regal authority and power to be conversant in, but of religion whole, and of whatsoever cause thereto appertaineth, kings may lawfully have charge, they lawfully may therein exercise dominion, and use the temporal sword."[84] Thus, in keeping with Erastian theory, the Duke's Laws, imposed in New York in 1665 and again in 1674, contained the following provision:

> To prevent Scandalous and Ignorant pretenders to the Ministry from introducing themselves as Teachers; No Minister shall be Admitted to Officiate, within the Government but such as shall produce Testimonials to the Governour, that he hath Received Ordination either from some Protestant Bishop, or Minister within some part of his Majesties Dominions or the Dominions of any foreign Prince of the Reformed Religion, upon which Testimony the Governor shall induce the said Minister into the parish that shall make presentation of him, as duly Elected by the Major part of the Inhabitants.[85]

Later in the colonial period, after the formation of the Society for the Propagation of the Gospel, Anglican missionaries could rely on English magistrates for assistance, as when George Keith praised Governor Francis Nicholson as an "Instrument of good both to Church and State."[86] The appointment of Van Rensselaer, then, may or may not have been a calculated attempt by the duke of York, a Catholic, to disrupt the colonial Dutch Reformed Church, but it most certainly represented a clash of ideologies.[87]

Van Nieuwenhuysen very quickly perceived that the events of the mid-1670s had exacted a price. "The church here does not now increase," he wrote. "I should not be surprised if a large portion of the Dutch citizens should be led to break up here and remove." The controversy surrounding Van Rensselaer had divided the Albany church—he garnered enough votes to win vindication in the consistory—and Jacob Leisler and Jacob Milborne doubtless spawned a growing animosity toward the English and a suspicion of their meddlesome high-church— even popish—tendencies as a result of the Van Rensselaer ordeal.[88] The case also placed Leisler and Van Cortlandt in a direct adversarial relationship, a foreshadowing of events to come. Leisler and Milborne perhaps even then harbored suspicions of the Dutch clergy, because although the New York ministers sat together with the Governor's Council at Leisler's hearing, there is no indication that the dominies came to Leisler's aid in his case against Van Rensselaer, despite their earlier initiative.[89]

V

Beyond the Van Rensselaer affair, the chronic shortage of clergy, and continued disaffection among the laity, the Dutch churches faced yet another challenge in the 1670s, when the consistory of the Dutch congregation at New Castle, on the Delaware River, asked the Dutch ministers of New York to ordain Petrus Tesschenmaeker, who had filled the pulpit on an interim basis, as their permanent minister. Initially the dominies demurred, for they realized full well that they possessed no formal authority to ordain ministers for the Dutch Reformed Church. But Governor Andros stepped in and directed Van Nieuwenhuysen and the other Dutch clergy to examine and ordain Tesschenmaeker, even though that procedure conflicted with Dutch Refomed polity.[90] The dominies complied, found Tesschenmaeker well qualified, and ordained him on October 9, 1679. Then, somewhat anxiously, they reported their actions to the Classis of Amsterdam.[91]

Dominie Tesschenmaeker's character and qualifications were beyond reproach. He held a divinity degree, had passed a preparatory examination back in Utrecht, had preached at the Hague, and had served ably as interim minister for the churches in the Esopus (Kingston). Plainly what gave the colonial clergy pause was not Tesschenmaeker but the arrogation to themselves of ecclesiastical authority which traditionally had rested in the Netherlands. The dominies used every conceivable argument to justify their actions to the Classis—the urgency of New Castle's request, Governor Andros's authorization, their rigid adherence to the forms and procedures used in Holland, even "the inconveniences of the winter season here; the dangers of the voyage, if the candidate should seek to obtain his advancement" in the Netherlands. The Classis, for its part, had little choice but to accept the ordination. They recognized the extenuating circumstances of the Tesschenmaeker case, while at the same time making clear that they had no intentions of surrendering the authority of ordination to the colonial churches.[92]

Amsterdam's chary response derived from the ecclesiastical situation back in Holland. The Netherlands church officials for some time had regarded with suspicion an antiauthoritarian religious movement in the homeland. As early as 1675, the Synod of North Holland reported on the activities of the Labadists and declared that they were "watching against that evil with all diligence."[93]

The Labadists, followers of Jean de Labadie, a radical pietist, refused to submit to the ecclesiastical authorities, and they established their own conventicles outside the Reformed churches.[94] After flirting briefly with Labadism and its separatist impulses, Jacobus Koelman, a minister at Sluis in Zeeland, carried on the pietist tradition of opposition to ceremonialism and formalism within the Dutch Reformed Church. Whereas Labadie had chosen separatism, Koelman sought instead to "purify" the Dutch church of what he considered the Roman Catholic accretions of prescribed prayers and liturgical worship. He insisted on conducting religious services and administering the sacraments without regard to written forms. The peripatetic Koelman even held services in the city of Middleburg, "under the eyes of the authorities," and proposed to the Classis of Walcheren the abolition of the festivals of Christmas, Easter, and Pentecost as "useless and unedifying." To counter this threat, Dutch Reformed Church officials tried to suppress a book written by Koelman "containing two sermons against the Forms of Prayer," forbade him to preach or administer the sacraments, and denied him a seat in any classis until he renounced his heresies.[95]

But Koelman and his followers persisted. Four years later, the Synod of North Holland reported that Koelman continued "his private gatherings in several places" and his opposition to the settled clergy. He refused to "subject himself to the Church-Order of this land," so the Synod admonished the churches "to be watchful against him and his conventicles." In 1679, two Labadists crossed the Atlantic to explore sites for a settlement in Maryland, from whence they set out on missionary forays to gain converts in the New World. Although in 1681 the Synod of North Holland reported that Koelman and his followers were "gradually losing ground in our home churches," it was only a matter of time before reformists of his persuasion, growing weary of the vigilant ecclesiastical authorities in Holland, would show up in the New World.[96]

The Labadists' opening came, it appeared, in 1682 through a series of developments that assaulted the Dutch Reformed Church in two of the areas in which it felt most vulnerable: the uneasy relations with Jacobus Koelman in the Old World and the shortage of clergy leading to Petrus Tesschenmaeker's deviative ordination in the New World. In September of that year, the Dutch church at New Castle wrote to the Classis of Amsterdam to report that Tesschenmaeker, their minister, had left them "without lawful reason" for a congregation in Bergen (East Jersey). The letter complained about the pernicious influence of

Lutherans and Quakers in their midst and earnestly implored the Holland authorities to send them another dominie. The people at New Castle, furthermore, offered their own suggestion. Having learned that Jacobus Koelman, a man of "ripe orthodoxy, knowledge, aptness to teach, and good character," currently held no ministerial post, they urged that the Classis consent to his call. Yes, the church at New Castle knew of Dominie Koelman's irregularities, that he "usually does not observe the printed forms of prayers or holydays; but we will not grow angry about that while we know that he is sound in doctrine and of a good life."[97]

A subsequent letter from Dominie Henricus Selyns, recently returned to the New World as minister of the New York City church, cast a fuller light on the proceedings at New Castle. Reduced to abject poverty by a salary dispute—now a familiar refrain—Dominie Tesschenmaeker left New Castle to find a better position in one of the other Dutch churches.[98] Having come up empty in New York, he continued on to Boston, where he met a similar fate. Returning now to New Castle, he sought his former position and asked the other dominies to intercede on his behalf. Selyns and his colleagues resolved that Tesschenmaeker should submit a formal apology to New Castle, with a view toward his reinstatement. In the meantime, however, New Castle had communicated with Koelman directly; he in turn proposed that he bring along with him about two hundred and fifty of his following, a considerable augmentation to New Castle's fifty or so congregants.[99] Accordingly, the congregation on the Delaware discharged Tesschenmaeker, and a couple of members went so far as to pledge the cost of transportation for Koelman and his family.[100] Selyns, clearly shaken by these events, described the condition of the church as "pitiable" and warned "of the approaching storm and of the threatened hurricane."[101]

Jacobus Koelman, it turned out, never crossed the Atlantic; about this time, he renounced Labadism altogether.[102] But the entire episode, nevertheless, demonstrated again the precariousness of the colonial church under English rule, its vulnerability to forces beyond its control. Selyns and the other dominies lacked the civil authority to prevent a schismatic preacher from entering the colony and lodging himself in one of their pulpits. They also had precious little control over Tesschenmaeker or the congregation at New Castle. The Classis of Amsterdam rebuked the church at New Castle for being quarrelsome, for endangering the liberty of the Dutch church, and, most of all, for failing to communicate with Amsterdam regarding the call of a minister.[103]

VI

The Tesschenmaeker case, the Van Rensselaer affair, and incessant salary disputes underlined the extent to which the Dutch Reformed Church reeled from the effects of English rule in the colony. Indeed, the successive changes in political control of the colony had left the Dutch community as a whole anxious and confused. The hardships visited upon ordinary Dutch by the English takeover in 1664 and the apparent liaison between clergy and merchant portended difficulties and conflict in the years ahead.[104] Accusations of treachery and re-criminations had begun with Stuyvesant's surrender to the English in 1664 and continued for several years. The Dutch Reconquest provided further evidence of this alliance when the new Dutch rulers explicitly sought local magistrates with two essential qualifications: wealth and allegiance to the Synod of Dort.[105] Although the sentiment behind this directive—the bias for wealthy magistrates—was nothing new or unusual, its forthright connection of religion and riches may have implied to Dutch communicants a collusion among the Dutch Reformed clergy, the political authorities, and the afflu-ent. Given the generally diminutive role they played in both civil and ecclesiastical government, less prosperous Dutch congregants might be pardoned for suspecting, as in the case of Stuyvesant's surrender, a confederation between the clergy and the merchant community, and when a zealous young dominie fresh from the Netherlands dared to challenge the status quo, the colony's senior minister quickly rebuked him for preaching against what the newcomer called the "improper gains and godless traffic" of the merchants.[106]

The paradigm of church-state relations emerging since the English takeover looked even more troublesome. The impetuous and desul-tory appeals of the Dutch clergy to the English magistrates had served only to heighten animosity and suspicion among their communicants. The English judgments in their favor on salary matters had provided the dominies with a shallow—and quite transitory—victory, for in asking the English to adjudicate the matter they had set an unsavory precedent. Not only were the dominies identified with English rule and their congregants nettled with additional taxes, but the English magistrates felt little restraint about interfering further in the administration of the Dutch Reformed Church.

The Van Rensselaer affair provided the best example. Here the English governor of the colony, on orders from the duke of York, installed a renegade Dutchman with Anglican orders and apparent Quaker leanings as minister in a Dutch church. The dominies initially felt powerless to prevent such a transgression of their religious autonomy, for they themselves had invited English intervention in the earlier salary disputes. Only a couple of years later, Governor Andros exercised his prerogative and urged the colony's Dutch clergy to usurp the proper channels and ordain Petrus Tesschenmaeker for the church at New Castle. The dominies complied, noting that "it would not be safe to disobey" the English governor, who was, after all, the legitimate temporal authority in the colony.[107]

Salary disputes, themselves a symptom of growing disaffection among the Dutch, together with the uncertain political climate, translated quickly into a shortage of Holland-trained clergy in the New World. The legally enforced collection of ministerial salaries had placed the dominies so at odds with congregants that many of the clergy asked to return to the Netherlands.[108] The difficulties of the New York ministers, doubtless well known back in the Netherlands, engendered a wariness among ministerial candidates, and few of them proved willing to risk the perils of an Atlantic voyage only to plunge into a cauldron of communicant dissent, the uncertainties of English rule, and altercations over wages.

Indeed, the dominies' reliance on English authority for clerical salaries placed the entire colonial church in a precarious situation. The ministers found themselves in no position to protest English interference in Dutch ecclesiastical affairs during the Van Rensselaer dispute, since they had earlier compromised the church's autonomy. Henceforth the Dutch could never be sure that the English would uphold the best interests of the Dutch Reformed Church. To complicate matters, since the dominies had in effect cast their lot with the English either out of theological conviction or in exchange for financial security, they had become dependent on English authority. In the years to come, when the Society for the Propagation of the Gospel began its assaults in New York, English governors less friendly toward Dutch Calvinism would suddenly withdraw civil support, thus leaving the Dutch Reformed Church vulnerable to the zealotry of Anglican missionaries.

Certainly the lack of clergy looked unsettling, but the latent disaffection between the dominies and their communicants was even more ominous, though perhaps not so visible. In some instances the connection between the ministers and wealthy merchants was explicit, as in the *Duke of York* affair or when Cornelius Van Ruyven, a Dutchman of considerable substance in the colony, argued in court for the arrears in salary due to colonial dominies.[109] The Van Rensselaer affair notwithstanding, salary disputes in the years following the English Conquest allied the Dutch ministers with English magistrates against Dutch communicants. Forced to support the dominies against their will—and perhaps beyond their means—Dutch congregants began to harbor suspicions and resentments which, like dry firewood, awaited only a spark to erupt into a conflagration.

Jacob Leisler, to extend the metaphor, had already cast his kindling into the tinderbox. The Van Rensselaer affair had shown him the invidiousness of the English and led him to suspect the Dutch clergy for their apparent dilatoriness in challenging the Van Rensselaer appointment. The dominies, however, because of the awkwardness of their own situation growing out of salary adjudications, could offer little help in seeking a redress from English authorities. Although the years immediately ahead would be relatively quiet and marked even by an apparent expansion of political liberties, disaffection among the Dutch lay just beneath the surface.

2

Religion in Great Danger:
Leisler's Rebellion and Its Repercussions

Early in the 1680s, the dominies enjoyed a respite from some of the contentiousness that had plagued ecclesiastical life in the period immediately following the English Conquest of 1664.[1] "Everything goes on well in our churches," the colonial clergy wrote in 1680. As late as 1684, Governor Thomas Dongan reported to England on the religious composition of the colony, noting that the "most prevailing opinion is that of the Dutch Calvinists."[2] When he returned to New York in 1682 after several years' hiatus in the Netherlands, Dominie Henricus Selyns reported with equanimity that the colony's churches operated with the same order of worship and church government as in Holland and that "religious services are held with quietness, and without any annoyances." Selyns later informed the Classis of Amsterdam that former "complaints and difficulties" in the New York church had been "adjusted and removed" and that his congregation "is now engaged in building me a large house, wholly of stone and three stories high. It is built," he said, "on the foundation of unmerited love."[3]

On the last day of 1682, Selyns and two of his elders proclaimed a day of thanksgiving, fasting, and prayer, because "God the Lord in his incomprehensible favor and undeserved grace" has visited "this Province, and especially this City of New York with abundant blessings." The proclamation admonished Dutch communicants to pray that the church might continue "in the enjoyment of the pure doctrines of the Gospel and the free exercise thereof" and to ask the Almighty's blessings on King Charles II and James, the duke of

28

York.[4] The clergy had adjusted well to English rule, as the fast-day proclamations suggest. Selyns praised Governor Dongan, a Catholic, as "a person of knowledge, refinement and modesty" and was heartened by the duke of York's pledge to grant the colonists "full liberty of conscience."[5]

I

In 1683, under some duress, the duke of York made good on his promise. After a great deal of equivocation and while virtually in exile following the Popish Plot, James instructed his governor to call a General Assembly which would provide the inhabitants "free liberty to consult and debate among themselves all matters as shall be apprehended proper to be established for laws for the good government of the said Colony of New Yorke and its Dependencyes."[6] The Charter of Libertyes, passed October 30, 1683, ensured quite explicitly that all inhabitants, provided they did not disturb the civil peace, shall "at all times freely have and fully enjoy his or their Judgments or Consciences in matters of religion throughout all the Province."[7] But by the time the Charter reached England for James's approval, the duke had ascended to the throne and had second thoughts about his earlier magnanimity. He vetoed the charter and then in 1687/8 decreed that New York be governed jointly with New England and share the same constitution.[8]

Throughout this period the process of Anglicization continued apace, and on November 1, 1683, the Assembly approved a measure that epitomizes the attempt to homogenize New York's ethnic diversity into an English identity. The bill, "An Act for naturalizing all those of forreigne Nations at present inhabiting within this province and professing Christianity, and for Encouragement of others to come and Settle within the Same," provided naturalization as English subjects for all Christian denizens of New York who took an oath of allegiance.[9] By 1686, English political structures had supplanted the Dutch system, even down to municipal governments.[10] Dutch judicial forms gave way to English as New York's legal code began more and more to resemble English statutory law.[11] The cessation of government support after 1664 threatened the rather impressive network of Dutch schools established during the New Netherland period, thereby imperiling also the future of the Dutch language in the New World.[12] Even the influence of Dutch merchants diminished with the recall of Governor Edmund Andros in 1680 and the strident incursion of London trading interests into the New York entrepôt.[13]

Anglicization clearly had a religious dimension as well. James II's instructions to Governor Dongan, which included his order to repeal the Charter of Libertyes, envisioned a more prominent role for the Anglicans in New York:

> You shall take especiall care that God Almighty bee devoutly and duely served throughout your Government: the Book of Common Prayer, as it is now establisht, read each Sunday and Holyday, and the Blessed Sacrament administered according to the Rites of the Church of England. . . . Our will and pleasure is that noe minister be preferred by you to any Ecclesiastical Benefice in that our Province, without a Certificat from ye most Reverend the Lord Archbishop of Canterbury of his being conformable to ye Doctrine and Discipline of the Church of England, and of a good life & Conversation.[14]

The Church of England henceforth would assume a more conspicuous profile in the religious landscape of New York.

The Dutch clergy, however, did not seem terribly dismayed by the news from Whitehall, and they continued to send encouraging reports on the health of the churches back to the Netherlands. "The Reformed Church of Christ lives here in peace with all nationalities," the newly arrived Rudolphus Varick wrote in 1668; "each pastor holds his flock within its own proper bounds." Varick also remarked on the change of governors which once again placed Sir Edmund Andros in charge of the colony as governor of the newly formed Dominion of New England. Both Varick and Selyns commented in letters back to Holland about the agreeable character of Andros, noting his fluency in the Dutch language and his friendly disposition toward the Dutch church.[15] In short, after the turbulent initial years of English rule, tranquility prevailed.[16]

II

The accession of William, the Dutch prince of Orange, to the English throne in 1688, however, shattered that tranquility and triggered a series of cataclysmic reactions in the New World.[17] In New England the citizens of Boston arrested Governor Andros. His lieutenant in

New York, Francis Nicholson, fled to England after trying briefly to suppress news of the Glorious Revolution.[18] Rumors abounded. The people of New York feared that the French in Canada—whom they regarded as papists, just like James II—were preparing to overrun the colony. To stave off an invasion, the militia, "having extraordinary apprehensions of danger," assumed control of the fort on May 31, 1689, and chose Jacob Leisler, one of the militia captains, "to command the fort and to uphold the rights of said royal government and its prescrvation."[19] Lcislcr promptly "allarmcd thc city and in onc half houre there came about 500 men couragiously in armes." He dismissed the mayor and aldermen, organized a Committee of Safety, initiated "demonstrations of Joy and affection" toward William and Mary, and speedily demanded oaths of fidelity to the new English rulers.[20] Bitterly opposed to James II and Roman Catholicism in general, Leisler, already alienated from both English rule and the Dutch Reformed clergy, insisted throughout that he was merely securing the colony on an interim basis for the new regime. Leisler and his council even "adventured to make a new seal altering the Duke of York's Coronet and putting the Crown of England in its stead."[21]

No issue aroused the suspicions and ignited the passions of Dutch colonists more than the fear of Roman Catholicism. Stephanus Van Cortlandt described the Leislerians as "being much against papists." Leisler's militia consisted of older, first-generation immigrants, doubtless reared on stories of William the Silent's heroic struggle against Philip, the Catholic king of Spain, a struggle that culminated in the triumph of Protestant Calvinism and the establishment of the independent Dutch Republic in 1579. For Leisler's followers, the threat of Catholicism meant not only the specter of heresy but also the yoke of political tyranny, and they explicitly identified William of Orange's triumph over James II with William the Silent's victory over Philip II of Spain a century earlier. The new king of England's "forefathers had liberated our ancestors from the Spanish yoke," they recalled in 1698, "and his royal highness had now again come to deliver the kingdom of England from Popery and Tyranny." The procrastination of the colonial government in proclaiming "Gods deliverance from the two greatest plagues of mankind, Popery and Slavery," could only confirm Leislerian suspicions that the English in power in New York favored papism.[22]

Though certainly exaggerated, fear of Catholic encroachment was not entirely unfounded and fed on periodic frontier skirmishes with the

French and the Indians.[23] Dutch colonists, moreover, had seen entirely too much evidence of popery since the English Conquest. In 1672, the duke of York, the colony's namesake and heir presumptive to the English throne, announced what everyone already had suspected—his conversion to Catholicism. The Popish Plot in 1678 unleashed a flurry of anti-Catholic sentiment in London, all related to the succession, and the Dutch found the duke's accession to the throne in 1685 trebly opprobrious: first on account of his religion, but also because James had played a role in engineering England's naval victory over Holland at the conclusion of the first Anglo-Dutch war, and because he had reneged on his promise of a representative assembly. "It was with great dread known, that the late King James was bound in Conscience to indeavour to Damn the English Nation to Popery and Slavery," one Leislerian recalled in 1698, and his placemen "were the tools to inslave their Country, who pursuant to their Commission did make Laws and Assessed Taxes accordingly, without any Representatives of the People." Leisler himself complained of the king's "illegal and arbitrary power" and the actions of James's appointees, who ruled "without having any regard to advice or consent of ye representatives of ye people."[24]

Leisler and his following believed that papism posed an imminent threat to the colony. On June 22, 1689, someone set fire to the fort in three different places. Convinced that the arsonist was Catholic, Leisler attributed their "miraculous deliverance" from that "hellish designe" to God's mercy.[25] But for the Leislerians this event fit into a larger pattern of Catholic intrigue in the colony. At least three Jesuit missionaries were active in New York in the 1680s. The Society of Jesus, Leislerians charged, under the pretense of teaching Latin, had established a school and numbered children of the "most influential" among their students.[26] In 1687, Thomas Dongan, the Catholic governor appointed by James, had promised to secure a priest for Indians in the colony's northern reaches.[27] Despite popular suspicions of popery, the New York colonial government openly honored James II. On October 2, 1688, Dongan (now retired) launched extended celebrations marking the birth of the Catholic prince of Wales. "The Great Gunns of the fort were fired, volleys of small shot from his Majesty's two Companys answearing them. And then all the Shipps in the harbour firred off their Gunns," a contemporary observed. "The people every where drinking and crying out God Save the Prince of Wales. During this Entertainment in the fort a Very larg Bonfire was made before the fort gate where his Excellence and all the Councill dranke the princes health." A similar fete followed in Albany, where "barrells of very stout beere Stood every wheare ready broachd at the head for men, women, and children to drink or drown as they pleased."[28] Leislerians greeted the prince of Wales's birth far less enthusiastically—as nothing less than "a mortal stab for the Protestant Religion in England, and consequently for ours."[29]

The Leislerians, who had grown restive under the steady encroachment of English culture, showed little restraint in their attempts to punish and harass the English and their sympathizers. "Confusion and Disturbance here," the Anglicized Dutchman Charles Lodwyck wrote to London in 1692, have "wholly impeded even our common Affairs, that for almost 3 years, we had enough to do to exercise all our brains to secure our ps'ons, and what little we had, from ye Cruelty and Tyranny of an ungovernable mobb."[30] The dominies' general posture of accommodation to the English and their petitions for guaranteed clerical salaries already had identified them with the English colonial government and, by extension, with James II. Dutch artisans, moreover, found other evidence of the clergy's collusions with papists. Selyns, who openly admired Thomas Dongan, had enjoyed free access to the Catholic governor.[31] Dominie Dellius of Albany faced charges from Leisler that he corresponded with a Jesuit missionary, "according to what we have long had reason to suspect him."[32] For the Leislerians, neither the magistrates nor the Dutch clergy showed sufficient fear of the French. They alleged that Dominie Varick of Long Island "said he would go out and meet them with a glass of wine and bid them welcome" and that Selyns sought "on every occasion to enlarge the power of France."[33] The dominies' refusal to sanction Leisler's action, undertaken "for the glory of the Protestant interest," to throw off the bonds of "popery and slavery," served only to reinforce popular suspicions of the Dutch clergy.[34]

For the duration of their rule (June 1689 to March 1691), Leisler and Jacob Milborne, who married Leisler's daughter in 1691, enjoyed widespread popular support among the Dutch, who applauded their vigilance against the prospective retaliation of the papists. But the approbation was less than unanimous. The upper classes, by and large, refused to participate in what they stigmatized as a preponderantly lower-class movement led, in the words of one antagonist, by "Boors and butterboxes." One contemporary asserted that "almost every man of Sence, Reputation or Estate" opposed the rebellion, and another characterized Leisler's following as "the meanest and most abject Common people."[35]

Leisler's rise to political power had displaced not only Lieutenant-Governor Nicholson but also the three members of his council, all prominent Dutchmen and members of the Dutch Reformed Church: Frederick Philipse, Nicholas Bayard, and Stephanus Van Cortlandt, mayor of New York and Leisler's erstwhile adversary in the Van Rensselaer case. After Leisler had seized control of the fort and the city, his followers vented their anger against these prominent English sympathizers. When Van Cortlandt refused Leisler's order to proclaim William the king of England, Leisler called him a traitor and a papist and, in Van Cortlandt's words, "made the people just ready to knock me in the head." Leislerians armed with swords ambushed Bayard at the customs house, "severall cutting at Coll Bayard but the croud being so thick cutt only his hatt"; he escaped the mob, went into hiding, and quit the city. Leisler warned Philipse that "if he should meet again the Divell should take him."[36] Leislerians identified the Dutch elite not only with the English but also with the Dutch Church. "Now it is to be known that most of the magistrates or those who were their friends," angry Leislerians complained, "were also elders and deacons and therefore heads of our church." Indeed, the anti-Leislerians dominated the consistory at the time of the rebellion.[37]

III

A series of events in June 1690 further illustrates the growing acrimony between the Leislerians and their wealthier adversaries. At City Hall on June 6, as the Leisler government prepared to announce additional measures to fortify the city and defend the colony against the French, about fifty anti-Leislerians protested that they would pay no further taxes. They demanded the release of prisoners from the fort and vowed to free them by force. "Whereupon severall threatening & seditious words were uttered by the said disturbers," according to witnesses, "and when those opposers had spoken that they would rise, they gave three huzaas and went away." On the way to the fort, armed with swords, carbines, and pistols, they encountered Leisler. They surrounded him, tried to wrest his sword (and succeeded in removing it "about half a foot" before he resisted), shouting all the while, "kill him, kill him, and knock him down," and taunting him "with ill language and Threats." Leisler's son, according to one account, "seeing so many people crowding in upon his father, drew his sword and began to hack right and left, but the people got hold of him and took the sword out of his hand and broke it in two." Leisler himself, smitten several times with a cane, barely dodged a "powerfull blow" to his head with a cooper's adze, which struck him instead on the chest. With the help of some partisans now on the scene, he struggled free, brandished his sword, and walked to safety.[38]

Confronted again several blocks away, Leisler and three comrades held their antagonists at bay until the alarm could be sounded "and a cannon fired to call the farmers to arms." As word spread of the attack on Leisler, "the Country People upon a Rumour that the Government was in danger, by a rising of the disaffected Party, Flockt to the City Armed in Great Numbers." Leislerians rallied to his defense. They threatened revenge, and, "with naked swords in their hands, ran like madmen through the streets and those who happened to be about and were not of their party were taken at once to the fort, thrown in chains and put on bread and water." Over the objections of the magistrates, the "enraged Multitude" forcibly confined other miscreants to their houses for two days until the Leisler government could convince them that order would be restored and several of the attackers imprisoned.[39]

At the conclusion of the Sunday-morning sermon two days later, Leisler passed a note to Dominie Selyns for inclusion with the other announcements. Selyns, according to a contemporary, refused to read the missive, whereupon Leisler, "standing up, motioned with his fist and told him to read it." Calling the minister a rascal, Leisler bellowed, "I want you to do it at once." Selyns grudgingly read Leisler's note, addressed to "all preachers of the Reformed Church." The proclamation read: "Whereas there are those who tried to murder the Lieutenant Governor, public thanks are offered to God for his deliverance, etc." After the service Leisler walked to the front of the church and engaged Selyns in some verbal sparring. He called the Dutch minister "a seditious man," to which Selyns replied that if he was so bad then he "was not worthy to occupy the pulpit" and that he would not preach anymore. Leisler ordered him to continue his responsibilities "and threatened, if he refused, to throw him into irons and to quarter soldiers in his house." That same morning, Dominie

Varick on Long Island had received a similar note to read to his congregation, "but in delivering the paper they got into an altercation, so that Dominie Varick did not preach."[40]

During the rebellion clergy and merchants alike felt the Leislerians' wrath. "The furor of the common people ran very high, so that every body who did not escape, was taken by the throat, or, on feigned pretexts, thrown into prison," Varick recounted in 1693. "Merchants were forcibly stripped of their goods in the name of the King," and on Long Island "many Englishmen, especially, were robbed." When the Dutch clergy attempted to defend the deposed authorities, "they only drew forth the same vituperative expressions upon themselves."[41]

What accounts for these tensions? New York had witnessed an increased social bifurcation in the years following the English Conquest, a cleavage felt nowhere more strongly than in the Dutch community. At the top sat a wealthy group of merchants who enjoyed commercial monopolies at the expense of small traders, artisans, and city dwellers.[42] The control of the colonial government rested securely in the hands of the wealthy.[43] Though English merchants were the most apparent beneficiaries of the 1664 Conquest, many of the Dutch traders had retained old privileges and even expanded their commerce with new access to England and its colonies.[44] By one reckoning, New York harbored three ships, seven boats, and eight sloops in 1678, but by 1694 that fleet had increased to forty ships, sixty-two boats, and sixty-two sloops.[45]

The incursion of the English had effectively denied the Dutch lower classes any chance of economic advancement in New York City. To a considerable degree, Leisler's Rebellion allied artisans and small traders against the merchant class, the less privileged against the urban traders, a generalization shared by contemporaries. During the confrontation between Leisler and his adversaries at City Hall on June 6, 1690, his loyalists summoned "the Country People" who "Flockt to the City Armed in Great Numbers." Michael Hanse, for example, captain of a foot company at Brooklyn, later testified that "he was commanded by Jacob Leisler to come over to New Yorke with his company who by order of said Leisler were quarter'd in the houses of divers of the Inhabitants of the town during the stay of his said company there, for the space of one day." One anti-Leislerian, disgusted by the "insolence of the Country People in the Citty of New Yorke" during the rebellion, asserted that "they were all called in by Leisler's Command."[46]

Leisler's following did not consist entirely of the commonalty. Samuel Staats, a physician and native of New Netherland, "rather than endeavor to make himself an Englishman, . . . left this Province and went to Holland, where he remained till a very little time before the Revolution; then he came hither, and joyned with Mr. Leisler." Leisler himself had been a merchant of some means, and he attracted such prominent figures as Abraham Gouverneur and Gerardus Beekman, another physician.[47] But by and large, Leisler failed to rally the better sort to his cause. "We cannot yet learn that hardly one person of sense and Estate within this City and Parts adjacent do countenance any of these ill and rash proceedings," the three Dutch councilors wrote in 1689, "except some who are deluded and drawn in by meer fear." Indeed, many of those initially inclined to support the rebellion quickly became disillusioned with Leisler and his obstreperous following. They condemned Leisler's arbitrary rule and branded him a usurper. "The members of the former Government," a Leislerian complained, "gave all the opposition they could to this Reformation, and have created a Faction in the said province."[48]

On May 19, 1690, New York merchants (including a minister, three deacons, and two elders from Dutch churches on Manhattan and Long Island) expressed their outrage directly to William and Mary. Their petition, on behalf of the "most oppressed and abused subjects in this remote part of the world," complained of mistreatment at the hands of Leisler. The aggrieved merchants thought little of his followers, "whom we can give no better name then a Rable, those who formerly were scarce thought fit to bear the meanest offices among us." They found it difficult to escape the wrath of the Leislerians: "several of the best and most considerable Inhabitants are forced to retire from their habitations to avoid their fury." Leisler's government, Richard Ingoldesby wrote in 1691, had "grievously oppressed the best sort of the Inhabitants."[49] Support for the rebellion, then, which amounted to a litmus test for Dutch resistance to Anglicization, extended neither to the wealthy Dutch merchants nor to the ministers of the Dutch Reformed Church.[50]

Leisler's appeal lay in his anti-Catholic rhetoric and his strident opposition to the wealthy, Anglicized elite; when the Leislerians came to power, for example, they released those imprisoned for debt.[51] The opposition of the Dutch merchants, therefore, at least moderately wealthy by contemporary standards, is understandable; surely they had much to lose during the Leisler uncertainties.

The reactions of the clergy seem, at first glance, a bit more enigmatic. The Dutch dominies, all of them bilingual, had clearly identified themselves with the colony's elite. Many, in fact, possessed sizable personal fortunes which were imperiled by the popular uprising.[52] But the clergy also had other, less avaricious reasons for opposing Leisler. Earlier in the decade, they had manifested a resignation to English rule, a posture that frequently approached overt Anglicization. A quiet acquiescence to the English, they believed, ensured that the integrity of Dutch worship would continue unchallenged. Although they remained subject to the Classis of Amsterdam in matters ecclesiastical, they recognized at the same time the dangers of misusing the political privileges granted them after the Treaty of Westminster. "As to the Church Rules observed in the Fatherland, and subscribed by us when there—they are observed by us in our services and churches here as carefully as possible," the clergy had written to Amsterdam in 1680. "It would be a great folly in us, and an unchristian act of discourtesy," however, "should we either misuse or neglect the privileges granted us by treaty by the English at the surrender of the country." The realities of the colony's political situation demanded caution. "We are in a foreign country, and also governed by the English nation," the dominies noted pointedly. "We must exercise much prudence in order to preserve the liberties granted us."[53] Such a stance also corresponded with the Calvinist notion of submission to temporal authorities.

The dominies' strategy of placating the English had paid off through the 1680s. On the whole, the magistrates permitted the Dutch to govern their own ecclesiastical affairs, and Dutch ministers even enjoyed an exemption from taxation on their dwellings.[54] So confident had the clergy become of their standing in the eyes of the English that the Dutch church of New York City in 1688 petitioned the governor for an independent charter.[55] Perhaps in this light the ministers' refusal to join their communicants in Leisler's Rebellion seems less confounding.

Indeed, the Dutch clergy had faced a real dilemma when Jacob Leisler seized the fort and expelled Nicholson in 1689. In light of Leisler's evident popularity among their communicants, the path of least resistance lay in recognizing Leisler as the legitimate magistrate and thereby avoiding the wrath of his considerable following. If the clergy chose this route, then their convictions as Calvinists mandated obedience to Leisler, for in Reformed theology only outright tyranny warranted resistance to a duly constituted government. In his public showdown with Selyns in the Dutch church over the reading of the

proclamation concerning his deliverance from his adversaries, Leisler
had forced Selyns to take this very step. If he had read the official
proclamation of his own volition, Sclyns would have tacitly acknowledged Leisler's legitimacy, and by his own theological scruples he
would have owed Leisler his obedience. Given the generally amicable
relations between the Dutch clergy and the English magistrates, however, Selyns and the other dominies elected instead to view Leisler as
a usurper and thereby deny him their loyalty. And, coincidentally or
not, many of the wealthier Dutch concurred.[56]

Writing to a colleague on November 30, 1689, a scant six months
into the rebellion, Dominie Varick of Long Island called urgently for
a meeting of the clergy "concerning these dangerous times." "Pray
for the peace of Jerusalem," Selyns wrote in 1690, referring to the
troubles facing the church during Leisler's tenure. Selyns fervently
hoped that William and Mary would "send over some one to take
charge of this government who can heal the ruptures, remove the
cause of dissension, and tranquilize the community."[57] The political
chaos of the Leisler years, the dominies feared, threatened to undermine the advances and legal perquisites the clergy had secured for
themselves and for the Dutch Reformed Church in the previous decade. Surely such insubordination to the established order would
bring stricter controls once English power was reestablished.[58]

IV

Jacob Leisler relentlessly castigated the clergy for their opposition to
the rebellion. "The Dutch Ministers of the Reformed churches within
this Province have not escaped the lash of his inveterate tongue," one
partisan observed. "Nor hath his endeavors been wanting to create
the same disorders and confusion in Church as he hath already done
in Government." The ministers' spirited resistance to Leisler also
incurred the wrath of their congregations, thereby causing deep and
lasting divisions in the churches.[59] Because of their limited number,
formal education, the extended nature of their ecclesiastical jurisdictions and responsibilities, and their social connections with the privileged, Dutch colonial dominies had claimed a higher status than their
communicants. This doubtless compounded the ire felt by the Leislerians when their clergy opposed the rebellion. Instead of enlisting in
the Protestant crusade against papism, the dominies utterly refused to

join the uprising and used their pulpits to rail against the rebellion. Henricus Selyns in New York, the most trenchant critic of the rebellion, "could not find in his heart to pray for their Majesties as was required, till Capt. J. L[eisler] did give him a forme." Albany's Godfridus Dellius, described by Leislerians as "bitterly against the Revolution," also refused to pray for William and Mary. Dellius, however, still prayed for the crown, an action interpreted as fealty to James II, the Catholic, rather than William III, the Protestant. Rudolphus Varick of Long Island "was by armed men drag'd out of his House to the Fort, then imprisoned without bayl, for speaking (as was pretended) Treasonable words against Capt. Leysler and the Fort," while his wife, "constantly threatened with pillage had to fly with everything."[60]

"I have lived under constant hatred and contempt," Varick wrote after the rebellion, "such as I cannot express." As early as 1690, Dominie Godfridus Dellius of Albany complained of the abuse the ministers and leaders of the Dutch church received during the rebellion. A subsequent appeal from thirty-six merchants and ministers to William and Mary alleged ill treatment at the hands of the Leislerians, including the opening of mail, the disruption of trade, and "Scandallizing and abusing our Ministers and Rulers of the Reformed Church here, seizing ye Revenues thereof so that our liberties are taken away, our Religion in great Danger, our Estates ruined." Writing later in the same year, Selyns lamented: "Dominie Varick and myself have suffered more than can be believed and are forced to cultivate patience." He urged the Classis of Amsterdam to intercede for them before the English throne; otherwise, "we have resolved to relinquish everything and return to Holland."[61]

Religion and politics became so intertwined that when Leisler finally surrendered to Henry Sloughter, the new governor, in 1691, consistory members of the New York Dutch church, armed with muskets, joined the procession retaking the fort. In the course of the transition, "a large piece of cannon loaded with musket balls and small shot in being pointed towards the Fort was fired imprudently, killing several people, among whom was an Elder and a Deacon, and deplorably wounding others."[62]

When the anti-Leislerians regained the reins of government under Sloughter, they wasted little time consolidating their power and punishing their foes. "The old Council who always have been our bitter

Enemies are now again set as heads and Rulers over us," Leislerians complained in 1693.[63] Anti-Leislerians assured the new governor that "in our hearts we doe abhorr and detest all the Rebellious arbitrary illegal proceedings of the late Usurpers." Leaders of the rebellion were imprisoned and haled into the court of oyer and terminer, where they faced their erstwhile opponents during the rebellion. When one defendant answered the charges against him in the Dutch tongue, he was commanded to speak English. Protesting that the trial was a mockery, the defendant refused to enter a plea, whereupon, in his words, "the Clerk violently seized me grasping his sword and threatening to stab me: I bared my breast and said he was a coward, that he dared not, that a child's plaything suited him better than a sword." But such posturings constituted a feeble legal defense. Convictions were handed down, and prominent anti-Leislerians, with considerable assistance from the Dutch ministers, persuaded Sloughter to set aside his misgivings and sign the execution warrants for Leisler and Milborne.[64]

The new English government together with the anti-Leislerians sought simultaneously to restore order and punish their adversaries. In 1691, for example, the Legislative Council recommended to the Assembly a "Bill for regulating the Extravagancy of tradesmen and labourers wages that work by the day in this Province." But such measures only aggravated the tensions and fed Leislerian alienation. On September 6, 1692, the Assembly reported to the governor "the people much impoverished by the late disorders and many of them so Debauched in their affeccons to their Matys Government that in lieu of being helpfull they have rather contrived to disturb it." The same message also hinted at some kind of organized protest on the part of Leisler's loyalists and expressed hope that the "malecontents" would "forsake their disobedience and returne unto their dutyes."[65]

But tensions persisted, and the political discontent of the Leisler era quickly found religious expression. In 1690, the Dutch consistory at Kingston had found among them "too many unruly spirits, who are pleased to fish in the presently troubled waters."[66] Several years after the rebellion, one Leislerian characterized an opponent's account of the revolt as "the production of a Monster begat by an Incubus on a Scotch Witch, who had kindled his malice against Truth from the flames he put to the holy Bible."[67] Other, less salacious testimony focused Leislerian discontent specifically on the Dutch dominies, perhaps the most conspicuous of Leisler's adversaries. Whereas Dellius had fled to Boston and Varick had been incarcerated during the rebellion, Selyns had mounted the most spirited and visible resistance to the uprising. Leisler had suspected him of harboring the opposition. After the restoration of English rule and while leaders of the revolt sat in jail, Selyns rather intemperately preached on a text from the Psalms, which read: "I had fainted unless I had believed, to see the goodness of the Lord in the land of the living."[68]

All of these actions did nothing to endear Selyns to Leisler's partisans. Leislerians in his congregation said that Selyns omitted "nothing that he knew could in the least exasperate the people, and flung from the pulpit everything that was suggested to him by the most furious partisans." After the restoration of English rule, the Dutch ministers, Leislerians charged, "exaggerated in the pulpit as well as in their conversation the pretended tyranny of Leisler" and pressured the government to make an example of Leisler and his lieutenants in order to quash forever the popular restiveness that the rebellion had embodied. Leisler's followers chided the dominies for their comportment during and after the rebellion. Instead of urging Leisler to moderation, they had opposed him outright. Selyns even insisted on breaking the news of their condemnation to Leisler and Milborne at suppertime, Leislerians alleged, "although he might well have been aware that such a message would take away all their appetite."[69]

On a rainy Saturday, May 16, 1691, after moving speeches defending the propriety of their actions and their loyalty to William and Mary, the two leaders of the rebellion swung from the gallows, hastily constructed of wood from the fort, and were then beheaded.[70] Those gathered at the execution site sang the seventy-ninth Psalm, a bitter lamentation and an unmistakable rebuke to Jacob Leisler's enemies:

> O God, the heathen are come into thine inheritance; thy holy temple have they defiled; they have laid Jerusalem on heaps.
>
> The dead bodies of thy servants have they given *to be* meat unto the fowls of the heaven, the flesh of thy saints unto the beasts of the earth.
>
> Their blood have they shed like water round about Jerusalem; and *there was* none to bury *them*.
>
> Pour out thy wrath upon the heathen that have not known thee, and upon the kingdoms that have not called upon thy name.

For they have devoured Jacob, and laid waste his dwelling place.

Let the sighing of the prisoner come before thee;
according to the greatness of thy power preserve thou those that are
appointed to die;

And render unto our neighbours sevenfold into their bosom their reproach, wherewith they have reproached thee, O Lord.[71]

Whether from genuine contrition or fear of mob reprisal, the proceedings affected even Dominie Selyns, the Leislerians' implacable
foe, who, according to one account, grudgingly "confessed that they
died as Christians, although he previously in great passion had said
that Leisler was a Devil in the flesh, and never could be saved."
Nevertheless, the clergy's opposition to Leisler and their role in the
executions further exacerbated the divisions in the Dutch church. As
a result of the rebellion and its aftermath, the people "began to feel
more bitter hatred against those who had instigated this murder, and
these latter, by their conduct, intensified this bitter feeling as much
as possible."[72]

All of this took its toll on the colonial Dutch church. "The people
got such an aversion to the public worship, that at first only a tenth
part enjoyed the Lord's Supper," Leislerians wrote in 1698, "and
some have to this day not enjoyed the same."[73] Leislerians unequivo-
cally traced the ecclesiastical infighting of the 1690s to the rebellion.
Shortly after Sloughter's arrival, Dominie Varick of Long Island
reported scarcely a hundred communicants out of a possible five
hundred at a recent administration of Holy Communion; Dominie
Dellius wrote that the Albany church "has diminished daily in the
number of members."[74] Church attendance plummeted. Ministerial
salaries, notoriously difficult to collect in the early years of English
rule, again fell deeply into arrears, as the dominies were subjected
to open ridicule.[75] Their dismal fortunes made it increasingly difficult for the Classis of Amsterdam to recruit ministers for the New
World.[76] In 1691, the Council of New York ordered "the Churchwardens to collect the arrears of the salary detained by his parishioners from Rudolphus Varrick."[77] Quite aware that the rebellion had
changed the attitudes of his congregations toward him, Dominie
Varick, himself imprisoned during the revolt, observed that "love
has been turned into excessive hatred. The cause was the change in
the government here, the common people have called their old authorities traitors, papists, etc."

V

Although the Leislerians stayed away from Dutch Reformed worship in the 1690s in order to protest the actions of their ministers, they nevertheless returned at least once a year during the fall to elect members of the consistory. An analysis of the successive consistories in the New York City church indicates that even though Leislerians felt betrayed at the hands of the merchants and clergy, they were not ready to surrender their identity as Dutch Calvinists.[78] Although Leislerians stayed away from the New York Dutch church in large numbers after Leisler's removal, church membership actually increased.[79] But the acrimonious ecclesiastical disputes attest that whatever characteristics may have marked Dutch religious life in the 1690s, serenity was not among them. The composition of the consistory provides a hint of the partisanship that characterized ecclesiastical life in the 1690s. In the initial years after the rebellion, the consistory elections reflected the dominance of anti-Leislerians in both political and ecclesiastical affairs. As the decade wore on, however, the Leislerians rallied. By 1697, they outnumbered anti-Leislerians in the consistory four to two. The next year, a dispute over the consistory election gave the consistory a three-three split, but in 1699, Leislerians prevailed six to one, and during the next two years no known anti-Leislerian (aside from Selyns, in his capacity as minister) sat on the consistory.[80]

A recrudescence of factional tensions in 1698 reveals the persistence of Leislerian resentment toward Selyns and his allies. Although both sides had agreed to hire an assistant to Selyns, they disagreed over procedure. In November 1698, a determined group of Leislerians, some of whom Selyns had excommunicated, accused him of "unfair and improper proceedings" in his handling of consistory elections and meetings concerning the call of a minister. Although Selyns denied any impropriety, the dispute touched off yet another round of recriminations. "We now see, it is impossible, that we or the congregation shall ever obtain anything from Dominie Selyns for the establishment of peace," they wrote, characterizing Selyns's actions as an "insufferable assumption of authority and tyranny." Eleven anti-Leislerians jumped to the dominie's defense and denied the charges against him.[81]

The increase in church membership in the 1690s, then, had less to do with religious piety—much less church attendance, as contemporary accounts indicate—than with Leislerians padding the membership roles in order to muster their troops for consistory elections and, ultimately, church control. Despite the clergy's antipathy to Leisler and, by their definition, to Dutch ethnicity, Leislerians wanted to maintain their formal religious affiliation. The real ethnic battles after Leisler's Rebellion were played out between Leislerians and anti-Leislerians within the Dutch church, and the rebellion had the effect of politicizing Dutch religion; people formerly indifferent to religion lined up on one side or the other on the church rolls.

Indeed, all the dominies encountered resistance from Leislerians in the 1690s. Licking their wounds after the rebellion, the three ministers—Selyns, Varick, and Dellius—reviewed the sorry state of the Dutch Reformed churches and clergy: "Our ministers have been cast under suspicion through slanders against them; while the populace, ever ready for any change, were advised not to contribute for the support of religious services or for ministers' salaries." With anti-clericalism rampant among the Leislerians, "choristers and school-masters have been encouraged to perform ministerial duties." Those who served on the councils of former English governors, "who were also mostly Elders of the church, have been saluted by the unheard of titles of traitors and papists," and "even the Sanctuary has been attacked by violence and open force." "We ministers," they wrote, "are treated with scorn, and paid in insults, and deprived of what is justly our dues, receiving no salary worth mentioning." Because of their opposition to Leisler and their tacit support for James II, the dominies never escaped suspicions about their sympathy to papists, and the deep wounds of Leisler's Rebellion festered well beyond the 1690s.[82]

VI

The popular veneration of Leisler and Milborne, even after their executions in May 1691, provides one index of the schism in the Dutch community and the residual animosities that marked Dutch ecclesiastical life in the 1690s. In the Kingston Reformed church, devotion to the rebellion prompted one set of Dutch parents to christen their son "Leisler" in 1698.[83] After reviewing the trial and executions, the English Parliament ordered the return of Leisler's and Milborne's property to their families, passed a bill legalizing their rule, and removed the attainder of treason. In 1698, the families, abetted by a good deal of popular support, obtained permission from the magistrates to exhume the bodies, which had lain under the gallows. They then petitioned the New York consistory to reinter the corpses in the Dutch church on Garden Street. Bowing to public pressure, three members of the consistory, all of them anti-Leislerians, declared "that we cannot consent thereto, but also that we shall not hinder it."[84] Though the ceremony took place, Dominie Selyns opposed the move so vigorously that only after his death did the consistory, now composed entirely of Leislerians, resolve that the bodies and a display of their arms should remain in the church.[85]

Contemporary accounts offer only a hint of the emotion attending the reburial of these popular heroes. The bones of Leisler and Milborne were exhumed at midnight, amid the "sound of trumpet and drumms." The bodies then lay in state for "some weeks" before burial in the Dutch church on Sunday, October 20, 1698.[86] Once interred, Leisler's and Milborne's "arms and hatchments of honor" were hung in the church. Anti-Leislerians characterized the funeral as a mob scene: "100 men in armes" led the procession, attended by "1500 men chiefly Dutch, the scum of [New York] and the neighbouring provinces." Another account placed the participants at twelve hundred and noted that the number would have doubled were it not for a "rank storm." Governor Bellomont, who approved the proceedings, reportedly "honored this funeral by being a spectator out of a window whilst the cavalcade marched by."[87]

In a city whose population totaled just over four thousand in 1697, a "great concourse" of fifteen hundred Leislerians, one hundred in arms, could scarcely fail to attract notice, especially when punctuated by the beating of drums, the blare of trumpets, and an occasional blast of thunder.[88] With "great pomp and solemnity," Leislerians paraded through the streets with the bodies of two insurrectionists who had been hanged and then beheaded seven years earlier—and all this took place under the benign gaze of the new governor. The whole scene "struck such a terror into the Merchants" and the "principal inhabitants of the City of New Yorke, that most of them were forced to withdraw and absent themselves for a time for their security."[89] Although the funeral passed without major incident, the Leislerians left an impression with their opponents. The episode demonstrated anew the cleavage within the Dutch community, betraying the intensity of popular veneration for Leisler and the implicit opprobrium directed toward the Dutch clergy and merchants who opposed him and sided with the English.

The inhumation of Leisler and Milborne in the Garden Street church represented a gesture of defiance against Selyns and the anti-Leislerian elite. As Leislerians laid the bodies to rest they symbolically laid their claim to the Dutch legacy in the colony and asserted their conviction that the Dutch Reformed Church should inspire fidelity to Dutch culture and identity rather than capitulation to the English. The Leisler contingent, after all, had been considerably older than the anti-Leislerians—old enough to remember New Netherland or even Holland itself.[90] Unlike the wayward clergy and the affluent merchants and landowners who had, in the Leislerians' view, sold out to the English and the popish James II, the Leislerians saw themselves as people who had stoutly resisted Anglicization and therefore, unlike the clergy, were the true heirs of Dutch religion. In 1698, the Leislerians who had opposed Selyns over the call of a second minister insisted they were the true Dutch, buttressing their claim by pointing to the dominies' cooperation with the English authorities in suppressing the rebellion and punishing Commander Leisler.[91]

VII

The dominies quickly learned that the mercurial changes in the English colonial government rendered it unreliable as an ally. Benjamin Fletcher's openly anti-Leislerian policies as governor (1692–98) eased the clergy's plight somewhat, enough so that, in 1694, Selyns reported to the Classis of Amsterdam an improvement in church attendance as the tensions eased, but even this improvement might have stemmed less from a mitigation of animosities than from Fletcher's coercion. In 1692, the governor had demanded of Dominie Varick a list of the Leislerian deserters from his Long Island churches "in order to frighten them." Varick complied, and Fletcher "spoke severely to certain ones." The immediate result of Fletcher's meddling was a modest increase in church attendance and a slight improvement in his salary payments, but Varick recognized the perils of such a policy. "As to my salary," he wrote, "I have long had authority from the government to enforce execution, but that would only embitter them still more." Furthermore, "although the letters and the threats of the Governor frighten them, they also provoke them."[92]

The arrival of Richard Coote, Earl of Bellomont, as governor in 1698 had created new problems for the clergy and quickened old rivalries. Once in office, the new governor "displaced most of the Council, Sheriffs and Justices of the Peace and put in their places mean, ignorant people, mostly of Leisler's party," according to an anti-Leislerian. Bellomont, a Whig who had openly supported the Leislerians back in England, approved the exhumation of Leisler and Milborne, calling their execution "as violent cruell and arbitrary a proceeding as ever was done upon the lives of men in any age under an English government."[93] Bellomont's sympathy had emboldened the Leislerians and sparked the renewed tensions of 1698 in the New York church.

But the dominies themselves deserved a large portion of the blame for the continued disaffection. In the eyes of their communicants they had aligned themselves on the wrong side of an ethnic Dutch movement, a distinction not lost on the Leislerians, who even many years later remembered the rebellion as pitting "those of a Dutch extraction (who are the most numerous, Loyal and Sober Subjects of that Province) and the few English (who were most averse and backward in the Revolution, but violent and bloody in the Execution of Capt. Leisler, as well as the most dissolute in their Morals)."[94] In the years after the rebellion, the clergy had done little to dispel popular perceptions of their collusion with the English, a league that their congregants found so odious. When Dominie Varick of Long Island died in 1694, Governor Fletcher and members of the Governor's Council attended the funeral.[95] In 1697, Benjamin Bullivant, physician and gentleman, recorded in his diary that he attended the Dutch church in New York City with Fletcher, where they were "mett by the Mayor & Sheriffe with theyr white staffes and so accompanied to Church In which his Excellency hath a stall on purpose, distinct and elevated, with a cloath of State & Cushion before him, on each side are Stalls for the mayor, Sheriff, & Aldermen & principall gentry." The mayor and the sheriff, he added, "have a Carpet of Turkie work before them"; and, not coincidentally, Bullivant also noticed that the Dutch commonfolk in 1697 "seeme not very strict in Keepeing the Sabath."[96]

The long-term career and fortunes of Albany's Dominie Dellius provide the most graphic example of the Dutch clergy's Anglicization. In the 1690s, Dellius accepted a grant of land from Governor Benjamin Fletcher estimated to exceed half a million acres.[97] When Lord Bellomont, Fletcher's successor, challenged the legality of the gift, Dellius fled to England to defend his claim and enlisted members of the Anglican Society for the Propagation of the Gospel in his defense. In 1702, recounting his tenure in New York, he boasted to the Society that, in addition to his work among the Indians near Albany, "I made great advances as well for the English Crowne." Eager "to promote the pious Designe of your venerable Society," Dellius offered himself for Anglican ordination and asked to be appointed to the Dutch church at St. James, recently become Anglican.[98] Dellius never received that appointment, but he nevertheless boasted that "nothing remains, but the Satisfaction of having shown my readiness to serve this Illustrious Society," and he later returned to New York as missionary to the Indians—this time under Anglican auspices.[99]

The dominies' penchant for Anglicization and their preceived tolerance of Catholicism clashed with the militantly Protestant impetus of Leisler's Rebellion.[100] Moreover, stigmatized after the rebellion as part of the insensitive elite, the dominies gradually lost touch with many of their communicants who became disillusioned with traditional religious authorities and turned increasingly toward charismatic, less educated clerical leaders willing to challenge the Dutch clergy. This cleavage between traditional and charismatic religious authority would manifest itself in deep and abiding schisms in the years to come. Old memories die hard, and although on the gallows Jacob Leisler pleaded that discord and dissension "might with our dying sides be buried in oblivion, never more to raise up to the inflammation of future posterity," the Dutch Reformed Church remained scarred for many years by Leisler's Rebellion.[101]

Deluded by several years of outward peace and tranquility, the Dutch ministers had been quite unprepared for the hostilities that erupted when news of England's Glorious Revolution reached New York. In Leisler's Rebellion, the nascent tensions building since the English Conquest finally surfaced, pitting Dutch artisans against the upper echelons of the Dutch community. On this issue, as on earlier salary disputes, the dominies found themselves at loggerheads with the majority of their communicants, pariahs among their own compatriots. Having decided in the early years after the 1664 Conquest to align themselves with English rule, and having found that their interests and aspirations paralleled those of the colony's elite, the clergy became increasingly alienated from their communicants. The dominies' cozy relationships with the English secured both guarantees of religious liberty for their church and personal perquisites for themselves, and so it is hardly surprising that they joined the English magistrates and the Dutch elite in decrying Leisler's Rebellion.

Dutch artisans, on the other hand, inspired by Leisler's anti-Catholic rhetoric, cast their lot enthusiastically with the rebellion and, stung by the clergy's apparent betrayal of Dutch interests, unleashed their anger against the dominies. With English rule finally restored and Leisler and Milborne safely dispatched, the Dutch Reformed Church itself became the focus of popular disaffection. Although the clergy's amicable relations with the English magistrates ensured, for a time at least, the institutional well-being of the Dutch Reformed Church, attendance plummeted and ministerial salaries once again fell deeply into arrears.

The dominies, in spite of popular suspicions, doggedly pursued the Dutch church's accommodation to English rule as the surest road to ecclesiastical stability. "I cannot sufficiently praise the kindness of the English and Dutch authorities of this Province," Dominie Varick wrote after the restoration of English rule, "in trying to rescue me from my troubles."[102] But English favor proved protean and unreliable, as Dominie Dellius could attest. The change of governors from Fletcher to Bellomont, who openly sympathized with the Leislerian party, placed the Dutch clergy on the defensive yet again. It was Bellomont who authorized the exhumation of Leisler and Milborne and who created difficulties for Dellius.[103] Late in the 1690s, the Albany minister faced the united opposition of Bellomont and the Leislerians, still angry over the dominie's behavior during the rebellion. They leveled all manner of charges against him (including the allegation that he was an agent of Louis XIV), deprived Dellius of his property in New York, and forced him to leave the colony.[104] A continued reliance on English authority would be precarious, as the dominies quickly learned.

"I find them a divided, contentious, impoverished people," Benjamin Fletcher observed shortly after Leisler's Rebellion. Dominie Selyns, writing to Amsterdam in the fall of 1698, summed up the situation thus: "Because of the political quarrels, it is impossible for us to live in peace; and where there is no political peace, ecclesiastical peace cannot exist."[105]

3

A Most Unhappy Division:
The Ministry Act, Demographic Changes,
and the Rise of Frontier Pietism

In 1697, honoring Cotton Mather's *Magnalia Christi Americana,* Dominie Henricus Selyns of New York wrote a long poem which contained a broadside against everything from Catholicism to Anabaptism and betrayed his intolerance for ecclesiastical schismatics:

> Then in the Old World see how sects uphold
> A war of dogmas in the Christian fold:
> Lo! Rome stands first; Fanaticism next,
> And then Arminius with polemic text;
> Then anabaptist Menno, leading on
> Spinoza, with his law-automaton.
> Who shall of sects the true meridian learn?
> Their longitude and latitude discern?
> We of the Western World cannot succeed
> In conjuring up such difference of creed,
> Or to Uncovenanted grace assign
> So many heretics in things divine.[1]

Selyns had already established himself as an implacable foe of pietism.
When two Labadists visited New York early in the 1680s, he observed
that "in order to lay the groundwork for a schism, they began holding
meetings with closed doors, and to rail out against the church and
consistory, as Sodom and Egypt, and saying they must separate from
the church." Early on, Selyns detected their schismatic tendencies.
"They could not come to the service, or hold communion with us," he
wrote. "Then they absented themselves from the church."[2]

51

Until his death in 1701, Selyns worked vigorously, even somewhat belligerently, to keep the colonial Dutch Reformed Church from splitting into factions and the disaffected party from slipping into pietism. But the demographic and political changes around the turn of the century coupled with the legal advances of Anglicanism and his own resistance to Jacob Leisler rendered his task increasingly difficult, as the fanaticism and sectarianism Selyns so deplored in the Old World began steadily to invade the New World.

I

King William III surely recognized that he owed his throne to an anti-Catholicism that infected not only England but also, as Leisler's Rebellion proved, the colonies across the Atlantic. With the restoration of order in 1691, William had dispatched Henry Sloughter to New York as governor and reinstated the Test Act, which required that all officials fully renounce any allegiance to Catholicism.[3] William also directed that the Assembly be restored, whereupon that body passed a law respecting liberty of conscience that, not unlike the 1683 Charter of Libertyes that James II had vetoed, guaranteed freedom of worship to all orderly persons, save Romanists.[4]

When Benjamin Fletcher arrived the next year to replace the deceased Sloughter, he worked aggressively to introduce the Church of England into the colony. For his opening gambit, Fletcher introduced a resolution that "provision be made for the support and encouragement of an able ministry, and for a strict and due observation of the Lord's Day." The Assembly, however, ignored it and refused also for several sessions to act on the governor's proposed ministry bill. When they finally relented, the truncated bill denied Fletcher the power to induct and suspend ministers as he had wanted. Exasperated, the governor summarily prorogued the Assembly after a testy speech in which he threatened to assume the powers he sought, with or without the Assembly's approbation.[5]

Fletcher's Ministry Act, which finally passed the Assembly in September 1693, provided that "there shall be called, inducted, and established, a good sufficient Protestant Minister, to officiate, and have the care of Souls" in six different ecclesiastical jurisdictions. These ministers' salaries, moreover, would be supplied by local assessments, and the legislation even established the amount of the salary in each of the districts. The bill provided for ten vestrymen and two churchwardens elected by the freeholders of each jurisdiction to oversee the process.[6]

Shortly after the passage of this act, Fletcher wrote to the Lords of Trade: "I have got them to settle a fund for a Ministry in the City of New York and three more Countys which could never be obtained before, being a mixt People and of different Perswasions in Religion."[7] The governor had ample cause for exuberance; he had just pushed through the New York Assembly a bill that, in his judgment, designated the Church of England as the established religion of the colony, even though the only Anglican minister in New York at the time was the chaplain to English troops at the fort. Although the language of the bill admitted of various interpretations, as the ensuing years would illustrate, Fletcher nevertheless had secured legal sanctions for the Church of England. The Ministry Act did not use the nomenclature of parishes and vestries, but the ecclesiastical jurisdictions it created closely resembled those in England. The cost of all this, moreover, would come from the pockets of *all* citizens, regardless of religious affiliation. Benjamin Fletcher had legally—if not effectively—established Anglicanism in New York City and in the surrounding counties.

Enforcement of the Ministry Act, however, met with opposition. The Dutch tried through a series of subterfuges to prevent the measure from taking Fletcher's desired course; in the outlying "parishes" they met with considerable success, so much so that in 1705, the Assembly, noting that "many disuptes Difficulties & Questions have arisen for the preventing and avoiding" the 1693 legislation, passed an additional measure to fortify Anglican claims to the public tax money.[8] Resistance in New York City proved more difficult. When in 1694 New York freeholders elected Anglicans to only three of the twelve seats in the vestry, the majority resolved "that a dissenting minister be called to officiate and have the care of souls for this city."[9] The governor was not amused. He nominated John Miller, Anglican chaplain to the troops, who promptly demanded "by virtue of his license from the Bishop of London, an induction into the living lately established for the maintenance of a Protestant minister in the city of New York."[10] The vestry refused, and the new vestry, elected the following January as mandated in the Ministry Act, contained only one Anglican instead of three. Yet, intimidated by Fletcher's threats, the vestry voted to call Willam Vesey, an Anglican reader on Long Island. Fletcher, however, loath to enforce an unpopular law, backed down for the moment and delayed the call. The vestry then appealed to the Assembly for an interpretation of the Ministry Act, whereupon the Assembly, much to the governor's chagrin, ruled that a dissenting minister could be called.[11]

In the midst of these maneuverings, the Dutch church in New York judged that cooperation with the governor might yield some benefit. The consistory—dominated by such anti-Leislerians as Jan Harberding, Isaac De Forest, and Nicholas Bayard, who had a history of currying favor with the English—resolved on April 18, 1695, "since all appearances are favorable, that endeavors should be used to obtain an Incorporation from his Excellency, Governor Fletcher and the Council, for our Dutch Church." Fletcher relented, and on May 11, 1696, nearly a year before extending similar privileges to Trinity (Episcopal) Church, the king granted a charter to the Dutch Calvinists in New York City.[12] The charter, which effectively exempted them from the English classification *dissenter,* provided full freedom of worship, confirmed church properties, and guaranteed that "noe person in communion of said Reformed Protestant Dutch Church, within our said City of New Yorke, at any time hereafter shall be in any ways molested, punished, disquieted, or called in question" for his religious beliefs.[13] In a letter to the Classis of Amsterdam, Selyns reported the news after first informing the Classis of his "most friendly relations" with two Anglican ministers. "My Consistory and I have for a long time labored, and taken much trouble to secure certain privileges for our Reformed Church here," he said. Their efforts had met with success, and the church now enjoyed certain legal autonomy, a circumstance, Selyns believed, "which promises much advantage to God's church, and quiets the former existing uneasiness." The ministers' tenacious courting of English favor had paid off, and the New York church presented Governor Benjamin Fletcher with a silver plate, valued at "seventy five pounds or eighty pounds," to express its gratitude.[14]

The benefits of a charter to Dutch Calvinism, however, paled next to the advantages of the Ministry Act to the Church of England. Though frustrated in their immediate attempts to effect the bill, the Anglicans of New York City secured land, began a building, and called William Vesey as minister. In their request for a charter the vestry of Trinity Church referred to itself as the "Church of England Established by Law," a phrase that recurs twelve times in the actual charter. More significantly, the money appropriated under the terms of the Ministry Act was assigned to the perpetual use of Trinity Church.[15]

Even though, decades later, a prominent Anglican described Fletcher as "the only Governor that ever seriously apply'd himself to promote the interests of ye Church in this province," Benjamin Fletcher would not remain in the colony to see the fate of his accomplishment, the Ministry Act of 1693; five years elapsed after the founding of Trinity Church before another Anglican church took root in New York.[16] Anglicanism never became the exclusive religion of New York, nor was its privileged legal standing fully appreciated until Lord Cornbury's administration, when non-Anglican churches struggled against the whims of a supercilious governor.

Because "dissenters" successfully delayed its implementation, the immediate significance of the Ministry Act lay not so much in legal establishment but rather in the English interpretation of the measure and in the extent to which it signified Dutch Calvinism's fall from political favor. The English believed quite confidently that the act had established Anglicanism in the colony, witness Fletcher's enthusiastic report to the Lords of Trade and the allusions in Trinity Church's charter. But more important, as a later generation of Dutch clergy squirmed under the interventionist policies of Lord Cornbury, they looked back on the Ministry Act as an index of the extent to which the political standing of the Dutch Reformed Church had declined. Once the established religion of New Netherland, the Dutch Reformed Church now enjoyed a preferred standing and certain legal perquisites under the English, but the Dutch Calvinists, already afflicted with internal dissension, also faced a spirited threat from the Anglicans. Cornbury's use of the Ministry Act in the next decade would finally convince the dominies that they could no longer consort with the English with impunity.

The charter for the Dutch Reformed church of New York, however, provided an illusion of security in the 1690s, an apparent surety against English interference in Dutch religious affairs. But virtually at the same time that Selyns exacted concessions from the English, demographic changes together with the Ministry Act and a change of governors began to erode the Dutch Reformed Church's standing in the colony.

II

The turn of the century saw the Dutch in New York finally fade into a minority. Although emigration from the Netherlands slowed almost to a halt with the English Conquest of 1664, the Dutch had managed through the remainder of the century to maintain their status as the colony's dominant ethnic group. In 1685, fully three-quarters of New York was Dutch, but by 1695, that number had dropped to fifty percent, and by 1703, less than half of the heads of households in New York City were Hollanders.[17]

The Dutch population in the Esopus-Catskill region and in New Jersey, however, increased steadily after Leisler's Rebellion.[18] The natural demographic growth in New York prompted this emigration— farms on Manhattan and Long Island no longer sustained an expanding population. New Jersey, by contrast, offered a veritable cornucopia. "The soyl of this Province is very rich and fruitful," a traveler wrote in 1681. One New Jersey denizen noted the abundance of "all the kinds of the fish and fowl of England" and added that "the land breeds good horses, good sheep and good deer, and swine in abundance, and as large oxen, and cowes as in any parts of England, and the flesh eats much better, especially the pork and venison." For these reasons, he concluded, "It will not now be long before New-Jersey be peopled."[19]

Governor Cornbury, writing to the Board of Trade in 1708, re-hearsed the reasons for the exodus of husbandmen from Long Island. "The first is because King's County is but small and full of people, so as the young people grow up, they are forced to seek land further off, to settle upon," he wrote. "The land in the Eastern Division of New Jersey is good, and not very far from King's County, there is only a bay to crosse: The other reason that induces them to remove into New Jersey is because there they pay no taxes, nor no duties."[20] The availability of land from East Jersey proprietors together with mini-mal governmental interference provided ample inducement for Long Island farmers. As early as 1693, Governor Fletcher, noting the lack of taxation in Connecticut, Pennsylvania, and New Jersey, com-plained to London that "our inhabitants flee thither for ease and leave us almost destitute."[21]

This migratory trend continued for more than two decades. In 1715, an Anglican missionary in Rye recorded the arrival of families from "Long Island, & other places that are full" so "they can have more room."[22] New York City itself faced a housing shortage after the turn of the century. "I have eight in family and know not yet where to fix them," an official wrote to the Board of Trade in 1701; "houses are so scarce and dear, and lodgings worst in this place."[23] Additional de-mands for land in and around New York City coupled with Fletcher's large grants to political favorites in the 1690s had escalated the cost of farmland and made the rich soil of Ulster, Dutchess, Westchester, and Albany counties, East Jersey, and even northeastern Pennsylvania quite attractive to restive Hollanders in Manhattan or on Long Island. The charting of baptisms at the Kingston Dutch church over four decades provides further evidence of Dutch population growth outside Manhattan and Long Island. From the years 1680 to 1689, Dutch baptisms averaged 44.5 a year and in the 1690s, 50.7. From 1700 to 1709, however, and from 1710 to 1719, the yearly number of baptisms jumped to 67.6 and 92.3, respectively.[24] In 1704, an Anglican clergyman noted that in Ulster County, "the greatest number of people are Dutch," and another observed nearly ten years later that in Albany County the Dutch dominated "this part of the province but few English."[25] Writing to the Council of Trade and Plantations in 1700, the earl of Bellomont, Fletcher's successor, observed: "The people are so cramp'd here for want of land, that several families within my own country are removed to the new country (a name they give to Pensylvania and the Jersies)." Bellomont understood the reasons for the migration. "What man will be such a fool to become a base tenant," he asked, "when, for crossing Hudson's River, that man can for a song purchase a good freehold in the Jersies?"[26]

The genealogical information in a Dutch family Bible also illustrates the move westward. On February 28, 1714, Gualtherus Du Bois baptized Geertie Beerman in New York City's Dutch Reformed church; she married Isaac De Reimer, a Leislerian, in New Jersey in 1736, with Theodorus Jacobus Frelinghuysen presiding.[27] Population statistics for New York, as Table 3.1 illustrates, confirm the exodus

TABLE 3.1.   Population in New York Counties, 1698–1723

	1698	1703	%	1712	%	1723	%
New York	4237	4436	4.7	5840	31.7	7248	24.1
Kings	1721	1915	11.3	1925	0.5	2218	15.2
Richmond	654	503	−23.1	1279	154.3	1506	17.7
Orange	200	268	34.0	439	63.8	1244	183.4
Westchester	917	1946	112.2	2803	44.0	4409	57.3
Queens	3366	4392	30.5	N/A	—	7191	63.7
Suffolk	2121	3346	57.8	N/A	—	6241	86.5
Albany	1453	2273	56.4	N/A	—	6501	186.0
Ulster*	1228	1669	35.9	N/A	—	4006	140.0

*Includes Dutchess County.

from New York City and Long Island.[28] Whereas in the period from 1698 to 1703, population in Kings County increased just over 11 percent and New York County only 4.7 percent, both Suffolk and Albany counties increased more than 50 percent, and Westchester 112.2 percent. Census figures for 1703 and 1712 show an increase of only ten people in Kings County, whereas from 1703 to 1723, the populations of Albany, Orange, Ulster, and Dutchess counties grew well over 100 percent.

A number of factors besides the availability and cost of land influenced the Dutch migration. As English and French immigrants arrived in New York late in the seventeenth century, the opportunities for advancement among the Dutch middle and lower classes had narrowed considerably. Within the Dutch community, moreover, wealth became increasingly concentrated in the hands of the elite, who retained their status in the upper levels of New York society.[29] The loamy soil of New Jersey offered an escape from this stratification. At the turn of the century, Philadelphia began to emerge as a formidable port city and thus an alternative trading center for farmers in West Jersey and eastern Pennsylvania. As early as the 1690s, colonists developed ports in New Jersey (Perth Amboy in East Jersey, Burlington in West) to avoid New York customs, a move vigorously opposed by the governors and trading interests in New York. This issue fueled the tensions between New York and New Jersey, and when officials succeeded in limiting New Jersey shipping, smuggling abounded, prompting complaints about captains who "attempted to Runn into private Creeks and harbours where there are noe officers, the better to Cover their Indirect practices."[30] Unrest among the Iroquois League and Queen Anne's War discouraged settlement to the north and west of Albany.[31] An epidemic of yellow fever—or "Mortal Distemper"—decimated New York City's population in 1702, prompting the Common Council to observe that "great Numbers of this Citty have left their usual habitations and Retired into the Country." This epidemic, following on the heels of a smallpox outbreak earlier that spring, further diminished the city's attractiveness, especially to those without large estates who could readily pack up and head west.[32]

But the Dutch exodus from New York doubtless had other roots as well. Leislerian and anti-Leislerian factionalism had tainted both political and ecclesiastical life in the 1690s. Leisler's Rebellion had so divided the people of New York, John Miller wrote in 1695, "that these injuries done by either side to their opposites have made a most unhappy division & breach among them which will hardly of a long time admit of cure."[33] During Leisler's rule, some of New York's wealthier denizens had fled the city and maintained a kind of shadow government loyal to James II. "Many resort to our neighbours in the Jerseys and Pennsylvania," Leisler's Council noted in 1690; "they assert Mr. Penn to be a man of undoubted sincerity, and say that King James's commissions are good to this day." Leisler himself later complained that the "raging spirit of malice obstructs us much in East Jersey."[34]

But Leisler's fall from power reversed this pattern. In 1692, after Leisler's execution, Killian Van Rensselaer testified that because of "the wicked proceedings of the said Slaughter and the misfortune of their imprisoned fellow citizens," New York's Leislerians "fled thence and left the province, retiring elsewhere for their own security." A contemporary noted that "by reason of the disorders in ye said province" after the restoration of English rule, "great numbers of ye Inhabitants did leave the same & withdrew into other parts."[35] Leislerians in the 1690s also complained of corruption and political repression at the hands of Benjamin Fletcher, who, they said, "made a fast friendship with the few Papists, Jacobites, and dissolute English of New York, who had opposed the Rebellion and revenged themselves on Capt. Leisler." Abraham Gouverneur and Jacob Leisler's son took their grievances to Whitehall on September 25, 1696. "Colonel Fletcher hinders free Elections," they charged, "espetially the last, by bringing Soldiers with their Captains disguised and armed, to vote as freeman: And Seamen with clubs to deter the Electors." The Council of New York reported to the Board of Trade in 1701 "the unhappy differences heats & animosities amongst the inhabitants" of the colony, urging that "due methods may be taken for the healing and composition of those animosities."[36]

Factionalism also plagued the churches, as Leislerian discontent extended into the religious sphere. During the early 1690s, the Dutch elite had consolidated their hold over Reformed worship, and Leislerians asserted their ecclesiastical influence only later in the decade. Writing to the New York church late in 1700, the Classis of Amsterdam correctly perceived "that there still remains an evil residue of the difficulties and strifes which previously existed."[37] When the Dutch church masters in New York City considered the Leislerian request to reinter Leisler's and Milbornes' bodies in the church, they reported being "pressed by both parties in the Congregation."[38] Some Leislerians had ceased attending church altogether. In 1695, John Miller observed the "wickedness & irreligion of the inhabitants" and "the great negligence of divine things that is generally found in most people." "If they go to church," he recorded, "'tis but too often out of curiosity & to find out faults in him that preacheth."[39] Since by his own reckoning Dutch Calvinists still outnumbered Anglicans and Huguenots in New York City, Miller's observations tend to confirm a growing popular disaffection with the Dutch Reformed establishment after Leisler's Rebellion.

Not all the lower-class Dutch fled New York, but while some Leislerians remained on Manhattan and Long Island, others headed west.[40] Fleeing the tensions of the post-Leisler era, some Dutch artisans and farmers sought to rebuild their lives on the frontier beyond the ken of anti-Leislerian politics and orthodox Dutch Calvinism.

Fragmentary church records in New Jersey and the difficulty of identifying individual Leislerians in New York beyond male heads of household render the task of documenting this migration virtually impossible, aside from broad demographic statistics and contemporary narratives.[41] The mere volume of documentary testimony, however, leaves little doubt that New Jersey functioned as a safety valve for Leislerian discontent. Writing to the Board of Trade late in 1698, Governor Bellomont recounted the exhumation of Leisler and Milborne and their reinterment in New York's Dutch church. "There was a great concourse of people at the funeral," he wrote. Twelve hundred Leislerians participated, "and would 'tis thought have been as many more, but that it blew a rank storm for two or three days together, that hindered people from coming down or across the rivers."[42] With the funeral conducted on Manhattan, Bellomont doubtless referred to the Hudson and East rivers, indicating that in addition to a residual population of Leislerians in New York and on Long Island, some Leislerians now lived across the Hudson (New Jersey) or would be "coming down" from the upper Hudson Valley. Another account of Leisler's reburial noted that many of those in attendance—about "1500 men chiefly Dutch"—came from "neighbouring provinces."[43] Colonel Lewis Morris's 1700 report "Concerning the State of Religion in the Jerseys" also corroborates this testimony. New Jersey, he wrote, "was peopl'd mostly from the adjacent colonies of New York and New England, and generally by Those of very narrow fortunes, and such as could not well subsist in the places they left." The people of Bergen, he noted, "are most Dutch, and were settled from New York and the United Provinces," while Passaic "was peopl'd from New York also, they are Dutch mostly and generally Calvinist."[44]

The Dutch population in New Jersey plainly increased at the turn of the century, fed by migrants from New York and Long Island, especially Kings County. During an ecclesiastical controversy along the Raritan in the 1720s, twenty-one of the thirty-two principal disputants (sixty-six percent) either came from Kings County themselves or had immediate family ties back on Long Island.[45] In 1704, four years after his earlier report, Morris commented on the presence of "three or foure Dutch townes in Jersie." In 1730, Jersey Dutch from Freehold and Middletown wrote to Amsterdam requesting a minister. "For more than thirty years now," they said, "divers families have come, from time to time, from New York to take up their abode in this adjoining province of New Jersey." "The country between Trenton and New York is not inhabited by many Englishmen," Peter Kalm noticed in 1750, "but mostly by Germans or Dutch, the latter of which are especially numerous."[46] The migration that began shortly after Leisler's Rebellion continued in earnest after 1700, as many Dutch commonfolk left Manhattan and western Long Island and fanned westward, from Albany and Ulster counties in the north and as far south and west as Pennsylvania.[47]

This region quickly emerged as the nexus of Dutch culture in the New World, as Dutch customs, farming practices, religion, and architecture appeared on the New Jersey and Hudson River landscape.[48] Manhattan and Long Island, however, steadily lost their Dutch character in the eighteenth century. By 1790 (the date of the first federal census), New York City's Dutch population had increased to only five thousand from its two thousand at the beginning of the century; Long Island's stayed at fifteen hundred, showing no increase whatsoever. Estimates of the Dutch presence in New Jersey, on the other hand, range from twenty-four to thirty-five thousand, with the Dutch comprising more than one-fifth of the state's population.[49]

III

With its unsettled and rapidly changing character, New Jersey around the turn of the century bore the markings of a frontier society. In East

Jersey "not a shadow of Government remains," a former governor complained in 1701, "and the King's interest in this state of anarchy by the total neglect of the Plantation Laws considerably suffers." A report prepared for King William the next year described New Jersey as a place of "great disorders" where "no regular government hath ever been established." Anglican John Talbot described New Jersey in 1704 as inhabited "with all sorts of Heathen and Hereticks," and in May of the same year the General Assembly of the colony passed "An Act for Suppressing of Immorality" directed against adultery, disorderly public houses, "Drunkenness, Cursing, Swearing or breaking the Lords Day."[50]

Riven by ethnic clashes and disputes between proprietors and nonproprietors over land titles, New Jersey had fallen into bitter factionalism.[51] In 1709, one settler lamented "all the Rebellions & Disorders that have been in this Province." Lewis Morris complained of a general lawlessness, caused by "persons unable to govern themselves," and Lord Cornbury characterized Jersey residents as "prone enough to throw off all Government."[52] In a speech before the New Jersey General Assembly on November 10, 1703, Cornbury urged his audience to "apply yourselves heartily and seriously to the reconciling of the unhappy differences which have happened in this province."[53]

The movement of settlers into New Jersey around the turn of the century, as Cornbury himself had attested, consisted largely of the younger sons and daughters of New Yorkers, those displaced by growing population and the attendant demands for land—those also without fortune who sought better opportunities and fewer taxes across the Hudson. Writing to the British secretary of state in 1707, Lewis Morris reported that the number of large landholders in New Jersey was "inconsiderable compared with ye whole."[54] In 1706, John Brooke, Anglican missionary in New Jersey, referred to "my Parishioners of Amboy, who are generally poor," a characterization that applied to many colonists and accounted for their resentment toward the wealthier New Yorkers.[55] Occupational pursuits further accentuated intercolonial differences. Unlike the situation of their commercial neighbor to the east, farming lay at the heart of the New Jersey economy. "This Province produces all sorts of Grain or Corn," the Board of Trade observed in 1721; "the Inhabitants likewise breed all sorts of Cattle in great quantities."[56] Contrasts began to emerge between the quiet, bucolic life in New Jersey and New York's urban, more cosmopolitan culture. "You have the advantage of your Native Country, a good Air, great plenty of all things Necessary," wrote a New Yorker to his brother in New Jersey in 1729, outlining the comparative virtues of life in the two colonies. "I dwell in a neat and cleanly City, among very civil People, have a due Freedom, am indifferently well supplyed, gain knowledge in Arithmetick and Bookkeeping, am in a way of attaining the methods of Merchandizing, and correspondence in sundry parts of the world, and many advantages."[57] Thirty years later, these contrasts still obtained. New Jersey "produces vast quantities of grain, besides hemp, flax, hay, Indian corn, and other articles," Andrew Burnaby observed; "they have some trifling manufactures of their own but nothing that deserves mentioning." In New York, "the people carry on an extensive trade, and there are said to be cleared out annually from New York, tons of shipping."[58]

As Table 3.2 shows, population in the frontier settlements of New York and New Jersey increased dramatically early in the eighteenth century, with Dutchess, Orange, and Ulster counties in New York and Somerset, Essex, and Bergen counties in New Jersey seeing the largest growth over the years 1723 to 1737.[59] Although the preponderance of migrants came from New York and Long Island, others,

TABLE 3.2.   Population Increases in New York and New Jersey Counties

	1723/26*	1737	Increase	%
New York, 1723–37				
New York	7248	10664	3416	47.1
Kings	2218	2348	130	5.9
Richmond	1506	1889	383	25.4
Orange	1244	2840	1596	128.3
Westchester	4409	6745	2336	53.0
Queens	7191	9059	1868	26.0
Suffolk	6241	7923	1682	27.0
Albany	6501	10681	4180	64.3
Ulster	2923	4870	1947	66.6
Dutchess	1083	3418	2335	215.6
New Jersey, 1726–1737				
Bergen	2673	4095	1422	53.2
Essex	4230	7019	2789	65.9
Somerset	2271	4505	2234	98.4
Middlesex	4009	4764	755	18.8

*New York figures begin in 1723; New Jersey, 1726.

notably immigrants from the German Palatinate, came directly to the rural areas of the Middle Colonies.[60] The arrival of the Germans underscores another characteristic of frontier society in New York and New Jersey, namely its ethnic diversity. Palatinate Germans joined well-established groups of Dutch, Scots, French, and all stripes of Englishmen. In 1721, the Board of Trade reported to the monarch that "the inhabitants daily increase in great Numbers from New England and Ireland."[61]

Beset by ethnic diversity, antagonism toward the urban center, a rapidly expanding population of younger people, and an agrarian economy, New Jersey and some of the outlying regions in New York took on the character of a frontier society. The Middle Colonies' religious complexion inevitably reflected these social conditions, especially among the Dutch.

IV

After Leisler's Rebellion, the cleavage within the Dutch community had shaken Dutch ecclesiastical structures to their very foundations. The New York clergy believed at one point that Varick and Dellius would be forced out of their posts and that Selyns would have to live on his own means. More ominously, they observed that the churches of "Bergen, Hackensack, Staten Island and Harlem have deserted us, yielding to the power of evil. They say that they can live well enough without ministers or sacraments."[62]

Anticlericalism on the frontier arose in part from religious confusion and from the failure of the churches to establish institutions capable of meeting the religious needs of an expanding population.[63] Less educated preachers such as Guiliam Bertholf stepped into the breach and fashioned their appeal in part by articulating their opposition to orthodox churchmen and the urban elite. With class antagonisms already festering among the Dutch, this message resonated easily with the denizens of New Jersey, but other preachers would fashion similar appeals and enjoy similar success. Conrad Beissel, radical pietist and mystic, collected a following and eventually established a semimonastic community in Ephrata, Pennsylvania. The Dunkers, and, later, the Moravians reaped a harvest among German immigrants who had fallen into religious confusion and disintegration after their arrival in the New World.[64]

In November 1701, Lars Tollstadius arrived in Philadelphia and announced that he was the new pastor of the Swedish Lutheran church in Wicaco. While in Stockholm, Tollstadius had heard of a ministerial vacancy in the New World and had applied for the position, but church officials learned about some unspecified trouble in his past and declared him "unsuitable for the position." Tollstadius came anyway, averring that he had left his credentials in New York. When Andreas Sandel, the accredited minister, arrived, Tollstadius conceded control of the church but then retired across the river to Raccoon, New Jersey, where he gathered disaffected members of the Wicaco congregation and eventually formed a new parish. Tollstadius also itinerated to other Swedish congregations and thereby aroused the ire of the established clergy, who condemned his schismatic tendencies.[65]

Likewise, for the Dutch dominies in New York, the storm gathering west of the Hudson looked troublesome indeed. The Dutch were perhaps the first to feel the effects of this frontier religion shaped by anticlericalism and energized by class antagonisms. Guiliam Bertholf, a farmer and cooper, had come to the New World in 1683 and settled in Bergen.[66] There he made the acquaintance of Dominie Selyns, who secured the young immigrant's appointment as a clerk and lay reader for the small congregation at Harlem. After a brief tenure there, Bertholf purchased a farm and settled in Hackensack, where he assumed the same positions in the fledgling Hackensack and Passaic (Acquackanonck) churches. Bertholf's responsibilities as lay reader included keeping official records, teaching, and conducting religious services in the absence of an ordained minister. Authorized to read the liturgy and a sermon from an approved collection, the lay reader's prerogatives, however, did not include the administration of the sacraments, something reserved to the ordained clergy, who generally visited three or four times a year.

Bertholf quickly endeared himself to the frontier congregations, many of whose members were Leislerians who had fled to New Jersey after 1691 to escape the heavy-handed rule of English magistrates and the Dutch clergy.[67] The Hackensack and Passaic churches soon began to balk at the expense of bringing Dominie Varick from Long Island for sacramental observances when their own lay reader, Bertholf, could do the job just as readily. As early as 1693, Varick recognized trouble across the Hudson, caused by the Leisler tensions. "Formerly I preached twice a year on Staten Island and at Hackensack, and also administered the Lord's Supper, but on account of the difficulties mentioned they do not ask me any more," Varick wrote to Amsterdam; "I hear now, however, from their neighbors, that there is a certain cooper from Sluys, William Bertholf, who is also schoolmaster and precentor there. He is a man well known to me, of courageous but stubborn spirit, a Koelmanist by profession. He has violently urged on the revolting party." Varick had also learned that Bertholf "is about to take ship at the first opportunity, to be ordained by some Classis, perhaps that of Zeeland, or Sluys. If he succeed there will soon more of his kind follow." And to underline the alienation that had taken place in the New York churches and, as Bertholf's success indicated, had extended also into New Jersey, Varick added: "Dominie Selyns is no more loved by the factious party, than I am; but his Reverence has more of the better element in his congregation, than I have."[68]

Varick's charge that Bertholf professed Koelmanist views hearkened back to previous disputes. During earlier difficulties in the New Castle church, both the Classis of Amsterdam and the colonial dominies feared that Jacobus Koelman, whom they regarded as a schismatic, would bring his following and settle in the Delaware Valley. Koelman himself never came to the New World, although others of his persuasion—including now Guiliam Bertholf—began to attract followings outside the traditional bounds of religious authority. Bertholf's appeal lay both in his summons to a life of personal piety and in his antagonism toward the Dutch clergy of New York, all of which represented the ecclesiastical elite that had resisted Jacob Leisler.

Although Bertholf already in effect served the Hackensack and Passaic churches, he still lacked official ordination. Knowing that the New York clergy and the traditionalist Classis of Amsterdam would never pass on his application, he collected letters from members of the Hackensack and Passaic churches and appealed directly to the Classis of Middleburg, an ecclesiastical body more congenial to pietism. Bertholf returned early in 1694 as a fully ordained minister in the Dutch Reformed Church.[69] The petition Bertholf carried with him offers a glimpse into the nature of his congregants in New Jersey. Only fourteen of the fifty-seven signatories appear in New Jersey wills, and, of those, ten identify themselves as yeomen (see Table 3.3). Six wills were proven later than 1746, an indication that these were probably fairly young men in 1694, and with only one exception the testators died no earlier than the 1720s. Twelve of the fifty-seven petitioners, moreover, signed with a mark and may be presumed illiterate.[70] Among this

TABLE 3.3.   Petitioners for Bertholf's Ordination, 1694

	Proved	Notations
Ackerman, Davijd	1724	"a house in N.Y. City"
Bradbury, John	1749	value: £1210
Hall, John	N/A	"yeoman"
Hansen, Folkert	1698	value: £4850
Mead, Peter Jansen	1747	"yeoman"
Pier, Tunis	1749	"yeoman"
Spier, John	1724	"yeoman"
Van Boskerck, Thomas	1748	value: £373
Van Houghem, Cornelius	1722	"yeoman," £154
Van Voorhis, Albert S.	1734	"yeoman"
Van Winckle, Waling J.	1729	"yeoman"
Van Winkle, Simon J.	1733	"yeoman"
Vreeland, Elijas M.	1748	"yeoman," £978
Vrelant, Michiel	1750	"yeoman"

young generation of farmers, many uneducated and most of modest means—the argument from silence here is probably significant; the majority, forty-three of fifty-seven, apparently did not acquire enough wealth to become testators—Bertholf enjoyed great success. He exercised considerable influence on the Dutch frontier, organizing churches in Tappan, Belleville, Tarrytown, and Oakland. Because Bertholf's congregations lay technically outside of their jurisdiction and because of more pressing problems of their own, the New York ministers were virtually powerless to check his advances.

The plight of traditional Dutch religion became all the more precarious with the deaths of Dominies Tesschenmaeker of Schenectady in 1690 (victim of a massacre by the French and the Indians) and Varick of Long Island in 1694.[71] These losses depleted the ranks of the orthodox clergy even further, leaving only Selyns and Dellius to fend off Bertholf and his kind. With the Schenectady and Long Island churches vacant, the pietists stood to make substantial advances. "He will now not neglect anything to carry out his designs," Dellius wrote of Bertholf. "I am informed that certain members of those vacant congregations wish to call him." The anticlerical sentiment among the Leislerians had advanced to such a point, Dellius feared, that other uneducated, unlicensed "prophets" would rise up to assume pastoral functions. "Ministers will be self-created," he wrote, and "soon some marvelous kind of theology will develop here."[72]

Dellius's observations could not have been more prescient. Drawing on latent disaffections building since the English Conquest, Leisler's Rebellion—and clerical opposition to Leisler—had galvanized Dutch farmers and artisans into an opposition force with independent religious leaders and an emphasis on personal piety new to the Middle Colonies. The changes convulsing the Dutch Reformed Church in the 1690s, as Dellius quite accurately predicted, would shape Dutch religion for the next half-century. Already the bifurcation in the church signaled an irreparable parting of ways, and the breach grew in succeeding years as other ministers of Bertholf's persuasion appeared in the New World.

The new pietistic congregations cropping up on the frontier, consisting largely of second-generation immigrants with no direct connection to Holland, disregarded the established ways of the Dutch Reformed Church—especially the Classis of Amsterdam—and evolved their own spirituality and ecclesiastical polity. As the orthodox clergy reserved to themselves the administration of the sacraments, the new congregations eschewed sacramental theology and emphasized instead the importance of piety and godly living. "They say that they can live well enough without ministers or sacraments," the orthodox dominies said of the churches at Bergen, Hackensack, Staten Island, and Harlem.[73] Having by now tempered their Anglicizing tendencies, these traditionalist ministers turned increasingly to the Classis of Amsterdam to help them out of their predicament. Bertholf, however, charged that the Classis consisted of unregenerate men, and he chose to ignore the Amsterdam hierarchy, all the while stressing the power of individual congregations to police themselves. Itinerancy emerged. The orthodox clergy chided Bertholf for his "running around," and Selyns noted that he "moves about and preaches everywhere."[74] Even the procedure for paying ministers reflected divergent approaches to church order. Alienated from the popular will and thus deprived of their salaries, the orthodox dominies sought other means to finance their livings. In 1695, Selyns and his wife (the widow of Cornelius Steenwyck) bequeathed Fordham Manor to the New York church and stipulated that the income be used "for the better support of the ministers," specifically those "called or hereafter to be called and come according to the Church-Order of the Netherlands."[75] Whereas Selyns sought to insulate himself and his successors from the vicissitudes of popular opinion, Bertholf, enjoying popularity with his congregations, needed no such structural security and relied instead on the continued, voluntary support of his congregants.

What constituted the best response to such a turn of events? The orthodox clergy cast about for answers. The beleaguered Selyns at one point conceded to Bertholf the Hackensack and Passaic churches but grew uneasy when the young minister turned his attentions to Bergen, one of the churches in Selyns's bailiwick.[76] For the most part, however, given the trouble in their own congregations, the dominies could mount precious little defense against Bertholf other than to implore the Classis of Amsterdam to send badly needed ministers to the New World.

V

As the dominies sought to shore up their defenses on the frontier, the Dutch Reformed Church in New York faced legal assaults from the Anglicans. The Church of England had made considerable advances in the 1690s, thereby laying the groundwork for future successes. The Ministry Act of 1693, which legally established Anglicanism in the southern counties of the colony, by far eclipsed any advantages of a charter to the Dutch. The measure, furthermore, constituted an overt threat to the Dutch Reformed Church on two fronts: first, by illustrating how dramatically the church had fallen from a privileged position of its own in New Netherland to merely one of several religions tolerated under English rule; second, by placing an added burden of taxation on Dutch communicants, already disinclined to support their own ministers as a result of Leisler's Rebellion. In 1699, the agent for New York had informed the Board of Trade that the English minister's annual salary of one hundred pounds "is levied, the greater part of it, on Dutch and French inhabitants."[77]

Quite apart from the Ministry Act, as the orthodox dominies looked around them in the 1690s, already they could discern palpable changes in the Dutch Reformed Church. By 1700, two distinct strands of Dutch religion had emerged: the traditional, orthodox Dutch Calvinism in the older areas of Dutch settlement, and the pietistic strain taking shape on the frontiers of New Jersey and New York. Guiliam Bertholf, a Koelmanist with ministerial credentials the orthodox dominies regarded as dubious, enjoyed considerable success with the frontier congregations. Whereas at the English Conquest in 1664 the umbrella of orthodox Dutch Calvinism sheltered thirteen congregations, after the Leisler troubles the dominies could count only one church within their

TABLE 3.4.   Dutch Congregations after Leisler's Rebellion

	Situation
	Orthodox
New York	Selyns against the Leislerians
	Pietist
Passaic, N.J.	Bertholf founded in 1694
Hackensack, N.J.	Taken over by Bertholf in 1694
Bergen, N.J.	Disputed by Selyns and Bertholf
Harlem	Under Bertholf's influence from 1691
Staten Island	Supplied by Bertholf from 1694
	Uncertain or Contested
Kingston	Nucella sympathetic to Leislerians
Albany	Leislerian majority opposed Dellius
Schenectady	Leislerian majority opposed Dellius
Brooklyn	Attendance declined after rebellion
Bushwick	Attendance declined after rebellion
Flatbush	Attendance declined after rebellion
Flatlands	Attendance declined after rebellion
New Utrecht	Attendance declined after rebellion
	Others
Stuyvesant's Chapel	Dissolved in 1687
New Castle, Del.	Became Presbyterian

orbit, as Table 3.4 illustrates, and even that congregation was buffeted by persistent factionalism. The defections of the Bergen, Staten Island, and Harlem congregations coupled with Bertholf's organization of the Passaic and Hackensack churches constituted a formidable opposition to traditional Dutch religion in the Middle Colonies.

Dominie Dellius of Albany and Schenectady faced considerable resistance from the Leisler contingent in his churches. When forced by Bellomont to defend himself against charges of malfeasance, Dellius collected "certificates of his piety and good life" from anti-Leislerians in his congregations, but, Bellomont reported, "I am told there are counter certificates signing by the Leisler party with four times the number of hands to 'em."[78] Kingston's loyalty remained in doubt; as the Leislerian and anti-Leislerian consistories feuded over the calling of an assistant for the New York City church in 1698, Kingston's minister, John Nucella, refused to back the Selyns party and allowed himself to be nominated by the Leislerian faction, which enjoyed the support of Governor Bellomont.[79] The clergy, moreover, could no longer be certain about the Long Island churches. Wracked by divisions following the rebellion, dissensions quieted somewhat with the arrival of a new minister in 1695, but the situation remained volatile enough to breed an even larger schism after 1700.

The fates of the New Castle church on the Delaware and Stuyvesant's Chapel on Manhattan provide a symbol of orthodox Calvinism's decline in the Middle Colonies. After Tesschenmaeker's departure from New Castle, Dominie Selyns warned of the changes taking place there and the steady demise of Dutch influence in the region. "A sermon is read on the Sabbath days," he wrote in 1683, "but the people are too few to support a minister." William Penn recently had arrived as governor, and Selyns advised the Classis of Amsterdam not to send a minister "amid the uncertainties of these present waves of enthusiasm." Anglican missionaries later reported that "the Dutch remained unsupplied with a preacher, the said Chapel was neglected, and at length tumbled down." Stuyvesant's Chapel simply closed in 1687, and the building eventually became St. Mark's Episcopal Church.[80]

The demographic changes after 1700 played nicely into the hands of Bertholf, whose summons to godly piety and relative neglect of sacramental observances appealed to erstwhile New Yorkers who had opposed Selyns and the wealthy elite. But, in addition to their own battles with Leisler's loyalists in the 1690s, the New York dominies also faced a continued erosion of their political influence, a loss of power felt most acutely when Edward Hyde, Lord Cornbury, assumed the governorship in 1702.[81] Here political and ecclesiastical matters became hopelessly entangled, as the dominies battled against both a schismatic preacher and a meddlesome governor.

4

Fit for Catechizing:
The Long Island Schism and the Society
for the Propagation of the Gospel

On the night of February 9, 1714, vandals broke into the north stee-
ple window of Trinity (Episcopal) Church, made their way to the
vestry room, and located the surplices used in Anglican worship services. They tore the sleeve off one of the surplices and ripped the
other completely to pieces. They then took the shredded vestment
into the churchyard, where, in the words of Trinity's rector, "having
spread the Surplice on the ground and put the common prayer books
and Psalm books round it left their ordure on the Sacred Vestment as
the greatest outrage and the most Villanous indignity they could offer
the Church of England and Her Holy Priesthood."[1]

The incident scandalized the colony's religious leaders, who publi-
cized their condemnations and offered rewards for the apprehension
of the perpetrators. But the event underscores the resentment fueled
by more than a decade of intense efforts by the English to Anglicize
the colonists in politics, social customs, language, and religion. Their
efforts met with varying degrees of success among the Dutch. The
Leislerian party continued as a political force into the first decade of
the century, until attrition by death and emigration decreased their
power. Well into the eighteenth century some Hollanders rejected
the primogeniture of English inheritance laws in favor of their own
custom, which gave precedence to widows and divided estates more
or less equally among heirs.[2] The virtual collapse of the Dutch school

system, however, did not augur well for the future of the Dutch language in the colony, and the English successfully exploited the divisions that had afflicted Dutch religion since Leisler's Rebellion.

The mounting pressures of Anglicization prompted a curious turnabout on the Dutch religious scene in the first decade of the eighteenth century. Whereas prior to 1700 the dominies had virtually led the movement toward Anglicization—witness their ready surrender and assimilation to the English, their opposition to Leisler, and their seeking of a charter from the English—events at the turn of the century radically altered their course. The actions of Governor Cornbury, the formation of the Society for the Propagation of the Gospel, and the arrival of a schismatic minister from the Netherlands all signaled difficulties for the Dutch Reformed Church and placed the dominies, once again, in a defensive posture.

I

Perhaps the largest disruption of Dutch Calvinism came from within. In 1699, the church at Albany, following the return of Dominie Dellius to the Netherlands, petitioned the Classis of Amsterdam for a replacement. The Holland authorities chose Johannes Lydius, erstwhile minister at Antwerp, but later learned to their astonishment that an Amsterdam merchant, one Willem Bancker, a wealthy man and patron to pietistic clergy, had taken it upon himself to commission Bernardus Freeman, a tailor by trade, for the Albany church. Because the Classis of Amsterdam had already refused Freeman ordination on account of his lack of formal education and his pietistic leanings, Bancker sent him off to the Classis of Lingen, in Westphalia. Complicating the situation further, Amsterdam proceeded to ridicule the young candidate, declaring that "it was impossible for us, with a good conscience," to commission Freeman, "who had only just come down from his cutting board, and who had neither ability for his own craft, much less that demanded of a pastor." Learning of Freeman's ordination, the Classis declared itself "surprised beyond measure that he ever passed his examination as a candidate, since with us he could not even pass an examination for a 'Krankbesoecker' [visitor of the sick]." Freeman tried to circumvent the Classis's jurisdiction further by seeking letters of authority in England, just as Nicholas Van Rensselaer had done.[3]

Though on different vessels, Lydius and Freeman sailed for New

York and toward a confrontation. The Classis wrote to the other colonial churches and entreated them to persuade the congregation at Albany "to receive Rev. Lydius in all love, and to send back Freeman, as having come in illegally, from another quarter, and not through the proper door." Amsterdam warned about the opportunities for mischief "when two pastors come, and possibly each seek his own adherents." Such circumstances, they feared, would invite further English intrusions. "This is just the way to allow all rights to be transfered to the English," they argued, "and to lose forever the council, aid and assistance of the Netherlands Church."[4]

Prior to the arrival of the two men, Dominie Selyns of New York and his assistant, Gualtherus Du Bois, decided to intervene. They thought it imprudent to send Freeman back to Holland, considering the desperate shortage of clergy in New York, so they settled the impasse speedily. Albany affirmed the legality of Lydius's call and installed him as minister; the neighboring church at Schenectady, without a pastor for a number of years, gladly accepted Freeman as their minister. But a vexing problem remained. To whom were Freeman and the Schenectady church accountable? Selyns and Du Bois anticipated this difficulty and asked that the Schenectady consistory affirm their allegiance to the Classis of Amsterdam. Upon learning of Freeman's settling at Schenectady, the Classis of Amsterdam fretted considerably over the arrangement. They offered to bury their differences with Freeman and ratify his appointment, provided he acknowledge their authority over the colonial churches. Stressing the urgency of the situation, the ecclesiastical authorities, writing to another New York minister, observed "that it would be very unprofitable for one of your churches to be outside the body of your communion, and in her church government be drifting toward the Independents."[5] Freeman, however, offered no response to Amsterdam's overtures.

Given his alienation from the Classis of Amsterdam and his predilection to pietism, the newcomer's desire to operate outside the bounds of traditional authority came as little surprise. As Freeman manuevered for a clerical appointment, another New York minister warned him that "such a way of doing things conflicted with all Ecclesiastical Regulations." The same minister later added, "it seems that he cares for nothing, if he can only earn a stiver somewhere by preaching." When Freeman delivered his inaugural sermon at Schenectady, another dominie noted that he "preached his installation sermon, but without regard to Church-Order."[6]

Less than three years later, Freeman became embroiled in a controversy that absorbed much of the church's energies in the ensuing decade. After the death of their minister, the congregations of Kings County, Long Island (Brooklyn, Flatbush, Flatlands, Bushwick, and New Utrecht), informed Governor Cornbury of their intention to petition the Classis of Amsterdam for a replacement. This procedure, perfunctory in previous administrations, received Cornbury's approval. Meanwhile, however, Dominie Freeman, "by earnest solicitations and intrigues had stirred up many in our congregations to call him" as minister of the five churches.[7] The idea of hiring Freeman gained momentum, and the congregations asked Cornbury for permission to hire him away from Schenectady. The governor refused on the grounds that Freeman "has misbehaved himself by promoting and Encouraging the unhappy divisions among the people of this province." Freeman nevertheless received a formal offer from Long Island on May 4, 1703. Although inclined to accept, he objected to one provision of the call and sought a change so that "he should not be bound to the Classis of Amsterdam." The Long Island consistories rejected this change as unpalatable; thus, Freeman remained at Schenectady, and the churches proceeded with their request that Amsterdam fill the vacancy.[8]

Because his intended wife, a resident of Long Island, refused to join him in Schenectady, Freeman visited Kings County some months later and persuaded the congregation at New Utrecht to offer him their pulpit on his terms, absent the pledge of loyalty to Amsterdam. When petitioned a second time, Cornbury reversed his previous decision, authorizing Freeman "to have & Exercise the free Liberty and use of your Religion" for "So Long Time as to me shall Seem meet."[9] With some misgivings and amid threats that Freeman might otherwise take his case to Guiliam Bertholf in New Jersey, Dominie Du Bois, now the senior minister in New York City, installed Freeman at New Utrecht with the clear understanding that he served the New Utrecht congregation alone and not the other Long Island churches. "According to his letter of call he was obliged, as minister of New Utrecht, to preach to that congregation twice every Sunday," the Long Island consistory wrote, "and no other congregation was mentioned." Furthermore, Du Bois agreed to the installation only after "Rev. Freeman had promised me again and again that he would certainly join himself to the Rev. Classis of Amsterdam."[10]

The Classis, in the meantime, unaware of New Utrecht's action, had commissioned Vincentius Antonides as minister to the Kings County congregations and had simultaneously appointed Henricus Beys to

Kingston. When Antonides arrived in Janaury 1706, Governor Cornbury denied him the legal authority to assume his Long Island
churches, claiming that a Dutch minister, Freeman, already preached
there. In addition, Freeman replaced the consistories in these churches
with members sympathetic to him. To provide the imprimatur of ecclesiastical legality, Freeman claimed to be acting according to the original call issued in 1703 from the five Long Island churches and not
merely to the subsequent 1705 call from New Utrecht alone. These
manuevers forced Antonides to minister to his congregations (those
not partisan to Freeman) outside the church dwellings and without the
benefit of a civil license. On the other hand, churchmen reported that
Freeman, like Nicholas Van Rensselaer three decades earlier, "boldly
relies upon his license, and boasts that he is the only legal minister,
being under the authority of Lord Corenbury." Writing to the governor, Freeman's consistory acknowledged that "Mr Freeman is Minister by Lisence from your Excellency."[11]

Freeman, however, owed his post to another circumstance that
indicates a great deal about the changing ecclesiastical climate of the
colony. Surely he needed Cornbury's sanction to complete his takeover on Long Island, but he also needed popular approbation. When
the duly elected consistory at Flatlands resisted popular pressure to
hire Freeman, his partisans formed their own consistory. A decade
later, they defended their action by arguing that the former consistory
had "set themselves in opposition to the people." The original consistory, they charged, "arbitrarily opposed the congregation, and refused to satisfy the desires of the people." In response, the Freeman
faction ceased to "regard them any longer as their officers." This
represented an important shift in the understanding of Reformed
polity. Just as Leislerians had politicized the New York church, Freeman's followers sought to transform the consistory, ideally comprised
of spiritual elders responsible for the religious well-being of the congregation, into a mere instrument of popular will. Indeed, in later
petitions to the governor, Freeman's consistories claimed to repre-
sent "the Major parte of the Freeholders of the Dutch congregations
in Kings County."[12]

Fragmentary records and the lack of uniform data make compari-
sons between the two factions difficult (see Table 4.1). For both sides,
the average age of those who signed the various petitions and documents was approximately thirty-seven years in 1700. Freeman mus-
tered the core of his following from Flatbush and New Utrecht; Antonides drew a bit better from Flatlands and Brooklyn, the oldest

TABLE 4.1   Freeman and Antonides Factions on Long Island

	Town	Age	Remarks
Freeman Party			
Fardon, Jacob	Utrecht		migrated to New Jersey
Hansen, John H.	Flatlands		0 slaves in 1698
Lott, Engelbardt*	Flatbush	46	5 slaves in 1698
Polhemus, Daniel*	Flatbush		Leislerian
Polhemus, Theodorus*	Flatbush		£79, no land in 1683
Remsen, Daniel*	Flatbush	35	1 slave in 1698
Sebring, Cornelius	Brooklyn		£98, 17 acres in 1683
Snedeker, Christian	Flatbush		
Snedeker, Jan	Flatbush		identified as yeoman
Van Brunt, Cornelius*	Utrecht		1693: 75 acres; 1706: 144
Vandewater, Benjamin*	Brooklyn	31	named son "Bernhardus"
Antonides Party			
Aertsen, Reynier*	Flatbush		£166, 40 acres in 1683
Amerman, Jan	Flatlands	26	sizable estate at death
Bennit, Jan	Flatbush	38	2 slaves in 1698
Bogert, Gysbert*	Brooklyn	32	1 slave in 1698
Cornel, Cornelius*	Flatbush	19	migrated to Pennsylvania
Cornel, Guiliam	Flatbush	21	migrated to Pennsylvania
Cornel, Johannes	Flatbush		identified as yeoman
Couwenhoven, Gerrit	Brooklyn		houses & lands in Bushwick
Couwenhoven, William*	Flatlands		migrated to Monmouth Co.
Dorland, John	Brooklyn		£123, 10 acres in 1683
Filkin, Henry*	Flatbush		0 slaves in 1698
Hansen, Joris*	Brooklyn	51	£110, 6 acres in 1683
Hansen, Michael*	Brooklyn	54	£148, 10 acres in 1683
Hegeman, Abraham	Flatbush		1 slave in 1738
Hegeman, Adrian	Brooklyn	20	
Hegeman, Benjamin*	Flatbush		0 slaves in 1698
Hegeman, Hanse	Brooklyn		
Hegeman, Isaac*	Flatbush		
Hegeman, Joseph*	Flatbush	33	Anti-Leislerian
Hooghlandt, Hermanus	Flatlands		1 slave in 1738
Mynderse, Frederick	Brooklyn		
Nevius, Pieter	Flatlands	37	£2, no land in 1698
Rapale, Daniel	Brooklyn	50	£158, 12 acres in 1683
Rapale, Jan	Brooklyn	27	owned several farms
Remsen, Isaac	Brooklyn	27	considerable landholdings
Remsen, Jeronimus*	Brooklyn	36	moved to New York City
Schenck, Martin*	Flatlands	39	2 slaves in 1698
Simpson, Alexander	Flatlands		0 slaves in 1698

	Town	Age	Remarks
Stevens, Luycas*	Flatlands	50	4 slaves in 1698
Stoothoff, Gerritt*	Flatlands		Anti-Leislerian
Strycker, Pieter*	Flatbush	47	£156, 50 acres in 1683
Terhune, Jan Albert	Flatlands		militia lieutenant, 1691
Van Arsdalen, Cornelius	Brooklyn		
Van Duyn, Cornelis*	Brooklyn	36	left estate over £485
Van Dyck, Nicholas	Brooklyn		1 slave in 1698
Van Torickses, Cornelius	Brooklyn		
Williams, Cornelius	Flatbush		2 slaves in 1698
Wyckoff, Cornelius	Flatbush		bought land in New Jersey

*Indicates magistrate.

Dutch settlement on Long Island. Both enjoyed the support of several magistrates. Any distinction between the two factions, however slight, lies in the value of their estates (although, once again, the small sampling and the absence of consistent records qualifies any conclusions). Freeman tended to attract fewer men of substance and more of the middling sort; Antonides likewise numbered several of modest means among his followers, but people such as Daniel Rapale, Jan Amerman, Reynier Aertsen, and Cornelis Van Duyn also gravitated to him.[13]

Whatever their fortunes, neither side demonstrated much restraint or decorum. Schisms opened in the Long Island churches. Antonides and Freeman exchanged recriminations. As late as 1711, the Governor's Council heard reports that "many violent proceedings are taken to the Great Disturbance of the Publick peace." Rival consistories each laid claim to legality—Freeman's consistories on the authority of the English governor and Antonides's on the authority of the Classis of Amsterdam. The dispute consumed the energies of the entire colonial Dutch clergy, who, writing to the Netherlands, lamented "how sadly the Long Island Church is despoiled, and how miserable is its condition, continuing, as it does, thus deplorably rent in twain."[14]

II

In the course of their second meeting back in England, the founders of the Society for the Propagation of the Gospel in Foreign Parts resolved that the mission's seal should depict "a ship under sail, making towards a point of Land, upon the Prow standing a Minister with an open Bible in his hand, People standing on the shore in a Posture of Expectation."[15] The formation of the Society with the stroke of William III's pen on June 16, 1701, may have excited the imaginations of London's Anglicans, but it portended a formidable threat to the Dutch Reformed Church in colonial New York. With this action the Church of England embarked on an ambitious missionary program in the New World.

Aided by the legal establishment of Anglicanism in 1693, the Society made significant advances in New York in the first decade of its existence. To satisfy growing demands, Anglicans began printing Books of Common Prayer in New York City as early as 1705.[16] By 1712, an Anglican missionary reported to London that "the number of my hearers & Communicants increase not a little." Commenting on the religious complexion of New York in 1704, a visitor from Boston exaggerated somewhat when she observed that "they are Generally of the Church of England," but she correctly detected the growing presence of Anglicans. In 1709, the French congregation at New Rochelle by vote of the "chief & principal Inhabitants" conformed to the Church of England, and the Society's missionaries expressed hopes that the church in New York City might soon follow. The Society also made substantial inroads into German congregations.[17] Cotton Mather conceded that the Anglicans had been highly effective on Long Island; in 1706, noting the Society's bold efforts there, Mather warned that "if such things proceed that noble Society for the Propagation of Religion in America will greatly wound religion & their own reputation which ought to be forever venerable."[18]

The Dutch Reformed churches, already in disarray, likewise fell prey to the Society's advances. When the Dutch church at Harlem found itself without a lay reader at the turn of the century, the Anglicans persuaded many of the Dutch in the neighborhood "into a good opinion of the Church of England." George Muirson of the Society reported a warm reception among the Dutch near Rye and 1708, and the Dutch families in nearby New Rochelle all presented their children for baptism to Church of England ministers. Aeneas Mackenzie on Staten Island wrote in 1705 that "such of the French & Dutch as understand English hear me preach" and that, in spite of some resistance, "the few Dutch prayer books I had with us have gained some of them already to a juster Opinion of our Form of Worship." Like other Anglican missionaries in the colony, Mackenzie believed the younger generation looked even more promising. "The French, some of the Dutch, and what Dissenters we have," he wrote in 1711, "allow their children to be taught the Church Catechism."[19]

Anglican missionaries fluent in Dutch fared even better. At Yonkers, John Bartow boasted "a large congregation of Dutch and English." "If we could have a Schoolmaster," he added, "it would be of great use to Instruct the Dutch children in English reading which I know they would be very glad of."[20] In 1710, Thomas Barclay of Albany County wrote to the Society's secretary in London that he preached regularly to "about sixteen English and about one hundred Dutch families" at Schenectady. "I have this summer got an English school erected amongst them, and in a short time, I hope, their children will be fit for catechising," he reported. "In this village there has been no Dutch ministers these five years and there is no probability of any being settled among them. There is a convenient and well built church which they freely gave me the use of. I have taken pains to show them the agreement of the articles of our church with theirs. I hope in time to bring them not only to be constant hearers, but communicants." At Albany "it hath pleased God to bless my weak endeavors," Barclay wrote, "for a great many Dutch children, who at my first arrival were altogether ignorant of the English tongue, can distinctly say our catechism, and make the responses at prayers." Barclay's report underlined the vulnerability of Dutch congregations without a minister. "At present there is no Dutch minister at Albany, neither is any expected 'till next summer," he continued; "in the meantime some of the Dutch children I have baptized, and married several, and other parts of the service I have performed in the Dutch tongue."[21] Barclay later cited a "daily increase" in the number of his catechumens and said that he lived "in intire friendship with those of the Dutch Congregation." Barclay had only recently received a shipment of books from the Society, including one Dutch psalter, several Dutch Bibles, and sixteen Books of Common Prayer. These, he said, "are already distributed."[22]

The Society also enjoyed considerable success with the divided congregations on Long Island. In 1704, with the churches still without a minister, William Vesey of Trinity Church sometimes supplied the pulpit, where he found "all the English and some of the Dutch well affected to the Church of England."[23] After Antonides's and Freeman's arrivals on Long Island, the schism there provided the Anglicans an opening. "The Church at Jamaica is of late very much strengthened by a violent division which hath for a considerable time been raging among the Dutch," the Society learned in 1712, "and their heats having grown to that degree that there is now no hopes of a reconciliation, many of those people have joined Mr. Poyer's Church [Anglican] which has not only increased the number of the auditors but his Communicants are augmented." The factious churches on Long Island had set the stage for the successful intrusion of the Church of England, and Thomas Poyer himself testified that "the number of my hearers & Communicants increase not a little."[24]

The advances of the Society for the Propagation of the Gospel proved costly to the Dutch. Prayer Books in the Dutch language had begun arriving in New York.[25] Anglicans took over Dutch missions to the Indians; John Frederick Haeger, Anglican missionary to the German Palatines, counted among his proselytes an Indian who spoke Dutch.[26] Admonitions to cooperate and maintain friendly relations conspicuously disappeared from the Classis's correspondence to America during this period. Divided against itself after Leisler's Rebellion and overmatched by an Anglicizing culture, the Dutch Reformed Church could not mount an adequate defense, and the shortage of ministers, a chronic problem in colonial New York, compounded the predicament.[27] On the other side, the Society enjoyed certain indisputable advantages, among them support from the crown, popular disillusionment with the dominies, and a colonial government sympathetic with its goals. The Society was well financed, a striking contrast to the penurious Classis of Amsterdam, which demanded reimbursements from colonial churches for the expenses incurred in finding and examining ministerial candidates. A Netherlands subsidy for fledgling churches was unthinkable. In all, colonial Dutch religion suffered mightily at the hands of the Society.

III

Although piqued at Freeman's effrontery in imposing himself on the Long Island churches, the Dutch clergy directed a good share of their anger toward the eccentric governor, Edward Hyde, Lord Cornbury. Believing that he bore a physical resemblance to his cousin, Queen Anne, and wishing to emphasize the likeness, Cornbury frequently dressed in female attire and paraded thus on the ramparts of the fort and through the streets of New York.[28] The governor, a notorious spendthrift described by one contemporary as a "peculiar but detestable magot," habitually spent his evening hours "at the bottle."[29] Cornbury's buffoonery and the risibility of his behavior, however, has tended to belie his political acumen. Throughout much of his tenure in New York, he proved himself quite skilled and unrelenting in accomplishing his political goals—and prominent among them was the advancement of the Church of England throughout the colony. As Edmund Andros had done in the Van Rensselaer affair during the 1670s, Cornbury used the full weight of his office together with an Erastian understanding of church and state to promote Anglicanism. Missionaries of the Society considered magisterial sanction and cooperation essential to the success of their enterprise. John Talbot wrote that his colleague in Rhode Island "does as well as he can there, but how can the Gospel be propagated, where no Christian is in Office in the Government?" Talbot gratefully referred to Queen Anne as "having promised to be always ready to do her part towards the carrying on so good a Work, which cannot be carryed on without a good Governour in Church and State."[30] Writing in 1705, another missionary praised Cornbury in particular and referred to government in general as "our great Asylum and Bulwark."[31]

For his part, more than any previous governor, Cornbury took an activist role in promoting Anglicanism with every means at his disposal. In 1707, he promised the Society "that nothing shall be wanting on my part to promote [the Society's] good and pious designs, to the utmost of my power and understanding"; on a number of occasions Cornbury himself appealed to the Society in London for more Anglican missionaries. But at the same time, Cornbury made it clear that he—not the Church—held ultimate authority in ecclesiastical matters. Cornbury chastened two Anglican missionaries (and the Society itself) for transferring posts without his approval. "Now if the ministers which the Honorable Society think fit to send over and maintain here, are to be Independent of the Government, under no controle, but at Liberty to do what they please, to go where they please, and to leave their Churches as they please," he wrote, "it is but reasonable that those who have the Honour to serve the Queen as Governors of the Provinces, ought to have it signifyed to them, that they may not intermeddle with them." Accordingly, the governor imprisoned one of the offenders in the fort.[32]

Cornbury's meddling in Dutch ecclesiastical affairs, then, fit quite decidedly into a larger pattern of Anglicization in colonial New York. Building on Benjamin Fletcher's Ministry Act of 1693, New York's Anglicans, at Cornbury's direction, launched a series of legal and tactical initiatives intended to bolster the Church of England in the colony. In 1703, the Assembly raised the taxes of all inhabitants for the support of New York City's Anglican minister. The 1693 Ministry Act had provided an annual salary of one hundred pounds, public money, for the rector's salary. The "Act for the Better Establishment of the maintenance [*sic*] for the Minister of the City of New York," passed June 19, 1703, mandated that taxes from all citizens "be Assessed, Levyed, collected and paid, for the Maintenance of the said Mr. William Vesey, Rector of the said Church, the Sum of One hundred and Sixty pounds."[33] Another measure, passed a year later, granted "Sundry Privileges and Powers" to Trinity Church, including "the patronage and advowson of the said church, and right of presentation after the death of the present Incumbent."[34]

Anglican contemporaries praised Cornbury as the source of these benefactions. "His Excellency my Lord Cornbury is a true nursing father to our infancy here," wrote two Anglican ministers in 1705. "His countenance & protection never wanting to us & next to heaven we may attribute the success of our endeavors to the favorable influence of his Government where inclination as a true son of the Church moves him zealously to support that interest."[35] William Urquhart wrote from Long Island: "We are very much oblig'd to my Lord Cornbury, who supports us all as far as lyes in his Power."[36] In October 1704, only twenty-nine months into Cornbury's administration, William Vesey, rector of Trinity Church, catalogued the governor's efforts in behalf of the Church of England. He listed the augmentation of his own salary, Trinity Church's "Sundry Privileges," and noted Cornbury's "resolve to use his interest to introduce a French Minister that shall have Episcopal ordination" at the Huguenot church. On Long Island, Vesey recalled, Cornbury had evicted two dissenting ministers and replaced them with Anglican incumbents.[37] Early in 1708, Robert Quary, who had just completed a tour of Anglican missions throughout the colonies, wrote to London that the New York City church "is the very best in all America," with the minister "well provided for by law in all respects." Crediting this success to Cornbury, Quary reported that the Anglicans in New York "are all well settled and provided for, by his Excellencys favour and kindness."[38]

Cornbury's assistance proved invaluable to the Anglicans. He fended off challenges to Benjamin Fletcher's Ministry Act and in 1706 obtained an Act of Assembly guaranteeing an Anglican's salary in Westchester.[39] He had a church erected at Jamaica "by a Publick Levy and Tax upon the Inhabitants."[40] In both New Jersey and Long Island, Cornbury licensed Anglican George Keith to speak in Quaker meetings and provided enforcement by justices of the peace.[41] On Long Island, Cornbury removed two Presbyterian ministers from their churches, and the ensuing episode illustrates the disruption of magisterial interference. Late in 1707, William Hubbard, one of the displaced Presbyterians, returned from Boston and sought to reclaim his congregation. On a Sunday morning, as John Bartow of the Society approached the meetinghouse, he found Hubbard already conducting services there. Bartow "went into the Church and walked straightway to the pew, expecting Mr. Hobbart wou'd desist, being he knew I had orders from the Governor to officiate there; but he persisted and I forebore to make any Interruption." Bartow, the Anglican, turned the tables for the afternoon meeting, beginning his service earlier than usual, whereupon Hubbard, after coming to the meetinghouse door, proceeded to organize his assembly in an adjacent orchard. He then "sent in some to give word that Mr. Hobbart wou'd preach under a tree." Bartow lost about half of his congregation, who carried their chairs with them. After the service, Bartow recorded, "we Lockt the Church Door and Committed ye Key into the hands of the Sheriff." The dissenters demanded the key to their meetinghouse and, when refused, broke a window, hoisted a boy into the building to open the door, and made off with the pew cushions. Bartow promptly sought recourse with Cornbury, who "summoned Mr. Hobbart, and the head of the faction before him, and forbad Mr. Hobbart evermore to preach in that Church for in regard it was built by a Publick Tax it did appertain to the establish'd Church."[42]

Cornbury's disruption of the Long Island Dutch churches, then, should be viewed against the background of the Society's strategy for Anglicizing the Dutch. The governor doubtless believed that his placement of a schismatic among them would weaken Dutch resistance to the Church of England. Freeman himself contended that "the Lord Governor ordered me, under threats of punishment, to go to Long Island."[43] But Cornbury's forcing of Bernardus Freeman onto the Long Island Dutch churches—surely the most subtle and cunning of his ecclesiastical meddlings—was not his first attempt to disrupt Dutch religious affairs. In 1704, he had appointed an Anglican, Samuel

Eburne, to the Kingston Dutch church, where he enjoyed considerable success, requesting, at one point, six dozen Common Prayer books in Dutch.[44] Dominic Du Bois, Selyns's successor in New York City, noting the differences between Cornbury and previous governors, remembered that "the churches of this province, if any of them were in need of a minister, and one was to be invited from Holland through the Classis, have usually simply given notice thereof previously to the Hon. Governor, but in no other sense than as a compliment and a token of politeness." At times, he continued, "they have even invited a minister without giving any notice thereof whatever to the Governor." Cornbury, however, sought to enforce a formal civil licensure upon all incoming ministers and even insisted that Dutch schoolmasters apply for a gubernatorial permit.[45]

At this the clergy grew indignant. They had grown restive under the caprices of a governor whose sympathies lay with the Church of England. The dominies and consistories urged Amsterdam to seek redress directly with Whitehall. When, on pain of banishment, Cornbury tried to force Dominie Beys to procure a license before assuming his church at Kingston, Beys, with the full support of his consistory, "thought that it was neither expedient nor advisable, in view of the privileges, laws and ancient customs of the Church, ever to accept of the license in the form in which it was drawn up." Beys refused to acknowledge Cornbury's authority in ecclesiastical matters, "lest hereafter, all Dutch preachers and churches should continually be subjected to the arbitrary will and caprice of his Excellency." His resolve to resist the governor soon spread to the other Dutch ministers, who agreed that "the acceptance of his license creates a dependence on his arbitrary will, and is directly contrary to the ancient customs of the Dutch Reformed Church, and the Acts of Parliament passed in the time of King William." Throughout, Beys insisted on the legality of his appointment on the authority of his commission from the Classis of Amsterdam.[46]

IV

The Society's efforts in the colony represented something greater than mere religious proselytization. The Church of England's subordination to the state in New York dictated that Anglicanization serve as an instrument of social control and political assimilation, especially among the Dutch, because the English, remembering Leisler's Rebellion and the Reconquest of 1673, still harbored misgivings about Dutch loyalties. "Our chiefest unhappyness here is too great a mixture of nations," Charles Lodwyck had written to London at the conclusion of the Leisler troubles, "and English ye least part," Many anti-Leislerians regarded the Rebellion as a *"Dutch Plott,"* noting the numerical predominance of the Dutch in New York and warning that they "threaten our ruine if ever the Government come into their hands again."[47] Although the English had controlled the colony since 1664, except for the brief Dutch Reconquest in 1673–74, they had yet to translate political gains into a strong cultural presence. In 1699, noting their abysmal failure to consolidate their hold on the colony, the churchwardens and vestry of Trinity Church observed that "though the English grew numerous, the government in their hands and the national laws took place, yet for want of a Temple for the public Worship according to the English Church, this seemed rather like a Foreign Province held by the terrour of a Garrison, than an English Colony, possessed and settled by people of our own Nation."[48]

By the turn of the century, Englishmen on both sides of the Atlantic felt it was time to address the problem of ethnic pluralism—and religion, they believed, could provide the vehicle. A letter from the Lord Bishop of London to the Society illustrates this clearly. Appealing for additional missionaries for New York, the prelate remarked that "the Dutch are generally inclined to come into our Communion, if they had any body to instruct them." This, he said "cou'd make much for the Security and peace of that Colony: because the Dutch are so numerous there that upon every Commotion they are apt to run into the worst side; as hath appear'd already by experience."[49] Englishmen in the colony echoed this view. In 1705, Thoroughgood Moore urged that the "Society may use their Interest towards making ye Dutch here better Subjects than they are." This could be accomplished, Moore believed, by outlawing Dutch schools and by prohibiting additional Dutch ministers from coming to the colony. Governor Cornbury, he added, had indicated privately that "if the Queen would only give him Leave he would never suffer another Dutch minister to come over."[50]

Cornbury himself shared the view that Anglicanization would foster Anglicization. Explaining to the Society his appointment of the Anglican Samuel Eburne to the Kingston Dutch church, he wrote: "Now I am of Opinion that if as ye Dutch Ministers dye, those Churches were supply'd with English ministers that would with schools be a means to make this Colony an English Colony, which I am afraid will not easily be done without it."[51] Cornbury requested a minister for Albany County on the same grounds. "This will be a means to make the growing Generation English men," he explained, "which they will not be without it."[52] Anglicans in the colony frequently linked phrases such as "the establishment of religion" and "good order" in the same breath, and Lewis Morris, arguing for additional missionaries, wrote that "the bringing over the Dutch will be of great use in this part of America, where their Numbers are so considerable."[53]

The Society's mission in New York, then, extended well beyond Anglicanizing those not in the Church of England's communion; the Society sought instead the complete Anglicization of the the colony in order to ensure political quiescence and to secure England's territorial hegemony. "I have ever been zealous for our Constitution in Church and State," one of the Society's more successful missionaries wrote in 1713, "and have taught my Hearers to be Obedient to Govornours, by my Example as well as Doctrine."[54]

The Society's strategy for subjugating the Dutch was simultaneously simple and cunning, and its success depended on the interaction of various factors. First, Anglican missionaries flooded the colony. More than sixty labored in New York at various times between the Society's founding in 1701 and the American Revolution; one missionary's sole responsibility, for example, was catechizing the colony's slaves.[55] The second strategy, acutely obvious to the Dutch, especially during Cornbury's tenure, involved the untrammeled exercise of political power in the interests of the Church of England. The Society's third tactic, Anglicization through the establishment of English schools in the colony, ensured the long-term success of Anglicanism in New York.[56]

This strategy fell into place shortly after Cornbury's arrival in the spring of 1702. On November 27, 1702, the General Assembly of New York passed "An Act for Encouragement of A Grammar Free School in the City of New-York," which provided "for the Education and Instruction of Youth and Male Children of Such Parents as are of French and Dutch Extraction, as well as of the English." Like the salary for the rector of Trinity Church, the "Orthodox" schoolmaster's annual stipend of fifty pounds, the bill mandated, "shall be Assessed, Levyed, Collected and paid" by New Yorkers of all confessions.[57] Anglican correspondence to London in the early years of the eighteenth century leaves little doubt about the Society's role in Anglicizing the colony. In 1707, Caleb Heathcote proposed "to have great numbers of Schools created in America, the masters whereof to be solely under the Government and Directors of the Society." These schools, he continued, would provide "the greatest service to the Church and State."[58] Aeneas Mackenzie on Staten Island knew well the importance of English education. With "most of the Inhabitants being Dutch and French," he wrote, "there will be but little Probability of doing much good among them without instructing their youth in ye English Tongue."[59] Thomas Barclay, Anglican missionary at Albany, understood his task as "catechising the youth and especially those of Dutch extraction."[60] The Society was prepared to ignore the older generation in the interests of Anglicizing the younger. "The Training up the Youth in the Doctrine and Worship of the best Churches," Barclay wrote, "I thought the surest way to Establish the Church here, for I found the Growne people ignorant of the English Tongue." Barclay paid the English schoolmaster in Albany out of church funds, and all schoolmasters in the colony reported ultimately to the Society in London.[61]

The curriculum in these English schools was unabashedly confessional. Barclay taught his charges the Church of England liturgy and distributed Prayer Books and Bibles "to the most deserving of the Schollars." "I teach them the use of the Common prayer," a Staten Island schoolmaster reported, "so that they can joyne with the Congregation in the Service"; and the schoolmaster at Westchester assiduously instructed his students "in the Principles of ye Christian Religion according to the Rules of the Church of England."[62]

V

Cornbury's administration marked a turning point in the history of New York's Dutch Reformed Church. Hitherto the Dutch ministers had accommodated themselves to English rule, often at the cost of alienating their own communicants. The dominies, to a man, had opposed Leisler's Rebellion and had insisted on the restoration of English rule, as even earlier they had urged Stuyvesant's surrender to the English in 1664 and had identified their own interests with those of the English magistrates and the colony's elite.

This collusion with the English, paradoxically, coincided with a steady diminution of Dutch ecclesiastical liberties. Despite guarantees of religious freedom in the 1664 Articles of Capitulation and in William III's Act of Toleration, the English regularly intruded into Dutch religious matters. At the duke of York's behest, Edmund Andros had installed an Anglican minister in Albany's Dutch Reformed church. Cornbury did the same at Kingston and succeeded in imposing a schismatic preacher among the Long Island churches.

Despite their erstwhile accommodation to the English government, in the years after 1700 the clergy could no longer abide further encroachments on their religious liberties, and their sudden resolve to resist the English prompted a shift in the colony's religious and political alignment. The same group who sought English guarantees for clerical salaries in the early years of English rule and who, not a decade earlier, had exulted in the procurement of an English charter now openly defied the governor: Antonides preached on Long Island, and Beys assumed the pulpit at Kingston. Cornbury's actions after 1700 forced both men to assume Dominie Selyns's old mantle of defending Dutch ecclesiastical prerogatives—but with one important difference. Selyns had railed against schismatics *within* the church, but political circumstances after 1700 directed the dominies' attention to forces *outside* the church as well.

This shift prompted other realignments. Seeing the success of Anglican schools and fearing that "the churches in the course of time" would decline, the consistories began for the first time to voice concern to the Classis of Amsterdam about the dearth of Dutch schoolmasters in the colony.[63] Their collusions with the English having failed them in the Bellomont-Cornbury years, the Dutch clergy appealed to Amsterdam for sorely needed ballast in the stormy seas they encountered at the turn of the century. The dominies abruptly abandoned their Anglicization and clung to Netherlands ecclesiastical authority and Dutch cultural traditions, such as the maintenance of the Dutch language. Their attitudes toward ecumenicity also reflect this change. When a Lutheran minister preached at Albany in 1684, for example, Dominie Dellius and members of the Dutch congregation had attended many of the services, and Dellius left the colony in 1699 with character references from one English and two Huguenot ministers. But by the 1730s, Lutheran ministers complained that "our opponents, the Calvinists," sought to proselytize Lutheran children, "urging them to become Calvinists, because the Lutherans are no good."[64] Whereas formerly "there existed excellent harmony between the English and the Dutch Churches," the dominies began opposing the Anglicans as best they could. In 1702, George Keith, the Quaker turned Anglican, wrote that "the Dutch Dissenters and all the Quakers, though differing from one another amongst themselves, yet agree in opposing with great zeal and malice, whatever tends to the honour and interest of the Church [of England]."[65]

Dutch ministers and church leaders eagerly expressed their dependence on the Classis of Amsterdam, a departure from their disposition immediately after receiving the charter. The dominies even sought Holland's approval for the "fraternal gathering once a year" of the colony's Dutch ministers, recognizing that an indiscretion on their part or an attempt to usurp the Classis's authority might force them "to hand back our commissions to you, and be compelled to deposit them on your Classical table." Beyond this sudden solicitude, the ministers' pronouncements against Freeman also reflect a change. They made no appeal to English law as their predecessors had done in earlier salary disputes; instead, the dominies deferred to the church order imposed by the various synods in the Netherlands as well as to traditional practice. They rebuked Freeman for preaching on the governor's authority alone.[66]

What prompted this reversal? Surely the change of monarchs in England must be taken into account. Queen Anne, perhaps the most Anglican of all British sovereigns until Victoria, would not likely be moved by Dutch Calvinist complaints about religious repression. When Thomas Poyer encountered difficulties claiming a parsonage and glebe on Long Island, the Society took his case directly to the queen, "lest, if he seek his remedy at law, and a cause of the Church be tried by Dissenters, he would not find justice."[67] With William on the throne, the Dutch churches had reason to believe they had a sympathetic ear in Whitehall and thus felt some assurance that the colonial government would not infringe on Dutch rights for fear of an appeal to England. Closer to home, English rule in the colony took the form of the transvestite Edward Hyde, Lord Cornbury. In his dealings with the Dutch clergy, Cornbury seemed bent on pursuing a course of meddling and provocation—first his appointment of an Anglican to the Dutch church at Kingston, then his vacillation on Freeman's call to Long Island, then his refusal to license Beys and Antonides. Cornbury, after all, had precipitated the schism on Long Island by finally lending his support to Freeman and his followers. His various sorties against Dutch Calvinism served to advance Anglicanism in the colony, and the dominies quickly learned that they could not trust the fortunes of their church to such a man.

In time, even fellow Anglicans came to detect a backlash from Cornbury's shameless officiousness and benighted policies. In 1709, after Cornbury had left office, Lewis Morris worried that the "pernicious effects of his arbitrary conduct" made the former governor the "greatest obstacle that either has or is likely to prevent ye growth of ye church in these parts." Morris described Cornbury as "a notorious breaker of his word" and "abusedly & openly unjust." Moreover, "the scandal of his life is such yt were he in a civilized heathen countrey, he would by the publick Justice to make an example to deter others from his practises." Even "in face of ye Sun & sight of ye town" Cornbury "rarely fails of being drest in womens cloaths every day, & almost half his time is spent that way." The governor showed up for Anglican worship thus attired and even attended his wife's funeral dressed as a woman. His "ill example" constituted "a great hindrance to ye growth of ye church, there being nothing more common in the mouths of ye enemies of our religion than ye instancing my Lord Cornbury as a Church man & one esteemed a great patron of it."[68]

Though less intrusive, English meddling in Dutch ecclesiastical affairs extended beyond Cornbury's administration. The orthodox fared somewhat better under the brief tenure of John, Lord Lovelace (December 1708 to May 1709), but suffered again during Lieutenant-Governor Richard Ingoldesby's one year in charge of the colony. Under Ingoldesby's rule, "the sheriff and his servants" in the fall of 1709 "publicly, and with violence" prevented Antonides and two hundred of his followers from conducting services in Jamaica. This injunction lasted eight months, until the arrival of the new governor, Robert Hunter, the following spring.[69] Hunter's administration, coinciding with the Whig party's rise to political dominance back in England, marked the end of coercive Anglicanization in New York, although various governors still dabbled in matters that the orthodox Dutch preferred to settle independently of English interference. In the 1730s, during an ecclesiastical dispute among the Dutch in New Jersey, those who opposed the Dutch religious establishment in New York benefited from the assistance of the "Governor and other officers of the English government."[70]

But traditional Dutch religion suffered its heaviest losses during Cornbury's administration. Although the rift between the people and the consistories paled next to Leisler's Rebellion, Freeman, who owed his very incumbency on Long Island to the Anglican governor, had siphoned off large numbers of Dutch communicants. His coming to Long Island built on divisions within the Dutch community and prompted rival ministers and rival consistories in each church to make conflicting claims to authority. Freeman clearly enjoyed greater popularity than Antonides; by his own account he preached to "great gatherings, which listen to God's Word with pleasure."[71] Even his detractors described him as a "good preacher." Because of his personal charisma, his defiance of an aloof clergy, and his evangelistic preaching, Freeman caught on with many Dutch communicants. And having earlier been jilted by the Classis of Amsterdam, Freeman understandably felt no allegiance to the hierarchy in Holland; Antonides's partisans wrote that Freeman "takes revenge for the wrong then done to him by the Classis." He "causes the church discipline in many points, to be despised," the consistories charged. "He pretends, that that only is the church discipline, which the congregations and the Consistory deem necessary."[72]

Thus, again early in the eighteenth century, the Dutch Reformed Church was divided, although this time the traditionalist dominies found themselves athwart the English government. Whereas Freeman and his followers were well satisfied with English rule, the orthodox Dutch clergy, on the other hand, resented the intrusions of the magistrates into ecclesiastical affairs. In contrast with their forebears' zealous defense of English authority during the Leisler troubles, the dominies in Cornbury's era found compliance with governmental formalities distasteful and an incipient threat to their religious freedom. The clergy's response to the difficulties yet ahead would be marked by a strong suspicion of English rule.

VI

The Freeman-Antonides affair on Long Island defied amelioration. The Classis of Amsterdam tried to mediate the dispute but found itself handicapped both by distance and by Freeman's refusal to submit to its authority. Through direct appeals to Whitehall, they sought unsuccessfully to restore colonial Dutch religious liberties. Freeman, contumacious as ever, still enjoyed the weight of civil sanction on his side, and the Classis felt keenly its legal impotence.[73]

Having failed repeatedly to settle the issue through ecclesiastical channels, both parties took their case to the English magistrates, so that suits and countersuits, charges and refutations, burdened the colony's courts. Here again the vicissitudes of English rule guided the fortunes of the Dutch church: the Freeman faction consistently received friendly rulings during Cornbury's tenure, while Antonides's partisans fared somewhat better in succeeding administrations.

But this too proved indecisive. In 1709, after forming a special committee to recommend a solution to the impasse, Lieutenant-Governor Richard Ingoldesby ruled that "from this time forward Mr Freeman and Mr Antoinides shall preach at all ye said Churches in Kings County alternately and divide all ye Profitts Equally." Both parties refused to abide the ruling, Antonides's on the ground that it violated "the Rules & Discipline of the Dutch Reformed Protestant Churches," and Freeman's because "the said Dominie Freeman has for sometime past been in full peaceable possession" of all the churches. The significance of this adjudication lies not in the decisions rendered but in the fact that once again an ecclesiastical matter had become so intractable that the disputants appealed to civil authorities. The right of governing the church, once so jealously guarded by the dominies, had again fallen into civil jurisdiction.[74]

After yet another fruitless appeal to the English, the Classis of Amsterdam again stepped in, this time a bit more forcefully. They responded petulantly to a letter from Freeman claiming his rights to Kings County by virtue of his license from Cornbury. "The fact that the Rev. Antonides was obliged to ask permission to preach on Long Island is a matter of a very different nature from your license," they wrote. "You compelled him to do this and thus prepared the way for the loss of liberty to all the churches." Antonides and the Classis steadfastly insisted that Freeman dismiss what they considered the illegally elected consistories and submit to the Classis of Amsterdam.[75] Freeman refused to disband his consistories, agreed only to maintain a correspondence with Amsterdam, and again disputed the legality of Antonides's call on the grounds that it lacked the "sanction of a magistrate." Once again the arguments sound familiar: Freeman appealed to the civil authority in the colony and Antonides to ecclesiastical authority in Amsterdam, and both sides claimed that their efforts at rapprochement had met with resistance."[76]

In 1710, the irenic Governor Hunter, "looking now with a fairer aspect towards a Reconciliation," ordered that Freeman and Antonides "preach to-morrow in the Respective Churches wherein in Course it is their Turn to preach and that no molestation be given to either of them therein." Hunter's directive prompted an uneasy peace between Antonides and Freeman. Both dominies agreed not to preach in the same town on a given Sunday if their rotations happened to conflict. Relations finally thawed on January 1, 1714, with both ministers scheduled at Flatlands. Antonides, who had priority, decided to strike a compromise as a gesture of good faith: instead of preaching both sermons—forenoon and afternoon, as customary—Antonides preached in the morning and then yielded to Freeman for the afternoon sermon. The effect was almost immediate. By midyear, Antonides reported to Amsterdam that "peace and unity, in all our external intercourse have become more real, and this shows itself daily among the people."[77]

Negotiations ensued, and according to the terms of their settlement the twin consistories at Flatlands and Brooklyn voluntarily resigned, and both ministers were, in effect, called anew to serve the churches jointly. "We are now busy going around, to invite the members to return to the Table of the Lord," wrote Freeman and Antonides. "For truly now, there is hope that, under God's blessing, the old love will flourish again in these congregations."[78] Dominie Du Bois of New York also expressed relief that the schism at last was over, noting that these "grievous evils" have "occasioned me, for many years, nothing but great anxiety, and have subjected me to much criticism." He proceeded to speak exuberantly about the accession of the House of Hanover as "the time of these wondrous changes in England" and hoped that it might bring for the Dutch Reformed churches in New York "the preservation of their ancient ecclesiastical freedom." With the settlement of the Long Island controversy and the Cornbury years behind them, an air of optimism prevailed; the Freeman-Antonides letter also included news that the Dutch congregations in New York "very plainly are increasing every day."[79]

VII

The "general satisfaction and joy" in which Dominies Freeman and Antonides exulted following the resolution of their impasse proved transitory. The same letter that carried the news of their reconciliation reported that the Raritan churches in New Jersey "are busy also in calling a minister."[80] Scarcely three years later, the Classis of Amsterdam, with considerable assistance from Willem Bancker, Freeman's patron, commissioned a minister, one Theodorus Jacobus Frelinghuysen, for the Raritan churches. Although he left Holland with the formal approbation of the Classis of Amsterdam, Frelinghuysen arrived in New York in 1720 amid rumors of his insubordination to the Netherlands ecclesiastical authorities.[81] Frelinghuysen's activities in the New World built on the same internal divisions that Freeman had exploited on Long Island. The orthodox clergy and wealthier elements opposed him to little avail, while Freeman, Bertholf, and the less affluent rallied to his cause. Once again the Dutch sought earnestly for peace, this time with less satisfying results.[82]

The years from the English Conquest through Cornbury's administration had plunged the Dutch Reformed Church into confusion and disarray. Divided against itself after Leisler's Rebellion, Dutch religion could mount precious little defense against the incursions of the English. The yoke of English rule became especially burdensome during Cornbury's tenure, as the governor sought unabashedly to impose the Church of England on the colony. His legal manueverings, his demands that the clergy seek his licensure, his encouragement of the Society for the Propagation of the Gospel, and his egregious meddling in Dutch ecclesiastical affairs all met with success. "Our whole ministerial service remains dependent on his Excellency's will and pleasure," the New York consistory wrote to the Classis.[83] Indeed, Cornbury's interference stymied the dominies' efforts to govern their own church; when Freeman took refuge in the governor's civil license, the clergy could do little to dislodge him as long as he retained popular support.

Dutch traditionalists feared that Freeman's maneuverings would leave the Dutch church vulnerable to other schismatics. "What troubles us might soon happen to the other congregations," Long Island churchmen wrote in 1713, perhaps with an eye toward New Jersey; "there is no lack of imitators, who try to intrude themselves in the congregations, to draw a part of the members to their side, and cause divisions thereby, taking no account of any Church Order, or of the Consistory." Cornbury's support for Freeman clearly had dealt a crippling blow to Dutch Reformed polity and left the church powerless to enforce internal discipline. Bernardus Freeman, a Reformed pietist minister, and Lord Cornbury, a high Tory dressed as a woman, formed an unlikely alliance, but the combined effects of their machinations sent the Dutch Reformed Church reeling in the opening decade of the eighteenth century. "We are now forced to acknowledge," the dominies wrote, that "no ecclesiastical sentence pronounced can be executed, because the overshadowing of political authority is necessary thereunto." "Our church will never be free from English politics," Dominie Casparus Van Zuuren had lamented back in 1681. Cornbury made him a prophet.[84]

The successive appellations assigned to the fort on the lower end of Manhattan might serve as a symbol of the political changes the Dutch endured in the first century after their settlement. It was named Fort Amsterdam throughout the New Netherland period, and the English conquerors in 1664 renamed it Fort James, after the duke of York. In the brief interim of Netherlands control from 1673 to 1674, it bore the Dutch designation Fort Willem Hendrick, only to revert to Fort James once the English again secured the colony in 1674. Upon seizing the fortress in 1689, Jacob Leisler shrewdly dubbed it Fort William in order to buttress his claim that he was merely securing the colony for the new English rulers, William and Mary. Signaling a subtler shift in the colony's politics after the turn of the century, Edward Hyde, Lord Cornbury, chose to rename the fort after his cousin, Queen Anne.[85] Rotating with the political winds, the fort, like a weathervane, charted the larger changes in the colony. Small wonder that the Dutch encountered difficulties in adjusting to the vicissitudes of English rule.

The plight of the orthodox ministers illustrates the difficulties facing the Dutch in general as a conquered people, and particularly the Dutch Reformed Church as it acclimated to free-church status. The dominies' response to magisterial fiats from the Conquest through the Cornbury administration required some rather awkward posturing: their jealous defense of ecclesiastical liberties led them to oppose the appointment of an Anglican to Albany but to defend English placemen during the Leisler uprising. They sought a charter from the English but later defied English rule under Cornbury. As the colonial government grew unfriendly after the turn of the century, the Dutch clergy allied itself ever more closely with the Classis of Amsterdam and deferred to its authority in handling the meddlesome Cornbury, the Society for the Propagation of the Gospel, and the Freeman affair.

The dominies may have believed that a retreat to Old World authority was the only avenue open to them. As the schism festered on Long

Island and as political relations with the English soured after 1700, the traditionalist clergy began increasingly to define themselves in contradistinction to their political and ecclesiastical opponents. While Freeman pointedly ignored Dutch Reformed polity in carving out his congregations on Long Island, the dominies reverted to an obeisance to the Classis of Amsterdam and lamented the decline of Dutch schools in the colony. For the next half-century, as the Dutch in New Jersey fell under the pietistic, evangelical influences of Frelinghuysen, the Dutch clergy in New York sought to maintain Batavian traditions and culture, a decided shift from their Anglicizing tendencies before 1700. As Cornbury's rule grew more and more inimical to Dutch religious liberties, the dominies began pining for the Netherlands, as when one minister longed "to enjoy our beloved liberty" back in Holland.[86] In the face of liturgical neglect and disorder in the outlying areas, the urban clergy began to emphasize the importance of historic creeds and sacramental theology. In 1700, Dominie Lydius of Albany published a catechism for those preparing "for admission to the Reformed Church and the Lord's Holy Supper."[87] During the Freeman dispute, Dominie Du Bois of New York City felt "compelled at the present time" to publish his "compendium of 'True Christian Doctrine' based on the Heidelberg Catechism."[88]

As Freeman, Bertholf, and, later, Frelinghuysen began to explore new frontiers of religious expression beyond the bounds of orthodox liturgy, other Dutch ministers took shelter in liturgical forms. These churchmen thereby sought order in the midst of chaos even as they reasserted orthodoxy in the face of pietism. In 1711, the consistory of the New York church resolved unanimously "that a little fence of the best kind be placed around the Communion Table of the Church, by the time of the next administration of the ordinance in order to prevent irregularity in those approaching." A year later, complaining of "the disorder of the Assembly, the dissatisfaction of many, and the grief of the overseers of the congregation," the consistory issued new and stricter rules governing the sale and use of pews in the church building and contrived an elaborate system for the administration of the Lord's Supper, to "preserve suitable order in such a holy service." "In acting thus no unpleasant crowding will disturb our pious thoughts," Du Bois declared, "but these will rather be aided by a seemly approach and an undisturbed departure."[89]

The Cornbury years had exacted a toll. By 1706, Dominie Henricus Beys of Kingston lamented "what a grievous state the Church is in, and how miserable and pitiable is her condition." But the dominies tasted one final, bitter irony in the waning years of Cornbury's administration, a tenure marked by such intense Anglicization. In 1709, they learned that the Church of England had won yet another convert from the Dutch—none other than Henricus Beys, the same minister from Kingston who had so tenaciously held his ground against civil licensure and whose lugubrious assessment had characterized Dutch Calvinism's "miserable and pitiable" state early in the eighteenth century.[90]

5

Flames of Contention:
The Raritan Dispute
and the Spread of Pietism

From 1664 through Cornbury's administration, the Dutch Reformed Church felt every major economic, political, social, and demographic crisis in the colony. The economic deprivation among lower-class Dutch following the English Conquest and the attenuation of the Dutch commercial empire gave rise to a dispute over clerical salaries and prompted the dominies' appeal to English temporal authority. When the duke of York preferred a political favorite to the Dutch church at Albany, he provoked the indignation of the colonial Dutch clergy and, later, Jacob Leisler and Jacob Milborne. England's Glorious Revolution triggered violent reactions among New York's Dutch and caused still larger repercussions for the colonial Reformed Church. Leisler's Rebellion brought to the fore the latent class antagonisms present in the Dutch community since Stuyvesant's surrender to the English, and it polarized the Dutch along social and economic lines. The political infighting between anti-Leislerian and Leislerian parties after 1691 together with rising land prices on Manhattan and Long Island prompted a Dutch migration—fraught with religious overtones—out of the older areas of Dutch settlement and toward the frontier of northern New York and eastern New Jersey. And finally, the Ministry Act, the advances of the Society for the Propagation of the Gospel, and Cornbury's meddling in Dutch ecclesiastical affairs caused an abrupt turnabout in the Dutch clergy's posture toward the English. No longer a benign force, English rule had turned hostile, and the dominies sought refuge from political chaos and popular opprobrium by proclaiming their allegiance to the ecclesiastical authorities in Holland and emphasizing the importance of Dutch cultural traditions and institutions.

With the orthodox Dutch Reformed Church in retreat after 1700, the Anglicans and the pietists divided the spoils. And once again, as with divisions in the church's colonial past, from the controversy over Stuyvesant's surrender to Leisler's Rebellion, the defections from orthodox Dutch Calvinism split generally along social and economic lines: the Anglicans attracted the better sort, and the pietists drew the core of their following from the less prosperous.

Because of the inroads of the Church of England, the ethnically based configuration of religious life in New York City began to skew around the turn of the century. Because of internal disputes, the desire to integrate into the colonial economy, and the lack of clerical leadership, the Huguenot church virtually disappeared. Political and cultural forces Anglicized the Dutch, although the addition of some Huguenot families and the loyalty of Dutch women kept the numbers on the Dutch Reformed rolls fairly constant.[1] Their husbands, however, whose economic survival now depended on their facility in English and their associations in an Anglicized world, deserted the Dutch Reformed Church more readily. Many of the Dutch who remained in New York after 1700 joined the Anglicans, perhaps because the high-church direction the dominies had taken in recent years differed so little from the Church of England that they could see no reason not to Anglicize. This course might have appeared especially attractive if they could simultaneously upgrade their social connections and escape the ecclesiastical tensions of the post-Leisler years.

The real conundrum lies in the overwhelming fidelity of Dutch women to the Dutch Reformed Church, even after their husbands deserted it or they had married English men. In the early decades of the eighteenth century, women comprised about two-thirds of the new members in the Dutch church. To some degree, however, the feminization of Dutch Calvinism had begun decades earlier. In the years following the English Conquest, many Englishmen had married Dutch women, and, with the Church of England not yet a presence in New York, Dutch wives reared their children in the Dutch church. In the list of contributors to the building of a new Dutch church in New York City in 1688, an unusually high number of women, at least 35 out of 294 (12 percent), appear as subscribers; more significantly, another 8 names are followed by the notation "for his wife," an indication that even though the husband did not care to contribute, his wife had prevailed upon him to subscribe to the building. Jacob Leisler himself, elected a deacon in the New York church five times between 1670 and 1681, dropped out of the Dutch church sometime in the 1680s, even though his wife and children appear on the membership rolls as late as 1686.[2]

A feminine loyalty to Dutch culture might also provide an explanation for the women's fidelity to the Reformed church and their insistence on rearing children in the church. The Netherlands was, by some accounts, the most advanced European culture of the seventeenth century. When Pieter Stuyvesant and the Dutch of New Netherland capitulated to the English in 1664, they had insisted on certain guarantees. In addition to Article VIII concerning religion, they also won the right to retain Dutch inheritance customs which, unlike the English system of primogeniture, gave precedence to widows and provided equal benefits to female heirs. Also, most Dutch women in colonial New York refused to take their husbands' names when they married, an indication that a Dutch wife customarily refused to be subsumed entirely into her husband's identity. With increased intermarriage between the Dutch and the English after 1700, however, the Dutch practice of writing joint wills—with more generous provisions for women, especially widows—virtually disappeared in favor of the English custom of primogeniture.[3]

Women enjoyed other prerogatives under Dutch law and custom, which traced its origins to the adoption of the Justinian code in parts of the Netherlands as far back as the seventh century. Dutch women could make their own wills, administer estates, operate their own businesses, and appear in court as independent agents—rights they exercised routinely when the Dutch controlled New Netherland. Dutch women dealt in both real and personal property. A good number, including Margaret Hardenbroeck and Maria Van Cortlandt, were business proprietors. But the imposition of English common law curtailed these customs, some of them markedly.[4]

It is possible, then, that female adherence to Dutch Calvinism in colonial New York grew out of a loyalty to Dutch culture as a guarantor of their rights. Membership in the Dutch church might imply a recognition that the status of women in Dutch circles was superior to that in English culture, and even though Dutch women could not prevent their husbands from Anglicizing and thereby exercising more domestic control under the pretext of English law and custom, they themselves could lodge a symbolic protest against the vitiation of Dutch culture in the colony.

The feminization of Dutch Calvinism mirrored other changes within the Dutch community. The conversion of Henricus Beys to the Church of England in 1709 may have signaled a trend among upper-class Dutch, particularly male church members, who found in Anglicanism a refuge from the chaos and disorder convulsing the Dutch Reformed Church since Leisler's Rebellion. Beys himself, installed by the Society for the Propagation of the Gospel at Harlem, "gained the most considerable of the Inhabitants" for the Church of England and drew Hollanders from both New York and Long Island.[5] Moreover, the "great divisions" among the Dutch on Long Island, Lewis Morris wrote in 1711, prompted several to invite Beys to preach among them, and Morris included in the same letter to London the happy news that "one of the most considerable dutch families in New Yorke" had embraced Anglicanism.[6] The Church of England also attracted affluent Hollanders in other parts of the colony. In 1709, Thomas Barclay of Albany and Schenectady counted "several of the better sort of the Dutch" among his auditors and two years later wrote that "some of the leading men of the Dutch Congregation have of late brought their Children to baptism."[7] Barclay's Dutch proselytes in Albany included present and former mayors, members of the Governor's Council, and the families of such prominent men as Peter Schuyler, John Schuyler, Killian Van Rensselaer, Robert Livingston, Jr., Evert Bancker, and Dr. Abraham Staats, "present Ruling Elder of the Dutch Church."[8] One New York missionary observed in 1709 that the Dutch "are very well pleased with the Liturgy's I lend them," another indication of the attraction that the ordered worship of Anglicanism held for upper-class Dutch New Yorkers. By 1724, New York's Trinity Church claimed "1600 families of English Dutch French and Jews" as well as a "great congregation" on Sundays.[9]

But in New Jersey and the rural areas of New York, among Dutch of generally lower social and economic standing, the Society's efforts foundered. William Andrews, Anglican missionary among the Indians outside Albany, faced opposition from some Hollanders whom he characterized as "a sordid base sort of People." These opponents accused Andrews of preaching a "Popish Religion," an epitaph reminiscent of the rhetoric surrounding Leisler's Rebellion.[10] One of the Society's missionaries in New Jersey expressed concern over the rise of religious enthusiasm and low-church sects, such as the Anabaptists and the Dutch Labadists.[11] In 1702, Lewis Morris opined that the majority of East Jersey inhabitants "could not in truth be call'd Christians," and another Anglican contrasted his church's success in New York with its poor showing in New Jersey.[12]

I

Shortly after Theodorus Jacobus Frelinghuysen's arrival on the Raritan, in a move indicative of their novel reliance on Old World authority and traditions, the New York clergy requested from the Classis of Amsterdam a complete set of Netherlands church minutes dating all the way back to the Synod of Dort, held from 1618 to 1619.[13] But as the orthodox New York clergy staked out ecclesiastical and theological positions closer to Amsterdam, their less traditionalist colleagues explored new media for religious expression and personal devotion. Under the influence of pietist ministers, Dutch spirituality in New Jersey, northern New York, and Long Island began to assume a character quite distinct from orthodox Dutch religion. In the absence of detailed contemporary accounts, recent sociological and anthropological writings provide insight into the rise and development of Dutch pietism in the Middle Colonies, from its rather inchoate beginnings under Guiliam Bertholf to its more refined manifestations under Theodorus Jacobus Frelinghuysen.

The sectarian impulse in religion rises out of some experience of social dislocation, in this case the political ferment of the post-Leisler years which resulted eventually in the exclusion of Leislerians from political and ecclesiastical office in New York. When conditions of social change render a particular group marginal to the broader society, that group reaches for a new interpretation of its social experience and turns very often to articulate, charismatic leaders who themselves are alienated in one form or another from the dominant social group.[14] This may explain Bertholf's appeal to the Jersey Dutch and Bernardus Freeman's ability to attract loyal followers on Long Island. Less educated than their orthodox counterparts, both men held ordinations from classes other than the Classis of Amsterdam, and both had run afoul of the traditionalist clergy in New York. Their congregants also harbored grievances against the Dutch religious establishment: the New York dominies had strenuously opposed Leisler's Rebellion and had insisted that leaders of the revolt be executed for their defiance of the English.

The charismatic leader acquires his authority outside of traditional channels and depends entirely on the approbation and devotion of his followers. The leader professes to some kind of "inner" calling which, if recognized by others, provides the only authority necessary for the exercise of leadership. No hierarchy or educational requirement intrudes on this process. In the 1730s, for example, a Lutheran clergyman in the Middle Colonies excoriated an itinerant who circulated in Reformed and Lutheran circles because he had "not even learned to spell." Charismatic authority, therefore, implies a repudiation of the past because traditional authority depends on precedent and formalized procedures, whereas the charismatic leader relies on an emotional, dynamic bonding with his community. Bertholf, Freeman, and Frelinghuysen all attracted loyal followings in part because their opposition to the traditional religious establishment struck a responsive chord among disenchanted Leislerians. Thus, sectarianism, which proliferates in periods of social unrest, became an outlet for the discontented.[15]

Having broken from the establishment, sects very often seek their definition by opposing the dominant religious group. The new sect requires the satisfaction of some criterion—such as conversion experience, knowledge of doctrine, or recommendation of another member—for inclusion in the movement. The sect views itself as an elect possessing some higher form of enlightenment. Whereas orthodox Calvinism held that the church consisted of those initiated into the faith by baptism and that the true elect were known only to God, the pietists, like New England Puritans, sought to determine for themselves who was or was not worthy of inclusion in the visible church.[16] As pietist congregations arose in New Jersey, the ministers recorded augmentations to their memberships not by baptism (as the orthodox had done) but by listing the names of those adults admitted "by confession of faith." A pietist minister in the 1740s insisted from his pulpit that "a believer ought to know the time and hour and place of his regeneration." Whereas the established religious group employs formalized procedures for admission, the sect emphasizes exclusiveness and strives to maintain its purity by the expulsion of those who fall short of the community's standards, as when Frelinghuysen withheld communion from those he judged lacking in piety. As the orthodox clergy began trumpeting the importance of doctrinal standards such as the Heidelberg Catechism, the pietists stressed the interiority of faith and relied on inner illumination.[17]

Not only did Freeman, Bertholf, and their allies protest against the traditional ecclesiastical establishment, but their religious leanings issued in a kind of iconoclasm against the blandishments of orthodox worship—liturgy and the sacraments. The orthodox Dutch placed a higher value on sacramental observances. In 1689, the staunchly traditional Henricus Selyns attested to the religious and moral character of

Stephanus Van Cortlandt and Nicholas Bayard (both virulent anti-Leislerians, incidentally). These "models of the orthodox religion," Selyns wrote, "do daily bind themselves by the sacrament of the Eucharist to preserve and protect the true faith."[18] Calvinist ministers, furthermore, believed the sacraments functioned not only as a means of grace but also as a means of social control. While appealing for additional clergy, for example, the colony's ministers reminded Amsterdam that "human hearts are like the soil of earth," which, if "uncared for, and left uncultivated, . . . generally produces nothing else than briars and thorns." In 1681, Dominie Casparus Van Zuuren of Long Island complained that the lack of Dutch ministers in the colony, together with the widely dispersed Dutch settlements, rendered the clergy's task of sacramental administration nearly impossible. Van Zuuren worried especially about "those who are scattered in small hamlets along the rivers and creeks." He was quite certain about the pernicious effects of sacramental deprivation: "This causes among many a condition of great rudeness, and a marked negligence in the use of the Sacraments by their children as well as by themselves."[19] A year earlier, the church at Kingston had implored the Classis of Amsterdam for a minister in order to "prevent all men from growing wild in doctrine and habits." The continued vacancy in their pulpit, they feared, would result in "negligence in the matter of divine service, as well as in all the duties of piety, and the breaking out of all kinds of excesses and prejudices."[20]

The Dutch migration out of New York after Leisler's Rebellion only exaggerated this problem. "For here and there, scattered in the woods, are little companies of settlers, consisting of ten, twenty or more families," the New York City Dutch clergy informed Amsterdam in 1746. "These, if they are not to grow wild altogether, living, as they do but little better than heathen, ought to have a religious leader." More often than not, pietist itinerants served these "country districts," and although these pietists did not ignore the sacraments altogether, about the same time that the New York City church erected an altar rail, churches in New Jersey argued that a layman could administer Holy Communion just as efficaciously as an ordained clergyman. Among the pietists, reception of the Lord's Supper evolved into a badge of regeneration, a subjective experience attended by the appropriate religious affections, rather than an objective means of grace, as the orthodox believed. In the 1740s, a pietist dominie on Long Island demanded to celebrate Holy Communion on a particular Sunday when it was not scheduled. When the consistory asked why, "he said, as he struck himself a heavy blow on his breast, 'I have an inward longing to do it.' " Frelinghuysen himself abhorred ecclesiastical liturgy, preferring spontaneity instead and thereby deviating from prescribed liturgical forms. In 1732, the Classis warned him against taking "too much liberty" in the administration of the Lord's Supper and enjoined him to follow "the Order of the Dutch Church."[21]

Preaching styles also reflected the divergence between the orthodox Dutch in New York and pietists in outlying regions. The traditional urban Dutch sermon, directed toward an educated audience, laid heavy emphasis on biblical exegesis and tightly reasoned argumentation. The preaching of the pietists, however, tended toward spontaneity. In 1758, a chaplain in a Massachusetts regiment during the French and Indian War wrote of a pietist dominie in Schenectady that he "preaches without notes, with little premeditation." Frelinghuysen's sermons to his rural audiences were emotionally charged and punctuated by vivid contrasts between the darkness of sin and the light of God's grace.[22] Moreover, those who, like the Jersey pietists, look askance at liturgies tend to value inner convictions and mistrust objective, external expressions. The year of his arrival in New York, Frelinghuysen preached against the "nominal and formal Christian" who "contents himself with the external performance, however diligent in the observance of the institutions of religion." Instead, Frelinghuysen proclaimed, God values "love out of a pure heart and a good conscience, and faith unfeigned." On another occasion, he numbered the "outwardly pious" among the wicked, those who were "externally and morally correct" yet lacking "the righteousness of Christ."[23] Attitudes toward liturgy, moreover, betray the structure of a given social group. In 1751, after preaching in a Dutch Reformed church, Heinrich Melchior Mühlenberg, a Lutheran pietist, commented that "the people are beginning to drop their unnecessary concern for external ceremonies." Because liturgical forms mark the boundaries between sacred and secular, purity and danger, a high regard for liturgy corresponds to groups with well-defined social boundaries; conversely, social groups with weak structure and fluctuating membership place a lower value on symbolic performance. Disposition to liturgy, therefore, often provides an index for social engagement, or its lack. Because liturgy serves as an elaborate form of communication, the individual within a close social group will value liturgical forms precisely because of their unitive and communicative functions. With the relaxation of social controls, however (as on the New Jersey frontier), the use of liturgy declines or is replaced by a new set of in-group ritual expressions. Religious conviction becomes internalized rather than expressed in outward symbols, and sin no longer takes the form of specific transgressions but becomes a matter of misguided or improper affections. Frelinghuysen spoke of the salutary effects of "inward dejection, through which the sinner is rendered entirely hopeless, and at a loss in himself, seeing naught but guilt and helplessness." Emotional fervor, unfettered by elaborate social conventions, thrives in such an environment.[24]

Alienation from society or from a dominant social group, then, issues in a desacralizing or devaluation of the dominant group's images, and God, no longer identified with the centers of power, becomes enthroned in the small group that is alienated. Social marginality thus pushes faith in the direction of interiority, where God speaks directly and intimately to the believer, wholly outside of instituted forms.[25]

Dutch religion, as Table 5.1 illustrates, began early in the eigh-

TABLE 5.1. Orthodox and Pietist Religion among the Dutch in America

	Orthodox	Pietist
Social status	established, elite	peripheral
Religious expression	formal, controlled, liturgical	informal, ecstatic, inner light
Membership	baptism	proof of conversion
Clergy	professional, education important	charismatic, pietism over learning
Polity	reliance on Old World authority	churches governed autonomously
Theology	doctrinal rigidity, old standards	doctrine less valued than illumination
Sacraments	means of grace	reserved to faithful
Sin	specific transgression	misguided affections
Symbols	emphasis on sacraments	sacraments incidental to spirituality
Identity	part of orthodox tradition	part of "inner elect"
Social ethic	engaged in society	relative withdrawal from world

teenth century to cleave into polarities. The extremism of one faction prompted a move to the opposite extreme by the other party. Walking the furrows that Guiliam Bertholf and Bernardus Freeman had cultivated, Theodorus Jacobus Frelinghuysen would enjoy bountiful harvests over the course of his long tenure in New Jersey.[26] Thoroughly schooled in Old World pietism, Frelinghuysen emerged as the apologist for those alienated from the Dutch religious establishment, as religious ecstasy and spiritual piety were aligned with political displacement, economic discontent, and ecclesiastical dissent.

II

By the end of the seventeenth century, the pietist movement in the Netherlands had gathered considerable force. Led by such figures as William Ames, Gysbertus Voetius, and Jodocus Van Lodensteyn, Dutch pietism arose as a reaction to the corruptions of wealth attending the growth of Holland's commercial empire and to the arid scholasticism into which seventeenth-century Reformed theologians had fallen. Small, private gatherings, or conventicles, provided the locus of a pietist spirituality, which emphasized religious fervor and godly living over theological precisionism and moral laxity. Nurtured with suspicions of stodgy conservatives and the urban elite, young Frelinghuysen found that the reprehensible conditons pietism had opposed in the Old World were present also in the New.[27]

Born in 1692 to a Westphalian minister and his wife, Frelinghuysen was educated at the Reformed *gymnasium* at Hamm and matriculated in 1711 at the University of Lingen, at that time a hotbed of pietism. Frelinghuysen there fell under the influence of teachers who styled themselves Voetians, followers of Gysbertus Voetius, pietist theologian at the University of Utrecht. Ordained in Westphalia in 1715, Frelinghuysen assumed his first pastorate at Loegumer Voorwerk in East Friesland from whence he accepted a position as co-rector of the Latin School at Enkhuizen. Shortly thereafter, Frelinghuysen, believing initially that Raritan was located somewhere in Flanders or Brabant, accepted the call from the Dutch churches in New Jersey's Raritan Valley. The Classis of Amsterdam, at Willem Bancker's behest, reordained the young dominie on June 5, 1719, at which time he agreed to maintain correspondence with the Classis. Frelinghuysen boarded the vessel *King George* in the fall of 1719 and, together with a schoolmaster, Jacobus Schuurman, arrived in New York early the next year.[28]

When the *King George* moored at Manhattan, Captain Jacob Goelet had much to say about the character and behavior of Frelinghuysen. Echoing Guiliam Bertholf's sentiments in the 1690s, "Rev. Frelinghuysen condemned most of the preachers in Holland as not regenerated men," the captain reported to Dominie Henricus Boel of New York City. Frelinghuysen, however, "had kept silent while there, so that they might not prevent his getting the call hither." But in the course of the Atlantic passage, Goelet insisted, Frelinghuysen had vowed to "come out boldly when in this country, according to the promise made to his Brotherhood, whose motto was, 'Be steadfast unto death.' " The orthodox dominies, according to the captain's report, could expect the arrival of other pietists. After Frelinghuysen worked "to secure a following in this country," then "immediately many more would come from Holland to his support, and would push their sect here, generally."[29]

Whatever the young pietist's other attributes, the colonial clergy found him wanting in circumspection. Upon his arrival in New York, Dominie Du Bois invited Frelinghuysen to his home, where the guest immediately noticed a large wall mirror and commented that even "by the most far-fetched necessity" it could not be justified.[30] On another occasion, Frelinghuysen chided Du Bois's colleague Dominie Boel for his lack of piety. "From my heart I wish that the all sufficient God will make you faithful in that weighty pastoral office by which so many eternal precious souls hang between salvation and damnation," Frelinghuysen said, "and that he will fortify you with his life giving Spirit, so that you, preaching the truth, might be unburdened, warmed and made free by that same truth."[31] Even Willem Bancker back in Amsterdam, patron to the pietist ministers in the New World, could not escape the dominie's censoriousness. Before Frelinghuysen's departure for New York, Bancker had praised his nephew Christopher as a "beautiful Christian, because he had secured for himself in Holland and New York a good name among both great and small." Frelinghuysen rejoined that the young Bancker's spiritual health stood in great peril, "because God's children are hated by most people, and well beloved only by those few who are God's own children."[32]

Frelinghuysen brought his penchant for judging the spiritual condition of others with him to the Raritan Valley. The newcomer proceeded to restrict access to Holy Communion to those who showed visible signs of regeneration, and he angered the more affluent of his auditors with his suggestion that "it has been very true that the largest portion of the faithful have been poor and of little account in the world."[33] His third sermon in New Jersey addressed the question of church discipline. Arguing that "the Church has become in this respect exceedingly corrupt, and greatly departed from its pristine purity," Frelinghuysen thought it the duty of ministers and elders "to exclude the scandalous and ungodly from Christian communication."[34] Freling-huysen lost little time imposing discipline. Within two months of his arrival at Raritan, he excluded Antje Smak from the Lord's Supper (the wife of a prominent member, Jan Teunissen).[35]

This action, together with other excommunications, prompted three of Frelinghuysen's congregants to approach Dominie Freeman of Long Island with their grievances on March 12, 1723. They charged that Frelinghuysen "did not teach correct doctrine," that he believed no one in the congregation "had exhibited true sorrow for sin." The dominie had refused baptism to a child, had accused his auditors of being unregenerate, and had taught that the congregation, because of their impenitence, "had eaten judgment to themselves at the Lord's table." Freeman, however, jumped to Frelinghuysen's defense. "I perceive that you are all affected by the spirit of hatred and revenge," he replied; furthermore, because Frelinghuysen "sharply exposes sin, you try to help the Devil, and to cause him to trample upon the Church of Christ." Freeman refused to convoke all the Dutch ministers so that Frelinghuysen's views might be scrutinized, reiterating the congregational principles of church polity that he had exercised so effectively on Long Island. "Suppose," he asked, "there were members here, in our congregation, who had a grievance against their pastors, would they go to Raritan or New York to offer their complaints?" No, he responded, "every church has its own Consistory."[36]

Freeman promptly reported this conversation to Frelinghuysen, whereupon the Raritan consistory demanded that the complainants, on pain of excommunication, come forward with their charges against Frelinghuysen. They defended their minister as an "earnest antagonist against the wicked conduct of many persons" and a man "who sufficiently proves his aim to be the winning of souls." Frelinghuysen's opponents, now seceded from the Raritan churches, promised that a formal complaint would be forthcoming, "as soon as it can be properly done." And, reminiscent of ecclesiastical confrontations in New York fifty years earlier, those dissatisfied with Frelinghuysen withheld their contributions to his salary.[37]

The dispute on the Raritan soon spread to the other Dutch Reformed churches. Having failed to enlist Freeman in their cause, Frelinghuysen's opponents took their case to New York City, where they found in Dominie Boel a sympathetic ear. Clinging, as Freeman had done, to the autonomy of individual congregations, the Raritan churches resisted this move, protesting that Boel and his brother, a lawyer, "have not been set over us as popes or bishops." On April 18, 1723, the Raritan consistory resolved unanimously (over Frelinghuysen's signature) "that we will never suffer or permit any church or pastor in the land to assume dominion over us." The consistory later chided the seceded members for going "to New York, inquiring with Pilate, 'What is Truth?' "[38]

Responding to several taunts from the Raritan consistories, Frelinghuysen's opponents finally issued their formal grievances in the form of the *Klagte van eenige Leeder der Nederduytse Hervormde Kerk* (Complaint of Certain Members of the Dutch Reformed Church), written on behalf of Peter Dumont, Simon Wyckoff, Hendrick Vroom, and Daniel Sebring by Dominie Boel and his brother Tobias, the attorney. With the appearance of this document protesting "the new and strange doctrine of their minister," the battle lines were drawn, as the Dutch Reformed Church once again plunged into schism and confusion.[39] Not surprisingly, those defending the pietist Frelinghuysen included Dominies Bertholf and Freeman, both of whom had written an introduction to a 1721 volume of Frelinghuysen's sermons, commending them to "all the pious and lovers of the truth" as "highly sound and scriptural."[40] Although Bertholf, New Jersey's pioneer pietist, died shortly after the publication of the *Klagte,* Freeman, who had initiated Frelinghuysen's call, issued a vigorous defense of Frelinghuysen, as did Cornelius Van Santvoord, pietist minister on Staten Island, who, like Freeman and Frelinghuysen, owed his commission to Willem Bancker back in the Netherlands.[41] Ministers in the older areas of Dutch settlement, including Vincentius Antonides of Long Island (Freeman's erstwhile opponent), Petrus Van Driessen of Albany, Petrus Vas of Kingston, and Dominies Du Bois and Boel of New York, all opposed Frelinghuysen.[42]

III

The *Klagte,* written in a scholarly Dutch uncluttered with Anglicisms, certainly had its meretricious qualities, but the substance of the document against Frelinghuysen included the following concerns. His opponents, now excommunicated by Frelinghuysen, accused him of having "departed from the pure doctrine and discipline of the true Reformed Church" by following the teachings of Old World schismatics Jean de Labadie and Jacobus Koelman. Indeed, like Labadie and Koelman, Frelinghuysen claimed the ability to discern whether or not someone was regenerate. The plaintiffs quoted him as having stated from the pulpit: "If one of you all says that he has been regenerated, I say, he lies. Or, if he says that he has *ever* repented of his sins, I say, *not one!*" Herein lay Frelinghuysen's departure from orthodox Dutch Calvinism. "The Reformed Church, by condemning the Labadists," writers of the *Klagte* argued, "*has rejected the doctrine of the perceptibility of one's regeneration,* and denied the ability to form a judgment on this subject."[43]

Frelinghuysen had combined his talent for discerning another's spiritual condition with his sacramental theology, which reserved baptism and the Lord's Supper to the faithful. Thus, he barred from Holy Communion those he found wanting in piety and, rather than baptizing infants into the church, insisted "that they *must first* grow to maturity and make confession of their faith."[44]

Frelinghuysen reserved to himself the judgment about who qualified to receive the sacraments, and here the writers of the *Klagte* detected no small amount of hypocrisy. Frelinghuysen readily excluded his ecclesiastical opponents from Holy Communion but acted quite differently on the matter of Jacobus Schuurman, his schoolmaster and associate. Shortly after their arrival in the New World, Schuurman—and, by extension, Frelinghuysen—came under suspicion of homosexuality. Several people in the Raritan Valley charged Schuurman (without apparent rebuttal) "with attempting scandalous undertakings by night, upon the person of more than one man with whom he happened to sleep." Schuurman, moreover, often slept with Frelinghuysen and, "both publicly and at home, often embraced him and kissed him." As soon as the scandal broke, Dominie Bertholf urged Frelinghuysen to disassociate himself from the schoolmaster and "cause inquisition to be made by impartial persons to determine if Schuurman was man or woman." Frelinghuysen refused and, to the chagrin of his opponents, continued to administer communion to Schuurman, averring that it was "more necessary that Schuurman should be prayed for, than that he should be censured, or publicly excommunicated." Even amid growing complaints about Schuurman's advances to male church members,

Frelinghuysen continued to allow the schoolmaster to sit in the consistory. The dominie was eventually married, in part to quiet rumors, as was Schuurman (to the sister of Frelinghuysen's wife), but the scandal over selective excommunications further convinced Frelinghuysen's opponents of his duplicity. "He proceeds with freedom and looseness in the administration of the two sacraments," they charged.[45]

The plaintiffs also expressed bewilderment over Frelinghuysen's low-church leanings and his disregard of Netherlands church order. "He introduces dangerous innovations and pretends that parents do wrong who teach their children the ordinary morning and evening prayers, and the prayers before and after meals," they wrote. As schoolmaster, Schuurman "did *not* teach the children the Lord's Prayer, *but even forbade their offering it.*" Likewise, Frelinghuysen "belittles the perfect prayer which the Saviour taught us, and makes the use of it arbitrary." Whereas formerly a lay reader would conduct services and read an approved sermon in the absence of an ordained minister, Frelinghuysen opposed this practice and "expressed from the pulpit the desire that liturgical prayers should be abandoned." Frelinghuysen's sentiments and his belief that liturgy served merely as a crutch call to mind Jacobus Koelman back in the Netherlands, who wanted to abolish the observance of all holy days, including Christmas and Easter. Indeed, Frelinghuysen never renounced his debt to Koelman; before coming to New Jersey, he had published a catechism in the preface of which he complimented Koelman.[46]

The case eventually found its way to the Classis of Amsterdam, where church leaders insisted on hearing all sides of the dispute before rendering a decision. Although the Classis found many of the arguments "very prolix," containing "many things worthy of no attention," they recognized also the "great divisions and estrangements" in the colonial churches. Their judgment rebuked all parties for their pettiness and urged moderation and reconciliation. In Frelinghuysen they detected "a very dictatorial spirit" and a tendency toward schism; the news about his kissing of Schuurman in public, the Classis said, "grieved us most of all." Moreover, in some of Frelinghuysen's statements, they observed, "gentleness is forgotten, charity is little sought, and the flames of contention are the more greatly fanned." But, the Classis hastened to add, "it also seldom happens in great disputes that the fault is all on one side." Amsterdam admonished both parties to settle their differences and asked, "Have you not quarreled long enough?"[47]

IV

The class antagonisms that had buffeted the colonial Dutch since 1664 continued throughout this period, as indicated by the alignments during the Frelinghuysen controversy. Frelinghuysen himself asserted that "not only uneducated wealthy country people, but also learned and acute divines" opposed him.[48] The four Raritan members who published the complaint against Frelinghuysen all held sizable estates. Peter Dumont, probably the least wealthy of the four, bequeathed a "large Dutch Bible" to his son John and fifty pounds to each of five sons. When Daniel Sebring died in 1764, he left his wife a house, five acres, a wench, and an annuity of twenty-five pounds. Simon Wyckoff left thirty pounds and a "negro woman" to each of five daughters, thirty pounds each to four grandchildren, and instructions to sell his real property and divide the proceeds eleven ways. In 1769, Hendrick Vroom's heirs received three plantations and well over three hundred pounds cash. Tobias Boel himself, author of the *Klagte* and brother to the minister in New York City, left an estate valued in excess of five hundred pounds. On the other hand, with only one notable exception, the seven Frelinghuysen supporters identified in New Jersey wills left little more than real property—presumably farmland—to their heirs, and four of these seven testators designated themselves yeomen.[49]

Frelinghuysen proved quite adept at exploiting to to his own advantage the social and economic divisions within the Dutch religious community. Within six months of his arrival in the New World, he had delivered a sermon on a text from Isaiah that read: "But to this man will I look, even to him that is poor and of a contrite spirit, and trembleth at my word."[50] "Believers are often poor as to this world," Frelinghuysen preached. "Riches are, frequently, a hindrance in following Jesus; not only because the heart is, usually, too much set upon them, and cleaves so tenaciously to them, but because they create such reluctance when it is necessary, with Moses, to prefer the reproach of Christ to the treasures of Egypt." Just as Long Island's Bernardus Freeman had argued that "Christ has left the pious poor in his place," when Frelinghuysen proclaimed that "the people of Christ are frequently obscure and lowly in their worldly condition," the lesson surely was not lost on his audience of preponderantly lower-class Hollanders.[51]

Accordingly, Frelinghuysen's opponents on the Raritan, generally more prosperous, appealed to the traditional sources of ecclesiastical authority in the Netherlands and New York City and claimed membership in "the true Reformed Church of Amsterdam, which was governed according to the discipline of the Synod of Dordrecht." In contrast to their own social status, they characterized Frelinghuysen's partisans as "stupid farmers" and "wholly illiterate." Frelinghuysen himself conceded that they "had not the necessary intelligence" to defend him.[52]

Frelinghuysen, however, realizing that he enjoyed the popular support to carry out his designs, never flagged in his zeal for bringing pietism to New Jersey. Shortly after his arrival on the Raritan, in an extraordinary gesture of both defiance and self-assurance, Frelinghuysen had the following sentiment painted on the back of his sleigh:

> No one's tongue, and no one's pen
> Can make me other than I am.
> Speak slanderers! Speak without end;
> In vain, you, all your slanders send.[53]

This imperiousness continued throughout the Raritan dispute and, indeed, throughout Frelinghuysen's tenure in New Jersey. He issued a veiled threat against one of his ministerial colleagues and repeatedly rebuffed the conciliatory overtures of his Raritan opponents, declaring at one point: "One might think from your long-continued and fruitless opposition to my preaching, that you had learned at least this much: that I am not compelled to allow you to prescribe laws for me."[54]

Frelinghuysen steadfastly refused to rescind the excommunications he had imposed on the complainants, despite several entreaties from Amsterdam, and the truculence of both sides prolonged the stalemate. The impasse finally was breached in 1730 during the course of one of Frelinghuysen's incapacitating, recurring mental breakdowns which left him "robbed of his reason" and "unable to perform the duties of the holy ministry." The Classis stepped in. After expressing sorrow that "Rev. Frelinghuysen is visited so heavily by God's hand," they annulled the excommunications, thereby restoring Frelinghuysen's opponents to the Dutch Reformed communion. But in a subsequent period of remission, Frelinghuysen again resisted the overtures for peace, and the Classis had to wait another four years before receiving news of a settlement on the Raritan. The eleven "Peace Articles," concluded during another of Frelinghuysen's bouts with insanity and read on successive Sundays in January 1734, cautiously reinstated

Frelinghuysen's opponents and acknowledged the Classis of Amsterdam as "our competent judge, to wit, in all things ecclesiastical."[55]

The Classis responded triumphantly: "Thus there is now a complete restoration of peace and unity in your congregations." The Amsterdam authorities, however, had seriously underestimated Frelinghuysen's effect on Dutch religion in the New World, especially in New Jersey. "We had no idea of the extensivenes of his influence," they conceded early in the 1730s. "We knew there was some restlessness and dissatisfaction in the congregation of Rev. Frelinghuysen, but supposed it was limited."[56] But the pietist's sphere of influence had expanded during the Raritan dispute; his ideas and the forces he set in motion now extended well beyond his own churches.

6

Peculiar Conversions:
Revival and Reaction
in New Jersey and New York

On January 9, 1726, after the Sunday-morning service in New York City's Dutch church, Dominie Gualtherus Du Bois detained his congregation for a few moments to address them on a matter of no small importance. "Inasmuch as under Divine Providence, we are all subjects of his Royal Majesty, George, the King of Great Britain, our most gracious Sovereign," he began, "and inasmuch as we are living in a Province where the English language is the common language of the inhabitants: there cannot but be a general agreement by each and all of us that it is very necessary to be versed in this common language of the people, in order properly to carry on one's temporal calling." But having in effect acknowledged English suzerainty, Du Bois continued in a much different vein. All who "prefer the worship of the Dutch Reformed Church" and "the devout hearing of pious sermons in the Dutch language," he said, also recognize the necessity "to be versed in the language in which God's worship is conducted and exercised." The dominie expressed regrets that, because of "a wretched carelessness of necessary things," his congregation had "now for some years neglected to have their children receive instruction in the Netherlandish tongue." Already, Du Bois claimed, their dilatoriness had resulted in a gradual attrition from the church among the younger generation (those, incidentally, most likely to have attended schools run by the Society for the Propagation of the Gospel). "If this shameless neglect continues," he said, "no one can attribute the sad condition of our religion and our Church, to anything else than our own carelessness."[1]

Du Bois, however, offered a solution. Prompted perhaps by his female congregants and their desire to retain the distinctives of Dutch culture, the dominie and his consistory had that very week concluded negotiations with Barent De Forest, who had agreed to assume the position of schoolmaster in a Dutch-language academy sponsored by the church. "The school is to open and close with prayer and singing," the consistory stipulated. "The children, according to their ability, are to be taught to spell, read, write, cypher; and also the usual prayers in the Catechism." And to underline their earnestness, the consistory pledged scholarship funds to any parents unable to pay the schoolmaster directly. Within seven years, De Forest found himself in debtors' prison, but the consistory gamely renewed its commitment to Dutch education by hiring Gerrit Van Wagenen to satisfy the need for "a good Dutch Orthodox Schoolmaster" whose primary task was "to advance the youth in the Dutch language." In announcing the appointment to the congregation, the consistory urged members to support the enterprise by "sending scholars to Mr. Van Wagenen's School of Orthodoxy" so that "the prosperity of our Church may be furthered."[2]

The consistory's concessions to the demands of English domination coupled with their almost defiant reassertion of Dutch language and culture illustrate the difficulties of maintaining a Dutch church in an increasingly English world. The consistory sought to establish careful boundaries, but this too proved difficult. In 1727, William Burnet, the British governor and a friend to the Dutch, presented an organ to New York City's Dutch church together with a "recommendation" that Hendrick Michael Kock be appointed organist. The consistory agreed, but only with the "definite understanding" that Kock play the organ "in the Zangtrant [song-style] of our Dutch Reformed Church."[3] The political realities of eighteenth-century New York made imposing demands on the Dutch, and the church fathers came, belatedly, to recognize the steady encroachment of English culture into their ranks, especially among the young. It was too late, perhaps, to reclaim from the Anglicans the task of educating the colony's youth; the Dutch could only hope to recover some of the losses within their own ranks and thereby forestall the eventual demise of their religion. In Du Bois's words, "all our hearts must be impressed with the necessity of instructing the young in the Dutch language."[4]

Dutch traditionalists, however, were engaged in a losing battle. The pressures to Anglicize proved too formidable, especially because the

Anglicans dominated the colony's schools and the Anglicization of the colony was well under way. Language provided only one indication of English influence.[5] Dutch men had deserted the Dutch Reformed Church in large numbers, and their practice of writing separate wills after 1685, rather than joint wills according to Dutch custom, reflects their adoption of English common-law practice. Marriage patterns also suggest ethnic changes. Whereas the Dutch had reckoned male majority at age twenty-five and the median age at marriage during the seventeenth century had been twenty-six, by the eighteenth century that average had dropped considerably, a concession to English standards, which placed the age of majority at twenty-one.[6] Material culture reflected the transition from Dutch to English custom in New York. After the English Conquest, the old Dutch tradition of vernacular architecture eventually gave way to more classical English forms. Between 1680 and the middle of the eighteenth century, the silver produced by Dutch silversmiths or commissioned by wealthy Dutch merchants copied the styles popular under successive English regimes.[7] In 1727, amid a resurgence in church attendance, the New York consistory met to discuss plans for a new church building. Shall the proposed edifice follow traditional Dutch style, "a plain octagon, or an oblong octagon"? No, they decided (for reasons never stated); the new church would be rectangular, "a four-sided oblong."[8]

While the Dutch in New York sought in vain to resist the advance of English culture, their compatriots in New Jersey began to assimilate with their British neighbors. In 1730, Francis Harrison, schoolmaster at Six Mile Run in New Jersey, published a Dutch-English grammar "whereby the Low-Dutch Inhabitants of North America may (in a short time) learn to Spell, Read, Understand and Speak proper English."[9] Frelinghuysen's partisans both heard and supported English Presbyterian ministers when their own dominies preached elsewhere. As early as 1737, the Classis of Amsterdam recognized that English "is in general use" among the Dutch on the Raritan, and doubtless Frelinghuysen's budding friendship with Gilbert Tennent, a Presbyterian minister, had much to do with the blending of Dutch and English cultures in New Jersey.[10]

Religion, especially pietism, provided the common ground between the two men, and late in the 1720s, Tennent began to serve, in effect, as Frelinghuysen's colleague. He offered prayers and then began preaching—all in English—at Dutch churches along the Raritan. "During these conjoint services of him and Frelinghuysen," a letter to Amsterdam reported in 1732, "he administers the Covenant Seals, mingling the English and Dutch languages with [each] other in the worship."[11]

Frelinghuysen forged a lasting friendship with Tennent and the Presbyterians, an alliance that served him well in skirmishes with his Raritan opponents and the traditionalist Dutch in New York. "The pious and faithful in the land have prayed for us, compassionated us in our affliction," Frelinghuysen preached in 1745, "among whom the English Presbyterian brethren have excelled." As Tennent's visibility increased, Frelinghuysen's erstwhile opponents on the Raritan (those who saw themselves as the guardians of Dutch orthodoxy) condemned this ecumenicity as inimical to the true Reformed religion and despaired for the future of their church. "We fear that it will become altogether irreparable," they wrote as early as 1732. "Now if those who belong in the Dutch churches persist in employing English Dissenters, they depart from the Holland Church-Order and Liturgy; for these belong to the Dutch alone; and certainly they are nowhere in use among the English over here." These traditionalists saw only one solution: "We must, therefore, be careful to keep things in a Dutch way, in our churches."[12]

These arguments failed to deter Frelinghuysen. Gilbert Tennent, he wrote, "is a Presbyterian, and they are surely orthodox." Then Frelinghuysen reverted to the old shibboleth employed by Bernardus Freeman's partisans on Long Island and used even as far back as the Nicholas Van Rensselaer affair in the 1670s, namely the futility of resisting England's policy of religious toleration in an English territory. "Ought we to oppose and persecute English Presbyterians in an English country?" Frelinghuysen asked. Indeed, his partisans added, "the English Crown gives them liberty not only in Scotland, but also in England and Ireland."[13]

No matter how vigorous their dissent, Frelinghuysen's traditionalist adversaries in New Jersey simply could not sweep back the tide of assimilation, and the rapidly changing religious climate in the Middle Colonies contributed mightily to this trend. Despite Amsterdam's expressed reservations about English-language preachers in Dutch churches, the practice continued. "The admission of English dissenters into our churches," Frelinghuysen's opponents wrote, "has already had most perilous consequences in other Dutch churches as well as ours." When Dominie Gerardus Haeghoort arrived from the Netherlands in 1731 to take the church in Freehold, New Jersey, he found "a congregation all in confusion, and scattered over a wide territory." He attributed the "distressful condition" of his church to the fact that "many had become almost wholly English, and had thus become estranged from the Dutch Reformed Church." Three other factors contributed, Haeghoort observed: the lack of Dutch schools, the bitter feelings occasioned by the Raritan schism, and Frelinghuysen's itinerancy. "His preaching at several times and places about here," he wrote, "has caused many to separate from this congregation, so that they were not willing to unite in the call of a minister from Holland."[14]

But the latter years of the 1730s saw other, broader changes affecting religion in the Middle Colonies. Pietistic, ecumenical Germans called Moravians began arriving in New York and Pennsylvania, amid warnings from the Classis of Amsterdam about such "errorists" who "hold many doctrines contrary to the fundamentals of our pure Reformed Church."[15] Gilbert Tennent's father, William, continued to turn out graduates from his Log College, an unprepossessing eighteen-by-twenty-foot structure in Neshaminy, Pennsylvania, devoted to the training of Presbyterian evangelists. Log College alumni, the Moravians, and Frelinghuysen's own machinations in New Jersey all paved the way for the arrival of the most famous itinerant of all, George Whitefield.

I

Whitefield's swing through the Middle Colonies met with resounding success. His open-air preaching attracted thousands; on Society Hill in Philadelphia, for instance, Whitefield preached twice on April 16, 1740, in the morning to six thousand auditors and in the evening to eight thousand.[16] The silver-tongued Anglican had attracted similar crowds elsewhere, even in more sparsely populated locales, and on Tuesday, November 20, 1739, he came to New Brunswick, New Jersey. Whitefield preached three times that day "to a large assembly" and commented on the presence of "several ministers, whom the Lord has been pleased to honour, in making them instruments of bringing many sons to glory." He singled out one of them for special note, "a Dutch Calvinistic minister, named Freeling Housen, pastor of a congregation about four miles from New Brunswick." Noting that Frelinghuysen "has been strongly opposed by his carnal brethren," Whitefield nevertheless acknowledged him as "a worthy old soldier of Jesus Christ, and the beginner of the great work which I trust the Lord is carrying on in these parts."[17] Similarly, Jonathan Edwards, apologist for the Great Awakening in New England, attributed the success of the revival in New Jersey to "the ministry of a very pious young gentleman, a Dutch minister whose name as I remember was Freelinghousa." Touring the Middle Colonies in 1759, Heinrich Melchior Mühlenberg, a Lutheran pietist, referred to Frelinghuysen as "a converted Dutch preacher who was the first in these parts to insist upon true repentance, living faith, and sanctification, and who had much success."[18]

The revival contagion spread quickly through the region, as the Great Awakening permeated what Frelinghuysen called "this so guilty land, the wilderness of America." The *New-York Weekly Journal* published Whitefield's sermon texts along with the observation that "he had Audiences more numerous than is seen on such Occasions; for it has been Observ'd that there were more on the outside of the Meeting House Wall, than within; and some oblig'd to return home, not being able to come near enough to hear him." Whitefield's success inspired imitators. "A Number of Ministers, in one Place and another, were by this Time formed into Mr. *Whitefield's* Temper and began to appear and go about preaching with a Zeal more flaming, if possible, than his," a Bostonian wrote to a friend in Edinburgh in 1744. On November 22, 1740, Thomas Colgan of Long Island informed the Society for the Propagation of the Gospel that "some itinerant enthusiastical teachers, have of late been preaching upon this Island."[19]

In 1747, Dominie Johannes Fryenmoet of Minisink, New Jersey, warned Amsterdam about the influence of the Moravians (Herrnhutters), who sought religious renewal across denominational lines. "The seeds of the soul-destroying and conscience-confusing and erroneous doctrines of the Herrnhutters, sown in two of our congregations have already taken root in some of our members," he reported. Dominie Du Bois of New York discerned that "a spirit of confusion is ever blazing up more and more." He proceeded to review the symptoms of religious unrest in the colony. "Everybody may do what seems right in his own eyes, so long as he does not disturb the public peace," he wrote in 1741. "Hence so many conventicles exist. Hence so many are perplexed and misled; while others neglect or scoff at the divine service not to speak of those who, on various wrong pretexts, entirely abstain from the Lord's Supper." Du Bois assured Amsterdam that he had "taken a stand" against the Moravians, and he complained about the disruptions caused by itinerant ministers. "They preach anywhere, in houses or in open fields," he said. "They also receive great credit on account of the peculiar conversions which they make, and for their own imagined holiness." Henricus Boel, Du Bois's colleague, denied Whitefield access to the Dutch pulpit "on account of his fanaticism," but Whitefield, similarly refused by the Anglican rector of Trinity Church, simply went "out of the city of New York, into the open fields."[20]

By 1740, the waves of religious enthusiasm had engulfed the Dutch. On his second stop in New Brunswick, Whitefield "preached morning and evening to near seven or eight thousand people," and the *American Weekly Mercury* reported "great Meltings in the Congregations." The crowd's emotional intensity surprised even the seasoned revivalist. "Had I continued," Whitefield wrote, "I believe the cries and groans of the congregation would have drowned my voice. One woman was struck down, and a general cry went through the assembly."[21] The itinerant Anglican, preaching in the fields and purlieus of the region, doubtless served as an impetus for revival in New Jersey, but even Whitefield himself recognized that Frelinghuysen's pietism had prepared the way. Frelinghuysen, in turn, was merely the latest in a line of clerical dissent and therefore shared responsibility with Bernardus Freeman of Long Island, who successfully challenged traditional ecclesiastical authorities, and with Guiliam Bertholf, whose perambulations among the Jersey Leislerians around the turn of the century forged an institutional alternative to the establishment orthodoxy of Leisler's wealthy adversaries. But if Bertholf, Freeman, and Frelinghuysen represented the older generation of pietists whose successive assaults had penetrated the fortress of Dutch orthodoxy, no one exploited that breach to greater advantage than John Henry Goetschius.

On May 29, 1735, the seventeen-year-old Goetschius arrived in Philadelphia with his parents and family. John Henry's father, a German Reformed minister back in Switzerland, had come to the New World to escape the scandal he had occasioned by impregnating a young parishioner. After an exceedingly stormy voyage, compounded by poor food and a martinet ship captain, the elder Goetschius fell ill and promptly expired on his arrival in Philadelphia, leaving the teen-aged John Henry to fend for his mother and seven younger siblings. Having studied theology briefly in Zurich, Goetschius began preaching in area churches, and in 1737, he appeared before the Presbytery of

Philadelphia to apply for orders. The Presbytery, however, found him "altogether ignorant in College Learning, and but poorly read in Divinity." They concluded, therefore, that "his ordination to the Ministry must at present be deferred." The lack of clerical credentials, however, did not deter young Goetschius, for he continued his itinerancy along the Delaware and preached the next year in Amwell, New Jersey, and on Long Island. "His conduct has been improper in each place," the Classis learned. "At present he is stopping at Fishkill, above New York, where he has been allowed to preach on his promise to abstain from strong drink."[22]

In October 1740, amid the turmoil of the Great Awakening, Goetschius scored his biggest success when the revivalistically inclined congregants on Long Island—those who admired his "preaching gifts"—called him as their minister. Although he still lacked formal ordination, Goetschius had studied theology in the "kitchen seminary" run by Peter Henry Dorsius, a Reformed minister in Bucks County, Pennsylvania, who also tutored two of Frelinghuysen's sons.[23] Despite the Classis of Amsterdam's repeated insistence that Dorsius and his academy lacked ecclesiastical standing—much less any authority to certify ministers—Dorsius, Frelinghuysen, and Gilbert Tennent ordained Goetschius as a minister in the Dutch Reformed Church on April 7, 1741, with Frelinghuysen delivering the ordination sermon. Bernardus Freeman, now an octogenarian, installed Goetschius at Jamaica, on Long Island, several days later. As both Freeman and Frelinghuysen had done, Goetschius dismissed the consistories opposed to him and installed his own. He further offended the anti-revivalists in his charge by preaching a sermon shortly after his arrival entitled *The Unknown God,* a rebuke to those lacking in experiential piety, who, according to its author, could not claim knowledge of God.[24] Goetschius reviled the practice of religion, which he contrasted with true spiritual piety, and he warned his ecclesiastical opponents that "you will experience your religion in hell, and not in heaven, as you had hoped."[25]

Among Dutch traditionalists, Goetschius evoked the same visceral reaction that Frelinghuysen had, and the Classis of Amsterdam, miffed about the Goetschius case in particular and about the colonial revival in general, appointed a committee of New York ministers to investigate Goetschius. The commission, headed by Dominie Du Bois, met several times at the Brooklyn ferry to consider the evidence against Goetschius and finally preferred formal charges on April 25, 1743.

They asked Goetschius to answer for his irregular ordination and for allowing unlicensed men to preach to his congregations. Furthermore, according to the committee's findings, Goetschius had insisted that those who come to the Lord's Supper "must first be assured of their regeneration and salvation" and that "no one can pray 'The Lord's Prayer' except the truly regenerated." Finally, "Rev. Goetschius had proclaimed publicly from the pulpit, and before the congregation, that a believer ought to know the time and hour and place of his regeneration." The committee's investigations also raised doubts about Goetschius's probity. Du Bois and his colleagues heard testimony that the young minister had made several untoward advances to Isaac Onderdonk's wife, Anitje, and his enemies on Long Island insisted that "Mr. Goetschius continues in and increases in perversities."[26]

When Goetschius refused to answer the charges—he declared at one point that any who opposed him "were plainly godless people"— the commission referred the case to Amsterdam and enjoined Goetschius from administering the sacraments until the Classis ruled on the validity of his ordination. Goetschius, however, ignored the committee's request, and when the Classis determined his ordination invalid, he disregarded this, too, and remarked that if it were not for the Classis of Amsterdam "this country had long ago been filled with pious ministers."[27]

In 1748, the Classis, attempting to defuse the situation, asked that Goetschius submit to an ordination examination and recommended that he seek a call from any church other than those on Long Island, because of the bitterness and partisanship that had surrounded his tenure there. Goetschius reluctantly agreed and accepted an appointment as an associate at the Hackensack church in New Jersey. But controversy followed him there, as Goetschius's pietism quickly clashed with the more traditionalist spirituality of Dominie Antonius Curtenius, his senior colleague. In nearby Paramus, Dominie Benjamin Vanderlinde complained that Goetschius visited the Paramus congregation almost weekly "in order to discover whether some people could not be inveigled into opposition to their own minister. Such people, then, he would attach unto himself, indeed, whole families of our congregation sometimes, who had been supporters of the church at Paramus. Then in houses and barns, he preached to them, and even administered the Sacraments."[28]

Nor did his removal quiet the factionalism on Long Island. "The congregation of Queens County has been so rent and divided," Amsterdam feared, "that nothing but scandal and offence can result, to the dishonor of God's name and cause." After 1748, the principals had changed—Johannes Arondeus represented the orthodox party, Ulpianus Van Sinderen the pietist—but the debate raged just as fervently, and once again it generally pitted wealthier, orthodox churchmen against their less affluent compatriots who had embraced pietism. Van Sinderen's party represented itself as "New Lights" and remarked "that from the Classis came none but evil-minded men, none but the scum of the sea and chaff," and when Arondeus left Long Island briefly for another post, "the principal people of the church" on Long Island, "those who have the most means in our counties," persuaded him to return.[29]

The Goetschius case coupled with the Arondeus–Van Sinderen differences sharpened the divisions between revivalist and nonrevivalist factions during the Great Awakening. "I soon found to my great sorrow that an extensive dispute and division had arisen in the Dutch Reformed churches here," Dominie Johannes Ritzema commented upon his arrival in 1744. "It does not exist so much in the city, where, since my stay, everything has gone on in a fairly quiet way; but it rages principally in the country districts, and especially on Long Island." At the center of the storm stood Goetschius, who had earned the enmity of his adversaries when he "endeavored to convert them." Frelinghuysen rallied to his defense. When Goetschius published *The Unknown God* in 1743, his bombastic sermon attacking enemies of the revival, Frelinghuysen contributed an introduction which defended both the validity of Goetschius's ordination and his orthodoxy. Like Frelinghuysen, Goetschius insisted that "an inward call through God's Spirit" was "superior to all external ordinations." Preaching styles reflected the divergent approaches and emphases of evangelicals and nonevangelicals. The Arondeus faction on Long Island testified that Goetschius "boasted that every sermon of his did not cost him more than an hour's study, as can be proved by those who heard him." Arondeus, however, eschewed the extemporaneous preaching preferred by the New Lights. "All the sermons he has ever delivered have first been written out in full," they said.[30]

But the pietists had little patience for the jejune sermons of the orthodox, preferring instead the extemporaneity of Goetschius and Van Sinderen.[31] Contemporaries regarded Goetschius as "a follower of Whitefield," and, indeed, "he went preaching to his adherents in barns or in open fields." At Hackensack in 1751, Heinrich Melchior

Mühlenberg found "a small group of awakened souls among the Reformed," and he identified Goetschius as "the intermediary through whom these awakenings take place." In 1740, Gilbert Tennent, one of the three ministers officiating at Goetschius's ordination, had published a tract called *The Danger of an Unconverted Ministry,* which lamented the sinful condition of the colonial clergy. Goetschius echoed this view with the charge that "most of the ministers in this country were unregenerate ministers" and, furthermore, that some of the Dutch clergy "had already preached many people into hell."[32]

Although certainly more of a charlatan than his pietistic forerunners, Goetschius shared with them a disregard for denominational boundaries, a fondness for experiential religion, a suspicion of high-church authority and traditions, and a disposition to take ecclesiastical matters into his own hands. In his introduction to *The Unknown God,* he declared that God had placed him "as a watchman on Zion's towers and walls to give clear warning to sinners." Goetschius condemned his theological opponents as those who "impose on many people, against their will, their old, rotten and stinking routine religion."[33] "He called himself and his adherents the truly regenerated ones, or God's people," one minister reported; "the others were the family of Cain, men of the world, and children of Belial, those who had been rejected." Goetschius and his partisans threatened to turn to the Presbyterian church should things not work out to their satisfaction with the Dutch. Like Freeman and Frelinghuysen, Goetschius abhorred religious formality and delivered himself of the view that "the reading of a sermon on Sunday, when there was no preacher was wicked." At one point, Goetschius stood "before the church door at Oyster Bay" and read a "well-known lampoon" discrediting one of his Dutch colleagues, and at Newtown he authorized his partisans to break into the church, thereby allowing Frelinghuysen to preach and Goetschius to install his own consistory, as he had done earlier at Jamaica.[34]

II

Wearied of the incessant bickering that plagued the colonial churches, the Classis of Amsterdam finally began to entertain the long-standing suggestions of Frelinghuysen and others that the American churches form an indigenous ecclesiastical federation. The Dutch colony of

Suriname had provided a precedent in the formation of a governing body, called a *coetus,* which ruled on colonial matters but retained its subordination to the Classis of Amsterdam.[35] Predictably, the pietists agitated most fervently for the coetus, because it would afford them greater autonomy from the Netherlands hierarchy, but the movement received its greatest impetus when the redoubtable Gualtherus Du Bois, senior minister at New York, threw his weight behind the proposal at about the same time that he made his peace with Frelinghuysen and appeared on the same stage with Whitefield. "The Dutch Reformed Church over here is not only robbed on all sides from without," Du Bois wrote, "but is also tossed about by those within, on the many currents of personal passion."[36] A coetus, he believed, might calm these storms.

Du Bois's more traditionalist colleagues, led by Henricus Boel, thought the coetus would only provide the pietists further opportunities to perpetuate their mischief, and when the American Coetus finally was gavelled to order on September 8, 1747, Boel and his confederates refused to attend, even though by the mid-1740s the Classis had come out strongly in favor of the idea. Amsterdam believed that such a body would provide an effective middle ground between utter dependence on the Classis and the kind of independent congregationalism that the pietists seemed to prefer. The anti-Coetus party refused to see it that way and insisted on continued fealty to the Netherlands. "We have no need of a Pope," they said, and in the face of repeated exhortations from Amsterdam to affiliate themselves with the Coetus, they replied that the Coetus was "prejudiced against us."[37]

Because of the reluctance of traditionalists to join with the Coetus, that body soon became dominated by evangelicals, and before long they sought to establish themselves as an American classis on a par with the Classis of Amsterdam. On September 19, 1754, the Coetus circulated a letter to the American churches seeking support for such a proposal, but a letter they sent to Amsterdam the same day offered no hint of this. The next spring, Theodore Frelinghuysen of Albany, son of the New Jersey pietist, citing "these days of Larger Vision," urged a meeting of the Dutch churches to consider not only the formation of an American classis but also an academy or seminary for the training of native ministers.[38] In part because two of his brothers had died of smallpox while crossing the Atlantic in quest of ordination in the Netherlands, Frelinghuysen adopted this cause as a kind of personal crusade, even though his conservative congregation in Albany took a dim view of the idea.[39]

From his first appearance on the American scene, George Whitefield had railed against the empty orthodoxy purveyed at the colonial colleges; other revivalists whom he inspired also took up this cry. "*Tennant* soon followed Mr *Whitefield's* Heels," according to a letter in the *Boston Evening-Post* in 1749, "and roar'd more fiercely than his Master, against *Colleges, Human Reason and Good Works.*" Just as Dutch pietists had established conventicles as alternatives to the traditionalist churches, so, too, pietistically inclined ministers had formed their own private academies for instruction in divinity, instead of following the inexpedient custom of sending candidates to the Netherlands for training and ordination. Frelinghuysen tutored several young revivalists in his home. Goetschius advertised his tutorial services in a New York newspaper, and at least fourteen ministers of the Dutch Reformed Church learned evangelical theology and piety from this man who himself had studied under Peter Henry Dorsius in Pennsylvania.[40]

Besides the convenience of offering theological training in the colonies, the pietists' desire for an indigenous seminary also had its roots in their dissatisfaction with graduates of the University of Leiden, who, the pietists believed, were deficient in personal piety, urbane in demeanor, and unnecessarily scholastic in theology. Indeed, the colonies' most traditionalist dominies—Henricus Selyns, Godfridus Dellius, Henricus Boel—had come from Leiden, whereas the Universities of Utrecht, Groningen, and Lingen more often produced pietists.[41] The most fervent pietists received their theological training at the "kitchen seminary" run by Dorsius, a product of Groningen, or under the tutelage of Frelinghuysen or Goetschius. The Coetus party, therefore, sought to secure a steady supply of evangelical ministers by providing for their education in America.

An academy in the colonies would also address the growing problem of language. By the middle of the eighteenth century, the Dutch spoken by ministers educated in the Netherlands could no longer be understood by the Dutch of the Middle Colonies, whose speech had become, in the words of one observer in 1744, a "medley of Dutch and English as would have tired a horse." "There is a vast Difference between understanding the common barbarous Dutch spoken in our Families, and the studied and ornamented Style of the Pulpit," the *Occasional Reverberator* noted in 1753. "The Generality of our People, that are well enough acquainted with the former, are almost totally ignorant of the latter."[42]

The issue of ecclesiastical independence and a colonial college immediately divided the Dutch clergy. The orthodox condemned the proposal as inimical to true Dutch Reformed traditions and polity. Once the intentions of Frelinghuysen and his colleagues became clear, Dominie Ritzema of New York City severed his ties with the Coetus and began to insist on continued subordination to Amsterdam, whereupon Frelinghuysen accused him of tergiversation and taking up "a position against true piety."[43] George Mancius of Kingston criticized Frelinghuysen for neglecting his own church for weeks at a time while he circulated among other congregations to rally support for his proposals. Mancius belittled Frelinghuysen's claims of optimism, astonished that he "called an irrational hubbub among the people 'the voice of God,' " and Mancius further concluded that "the making of ministers here will also have for its inevitable result the separation of our churches from those of the Fatherland."[44] Dominie Curtenius set forth a scenario outlining the effects of an American classis and college. "I am afraid that a bad use would be made of them," he warned. "Independent Presbyterian students will then also be admitted for examination. Our Dutch Churches in a short time will be governed after the Presbyterian fashion. If, in that case, we should complain about anything to the Classis or the Synod, that our Dutch churches were not regulated after the manner of the churches of the Fatherland, it would be said, 'Oh, the people of Holland govern *their* churches in *their* own way, and *we* find no fault with them; and *we* govern our churches, and we are no longer under obligations to give account of our doing to them.' "[45]

More than one conservative, then, posited a connection between ecclesiastical and political insurrection. Frelinghuysen himself acknowledged that his proposal for an indigenous classis had stirred the opposition of the antirevivalists: "They mock us and derisively say, 'What is this thing that you are doing? Will ye rebel against the king?' "[46]

The question of an American classis, and especially an academy, sharply delineated the differences between orthodox and pietist views of English and American culture. Pietists saw a college as a way to maintain the supply of evangelical ministers who would perpetuate evangelicalism in the churches and also provide an alternative to the decadence of the orthodox dominies (in the course of the Awakening,

the pietists had accused several ministers of drunkenness and dereliction of duty).[47] An academy in the colonies would also stanch the
attrition of congregations to other denominations because of the lack
of clergy, although the pietists repeatedly acknowledged their willingness to join forces with the Presbyterians.[48]

The orthodox also recognized the need for colonial religious education, but they followed a different tack. As plans progressed for the
establishment of King's College, the New York clergy, ever cognizant
of the need to placate the English authorities, supported the proposal
and won in return the right to appoint a Dutch Reformed professor in
the Anglican school. Such circumstances offered many advantages, for
they allowed the traditionalists to maintain their subordination both to
the Amsterdam ecclesiastical authorities and to the colonial political
authorities. They viewed pietist refusals to endorse this salutary arrangement as detrimental, considering the close ties between the
Dutch and the English in New York. "Opposition to it, therefore, can
only be regarded as the work of schismatical people, and would turn
our friends into enemies," Curtenius and Ritzema wrote in 1755. "It
would also furnish them occasion to use their power against us, and as
much as possible to hamper us in our liberties." The orthodox dominies cited the "close alliance" of the Dutch Reformed and the Anglicans in New York as reasons for cooperation in the matter of King's
College. "In this city, at present, one, it may be the husband, or it may
be the wife, is a member of the Episcopal Church, and the other
belongs to the Dutch Church. The same holds good with the children.
Thus families would be torn asunder, where now, for the most part
hands are joined." Whereas the pietists sought additional freedoms in
the formation of an American classis and college, the orthodox contended that the path to true liberty lay in continued solicitude toward
Anglicanism and the English political establishment.[49]

On October 14, 1755, the Coetus in effect declared itself a classis,
arguing that "not only the peace but especially the preservation of the
Dutch Church in New York, keeping it from going entirely over to the
English demand that we should have something more of organization
than we now have."[50] When the Classis of Amsterdam learned of this
insubordination, they regarded it as chimerical and responded with a
mixture of indignation, ridicule, and cynicism. "How large an under-
taking! What wonderful plans!" they wrote. Referring to the American
scheme as an "airy castle," Amsterdam continued: "Indeed, the
Classis, not having been at all consulted in the matter, is not obliged to

weary its brains in seeking to interpret this enigma; especially since the opportunity is given to exercise patience, and to wait for the time when this new phenomenon shall appear in the American Ecclesiastical Heavens."[51] The Coetus party responded in kind, chiding Amsterdam for its dilatoriness in approving American ordinations. A letter dated 1758 opened with this rather ponderous rebuke: "As hope deferred makes the heart sick, so expectations, without help or issue, must die." The Coetus then detailed the defection of the Stone Arabia congregation from the Dutch Reformed ranks because they were unable to secure the ordination in America of Mauritius Goetschius, John Henry's brother. This church, they wrote, "has now become prey to confusion and to German tramps."[52]

By the late 1750s, the divisions within the colonial Dutch Reformed Church had hardened. The Coetus group insisted on its power to ordain ministers and in 1760 outlined a proposal for, not one, but five American classes. Their traditionalist opponents insisted on close ties with the Netherlands. "Our object," two of the orthodox ministers wrote, "is that the tie between us and the churches of the Fatherland, instead of being broken, may become stronger and stronger."[53] The clerical alignments over the Coetus question provide a rough index to the pietist and orthodox factions among the Dutch clergy during the Great Awakening. As Table 6.1 indicates, the Coetus party drew primarily from the evangelicals located in settlements west of the

TABLE 6.1. Supporters and Opponents of the Coetus

Coetus		Anti-Coetus	
Erickzon	Freehold	Curtenius	Long Island
Frelinghuysen	Albany*	De Ronde	New York
Goetschius	Hackensack	Fryenmoet	Minisink
Hardenbergh	Raritan	Haeghoort	Belleville
Leydt	New Brunswick	Mancius	Kingston
Marinus	Passaic	Ritzema	New York
Meinema	Poughkeepsie	Rosenkrantz	New York
Romeyn	Long Island	Rubel	Long Island
Schuneman	Catskill	Schuyler	Hackensack
Van Sinderen	Long Island	Vanderlinde	Paramus
Verbryck	Tappan		
Vrooman	Schenectady		

*Frelinghuysen supported the Coetus over the objections of his Albany congregation.

Hudson (the areas into which the Leislerians had migrated half a century earlier). Opponents of the Coetus concentrated primarily in the older areas of Dutch settlement, such as New York, Albany, and Kingston. Long Island remained divided, with clergy represented in both parties.[54]

The clarion call to revival resonated more clearly among the Dutch in New Jersey and Long Island than among the Dutch in the upper Hudson Valley. What accounts for this disparity? First, the Leislerians who had migrated to the upper Hudson around 1700 joined an already established Dutch society, whereas those who ventured into New Jersey were compelled to begin anew, to form new communities, new farms, new churches. Emigrés to the upper Hudson also established new congregations but not with the same rapidity as their compatriots to the south, and the presence of older churches doubtless served to check some of the more rampant religious extremism, a brake not available in New Jersey. The second factor that modulated the responses of the Dutch in the upper Hudson Valley was the lack of any openly pietistic clergy. In New Jersey, on the other hand, the perambulations of Guiliam Bertholf from 1694 to 1724 placed an unmistakably pietistic stamp on the colony's religious character and prepared the ground for Theodorus Jacobus Frelinghuysen, who served as the immediate catalyst for revival. Finally, the proximity of Presbyterians both in New Jersey and on Long Island helped to pull the Dutch into the evangelical camp. In New Jersey, Frelinghuysen's liaison with Gilbert Tennent pried open the door of Dutch pietism and exposed it to New Light Presbyterianism.[55]

III

By the early 1750s, the momentum of the revival had slowed somewhat, and opposition began to mount. "The storm is gathering apace," George Whitefield had written in 1740. "As the word of God increases, so will the rage and opposition of the devil."[56] Indeed, in the judgment of many, the Awakening had careened out of control. Early in 1742, the itinerant James Davenport and others had banded together to form the "Shepherd's Tent," a seminary for radical evangelicals in New London, Connecticut, and on the afternoon of March 6, 1743, Davenport and his minions pitched the classics of Puritan theology into a bonfire built precisely for that purpose. Itinerants such as Davenport and Andrew Croswell had so riven the social fabric of New England that a conservative reaction set in.[57] The Middle Colonies also had a surfeit of itinerants. In 1746, Amsterdam declared itself "saddened at the shepherdless conditions of many churches in those regions, for the scattered sheep are constrained to seek strange shepherds for themselves." Conrad Weiser of the Moravians, Heinrich Melchior Mühlenberg of the Lutherans, the Presbyterian Gilbert Tennent and Log College alumni, Frelinghuysen and Goetschius among the Dutch—they all traveled about, preaching wherever they could gather an audience. George Whitefield addressed Dutch congregations on Long Island and along the Raritan.[58] In 1749, Dutch antirevivalists complained about a dominie who "runs about as though he would say, 'Who will have me?' " An itinerant named Johann Bernhard Van Dieren circulated in Lutheran and Reformed circles from Hackensack as far north as Tappan, New York, and south to the Swedish settlements on the Delaware River. Van Dieren failed in his several attempts at ordination, and, when asked for his license in an appearance before Dominie Antonides on Long Island, he responded by raising a newly purchased Bible and saying "that that was his license."[59]

Though perhaps less spectacular than the Shepherd's Tent episode in Connecticut, the Awakening visited its share of excesses on the Dutch as well. "Every one does about as he likes," one dominie complained in 1747. Unlettered preachers such as Van Dieren, who claimed spiritual illumination as his sole credential, had altered the fabric of American religious life. "The single test-question now is as to whether they have the Spirit," Dominie Ritzema lamented. "Learning is not of so much consequence. And, what is infinitely worse, such men are called Independents. Already a well-thought-out sermon is getting to be called 'literary work'; but to preach extempore,—that is the preaching of the Spirit, even if the Spirit is contradicted to His face."[60] In Hackensack, Goetschius established conventicles and "advised those who had been awakened to meet by themselves every week and engage in exercises of piety." But these gatherings soon got out of hand, consumed by their own enthusiasm. Mühlenberg, the Lutheran pietist, worried that the participants in these Hackensack meetings "used all kinds of offensive expressions in their prayers, they set up false marks of conversion, and they fell into all kinds of extraordinary practices which easily resulted in rash judgments and condemnation of others who do not share their feelings." All this resulted in "a deplorable split in the Reformed congregation, both parties being guilty of sin," he wrote. "The awakened looked upon those who were outside their circle as publicans and sinners and called the old preacher a dead literalist."[61] A lack of restraint afflicted both sides, pietist and orthodox. "Van Sinderen is a fox in the Lord's vineyard," the Arondeus faction on Long Island declared, and "he can expect a new call just about as certainly as that a roasted pidgeon should fly into his open mouth." The evangelical party, in turn, characterized Arondeus and his followers as "opposed to real heart piety," and Van Sinderen himself conducted an elaborate "funeral" in the Flatbush cemetery for one of his clerical adversaries, denouncing him as "an old rogue"—a full six months before the subject actually died.[62]

Dutch traditionalists sought to curb the turmoil and leveling impulses of the Awakening. Dominie Curtenius of Hackensack, according to Mühlenberg, declared "that he was not at all opposed to the exercises of piety, but he demanded nothing but good order, and that he and the elders had accordingly prepared and published certain rules for the conduct and control of the exercises; but his colleague and his adherents were too hot-headed."[63] In 1752, the New York consistory addressed the "various complaints" from "owners of sittings and chairs in each of our churches, that these are taken and occupied by those who have no right to them, and this not by chance, but is constantly recurring, so that their owners who have bought and paid for the same for their own use, are often compelled, to their great inconvenience, to look out for another place." The consistory, anxious that "good order will be preserved," condemned the practice and in the same resolution asked that "the chairs for the Magistrates be kept in proper honor."[64] In 1741, Thomas Colgan, Anglican missionary on Long Island, wrote that several of the revivalists had been "found guilty of the foulest immoral practices," and others had "wrought themselves into the highest degree of madness." Accordingly, enthusiasm, "once very prominent amongst us," now found itself "in a declining state." John Frelinghuysen, who replaced his addled father in the churches along the Raritan, pictured Reformed pietism as surrounded on all sides by its enemies. Dutch Calvinism was "a church which, in the rear, is attacked by the Anabaptists, whom many go to hear," he commented in 1753; "in front, by the Church of England, whose Pelagian principles and political bulwarks are so agreeable to the corrupt nature; in the flank, by that fanatic, Arondeus; and within by ignorance, etc., and all those monsters of the night."[65]

Indeed, the revivalists' difficulties worked, in many instances, to the advantage of the Anglicans. In 1743, Colgan reported: "Our Church here is in a flourishing condition her being depressed of late by those clouds of error & enthusiasm which hung so heavily about her, has in effect tended to her greater illustration & glory," And the next year, Colgan penned an even more optimistic appraisal to London. "The several Churches now belonging to my Cure (as those of Jamaica, Newtown & Flushing) are in a very peaceable and growing state," he wrote, "whilst other seperate [sic] Assemblies in this parish are in the utmost confusion." Independency, therefore, "is now by the providence of God in a very faint & declining condition."[66]

The excesses of revivalism, then, touched off a conservative reaction, and the Church of England became the main beneficiary.[67] But Dutch Calvinism, as Dominie Du Bois noted in 1741, lost followers to both sides during the Awakening—to the high-church Anglicans on the one hand and the low-church evangelicals on the other. Revivalists attracted the "rabble," those disgruntled with the Dutch religious establishment, whereas the Anglicans drew from the upper classes, the urban elite. The Church of England lured the affluent Dutch, Du Bois believed, because of its theological latitudinarianism and "for worldly reasons," most likely a desire to enter the mainstream of Anglicized culture, trade, language, and religion.[68] Religious affiliations among the Dutch in New Jersey illustrate this even further. Jonathan Arnold, Anglican missionary to New Jersey, informed the Society in 1741 that he preached regularly at Newark and attracted a considerable audience, "the Number of attendants and Communicants being over doubled within these Twelve months." Arnold drew his auditors "Especially from Second River," one of Frelinghuysen's strongholds, "from where comes Considerable part of the Congregation, some of Which are Persons of ye greatest worth and Distinction in any of These Parts." Before long, Arnold enlarged his circuit to include Second River, and he and his colleagues began seeing further increases from among the higher classes. "Several Proselites have been added to the Church from Second River new Barbadoes Neck & Acquacknong," they wrote, "as well as Dutch as English Dissenters who attend constantly at our Church when Divine Servis is perform'd."[69]

Menaced on the one side by pietism and on the other by Anglicanism, the plight of orthodox Dutch Calvinism once again became tenuous. "Arbitrary religiousness and frightful superstition contend for the upper hand," the New York consistory wrote in 1745. Long

Island churchmen fighting the advances of John Henry Goetschius found themselves "assailed by unspeakable deceits and falsehoods." The Classis of Amsterdam, ever wary of itinerants, worried about "those who, according to reports sent to us, to our great grief, run about your regions without being sent," and Amsterdam enjoined the Raritan churches "diligently to ferret out those who incline toward schism through fanatical or false doctrine" and "induce them, with the Lord's blessing, to return to the pure doctrine of the truth, laying aside their errors."[70]

IV

The admonitions from Holland, however, drew scant attention, and even the best efforts of the orthodox dominies could not stem the tide of revivalism. Larger, inexorable forces were at work, set in motion by the English Conquest, Leisler's Rebellion, and the frontier environment of New Jersey. More than one orthodox minister, such as New York's Dominie Ritzema, detected an undercurrent of subversion and a thirst for independence in the agitation for an American classis. "The ministers take the lead. and the farmers follow," Ritzema observed, and he characterized their arguments thus: "The yoke of the fathers had better be shaken off. The Classis has no power over *us*. Of what good is its power to *us?* It is useless. Where did it get the power to make promotions [ordinations]? Did it not take it? We are all brethren, and are as well able to do things as they are."[71] Preaching his brother's funeral sermon in 1758, Theodore Frelinghuysen apparently used the occasion to advance the call for ecclesiastical independence, "saying that they who recognized a foreign authority were in danger of falling into the hands of the King's counsel."[72] Even Thomas Secker, the archbishop of Canterbury, worried about the unrest on the American scene. "The dissenters in America are so closely connected with those in England," he wrote to Samuel Johnson, president of King's College, "and both, with such as under colour of being friends to liberty, are many of them enemies to all Ecclesiastical Establishments, and more than a few to the Gospel Revelation; that we have need to be continually on our guard against them."[73]

By 1760, the lines of division in the Dutch church between evangelical and orthodox, revivalist and traditionalist, were sharply drawn. When George Clinton arrived in 1743, the New York consistory, a stronghold of orthodoxy, hastened to assure the new governor of the congregation's "loyalty, fidelity and obedience to his most sacred Majesty, George the Second,"[74] As early as 1754, Dutch traditionalists reacted somewhat defensively to the pietists' taunts. "Some style our relationship to your Revs.' Assembly a father's yoke, which must be shaken off," they wrote to Amsterdam. "Yea, indeed, a spirit of independence is clearly manifest" in the proposals for an American classis. Belatedly, the conservatives began to discern a spirit of voluntarism which had appeared in various guises dating back to the salary disputes following the English Conquest and the massive attrition of Leislerians immediately following the rebellion—the same impulse that Gilbert Tennent had articulated most forcefully in his famous Nottingham sermon of 1740, which posited the right of congregations to choose their own ministers. "If we force ministers upon congregations against their will, who yet are to pay these teachers, the plan will never succeed," opponents of the Coetus acknowledged in 1758. "Men will rather go over to other churches, or else live without public worship, as is the case now with hundreds, if not thousands, of so-called Christians in this land, to the grief of all who love the welfare of Zion."[75]

Theodorus Jacobus Frelinghuysen and his pietistic colleagues could hardly have asked for more fertile soil in which to nurture the seeds of pietism, and by 1740 the time of harvest had come. The popular disaffection with the established Dutch clergy was pervasive. Declining opportunites for social advancement in New York, moreover, combined with the factious and disruptive politics of the post-Leisler years, had prompted a migration westward to the Raritan Valley. While the wealthy and monopolistic Dutch traders stayed in New York to enhance their fortunes, many of their compatriots began to build their lives away from what they considered the confining orbit of the merchants, the treacherous clergy, and the ossified, traditional Dutch religion that harbored them both. In this environment Frelinghuysen enjoyed virtually unbounded success, and his activities on the Raritan contributed significantly to the Great Awakening.

But for the Dutch of New Jersey the Great Awakening served a broader purpose than merely providing an outlet for their discontent; it ushered them into the mainstream of evangelical culture in the Middle Colonies and soon prompted calls for ecclesiastical parity with Amsterdam as well as ecumenical relations with other evangelicals. "Oh, that the partition-wall were broken down," George Whitefield wrote in 1739, "and we all with one heart and mind could glorify our common Lord and Saviour Jesus Christ!"[76] Frelinghuysen's liaison with Tennent provided only the most visible barometer of Dutch cooperation with other ethnic groups. Heinrich Melchior Mühlenberg often preached in Dutch churches, and Frelinghuysen's party supported Lutheran evangelicals.[77] In the ferment of revival, ethnic distinctiveness and denominational identities began quickly to erode, as evangelicalism provided the common language for their discourse. Contact with Huguenots, Quakers, Moravians, Lutherans, and especially Presbyterians functioned as an assimilating force among the Jersey Dutch.[78]

Theodore Frelinghuysen of Albany in many ways exemplified the confluence of evangelical and assimilationist impulses within Dutch Calvinism. Frelinghuysen, who had agitated so fervently for an American Coetus, preached to New England troops during the French and Indian War. In a style reminiscent of New England clergy, he invoked millennial themes and blamed the war on spiritual decline. "Our Sins and Abominations are exceeding great," he intoned, including "Enmity against real and experimental Religion." Then, sounding more English than Dutch, he recalled the piety of the Puritan founders: "Never forget how dear and precious, our venerable and pious Ancestors esteemed their Religion, and the Liberty of worshipping God in Spirit and in Truth, that they emigrated out of their Native Country, on Purpose to enjoy the free Exercise of it here, when the whole of this Land was nothing else than a vast Desart [sic], and an howling Wilderness."[79]

While Frelinghuysen cavorted with New Englanders, many of the traditionalist, urban Dutch back in New York sought refuge in the dominant Anglican religious culture, and by the middle of the eighteenth century, those who remained in the Dutch Reformed Church found that Anglicization had pervaded even this last stronghold of Batavian culture. During the Awakening, the traditionalist Dutch and the Church of England united against evangelicalism, a common enemy. Dutch cooperation in the establishment of King's College as an Anglican school indicates that by 1754 they considered their commonalities with the Anglicans more important than their differences.[80] In the 1760s, responding both to the demands of their congregants and to the loss of members to the Church of England, the New York consistory took steps to introduce the English language into Dutch worship.

The English Conquest and Leisler's Rebellion had caused cleav-

ages within the Dutch church—in economic status, political affiliation, liturgical preferences, geographical location—and the Great
Awakening divided them even further. For the pietistic Dutch in New
Jersey, the revival functioned as an assimilating force which brought
them into contact with other ethnic groups. For the orthodox Dutch
in New York, the Awakening served to Anglicize them further, as the
Church of England provided a shelter from the obstreperous revivalists. The evangelicals, although they retained many of the distinctives
of their Dutch culture, joined the mainstream of New Light evangelicalism, while the conservatives succumbed to the allure of the dominant English culture. By the middle of the eighteenth century, their
adopted language may have been the same, but their cultures, their
religion, and their politics could not have been more different. One
segment of the colonial Dutch community had Anglicized, the other
had accommodated to the more heterogeneous evangelical culture of
the Middle Colonies, and the magnitude of that divergence would
become abundantly clear in the coming decades.

7

Consumed by Quarrels: Dutch Religion in the Revolutionary Era

On Wednesday, November 2, 1748, the avuncular Gualtherus Du Bois penned his final letter to Amsterdam. Having spent forty-nine of his seventy-eight years as minister to the New York church, Du Bois indulged in some ruminations about the condition of the colonial Dutch churches. He took considerable pride in the establishment (with Amsterdam's blessing) of an indigeneous, yet subordinate, ecclesiastical tribunal in America, the Coetus. But other, less salutary conditions also caught his attention. A personality conflict between two dominies on Long Island continued to vex the churches there, and the congregation at Tappan was divided. "In some congregations, the difficulty lies quite as much with the minister, as with members of the church," he wrote. "Here, even as in other places, many earnest and peaceable ones are found; but also many quarrelsome ones." Du Bois feared the further unraveling of the colonial Dutch Reformed Church. "For the Dutch churches here are gradually beginning to languish; both on account of internal strife in some of them, and because of the distaste of true piety in others; and not less, on account of the fact that the Dutch language is gradually, more and more being neglected." Anglicization had so overwhelmed the Dutch, Du Bois recognized, that several in the New York church "begin to speak of calling a minister, after my death, to preach in the English language."[1]

William Livingston, writing in the *Independent Reflector* in January

1754, added his thoughts about the decline of the Dutch Reformed Church in the colony. "Their once crowded assemblies now scarcely existed, save in the sad remembrance of their primitive glory," he lamented. "Their youth, forgetting the religion of their ancestors, wandered in search of new persuasions; and the most diligent labors of those who were set over them, proved ineffectual to attach them to the profession in which they were educated." Livingston, who himself had left the Dutch church for the Presbyterians because he could not understand Dutch sermons, discerned the cause of this "melancholy declension." "In all the British colonies, as the knowledge of the English tongue must necessarily endure," he wrote, "so every foreign language, however generally practised and understood for a time, must, at length, be neglected and forgotten." And so the Dutch tongue, "once the common dialect of this province, is now scarcely understood, except by its more ancient inhabitants."[2]

I

How completely had English culture eclipsed Dutch culture in the colony? The conclusions of a committee appointed in 1763 by the Dutch Reformed consistory in New York provide eloquent testimony. "For some years past," the committee wrote, "the inhabitants of our Province in general, and the city of New-York in particular, by far the greatest part consisted of Dutch people, who adhered to the doctrines of the National Synod of Dort." The Dutch formerly claimed "the greatest share (at first the whole) in the administration of government," including officers of the militia, judges, justices, members of the Governor's Council. "In short, our influence in Church and State carried a superior sway in nearly all the counties of the Province." The English Conquest of 1664, however, changed all that, and the Reformed church felt this transition acutely. "We have daily the mortification of seeing the offspring of the wealthiest members of our congregation leave our divine worship, not being able to apprehend what is taught." This attrition so eviscerated the Dutch that "the respective English congregations among us at present, for the greatest part consist of persons who are descendants of parents, who were formerly communicants in our Church." The mantle of both political and religious influence had passed from the Dutch to the English. "Our congregation has, therefore, for some years, been a nursery for the English denominations of Christians in this city, and these chiefly from our principal people," the report concluded. "It thus happens, that most of those now in power belong to other congregations, though lineally descended from Dutch ancestors."[3]

While the wealthier members of the Dutch Reformed church in New York City defected to the Church of England or Presbyterianism in search of English preaching, Dutch congregations elsewhere also lost members to English-speaking churches. Writing from Freehold, New Jersey, in 1764, Dominie Reinhardt Erickzon, a conservative who frequently clashed with his evangelical congregations, protested that his ministry would be more successful "if the Dutch language had been spoken more generally, and if the Dutch schools had not ignored it as they did; and above all, if the parents had more generally spoken it at home, and had taught their children to read Dutch." Consequently, the younger generation "preferred to attend English services, whether it were with the Mennonites, with the Church of England, or with the Independents."[4]

In the 1760s, after a century of English rule, the Dutch Reformed church in New York City finally faced the inevitable and authorized the hiring of an English-speaking minister. The consistory's letter to two Scottish clergymen in Amsterdam catalogued the demise of Dutch power in the colony and the "diminution of our once flourishing congregation." In times past, they wrote, "our influence in church and state carried a superior sway in all the counties of the Province." But under the English, "all matters of government, courts of justice, and our trade and traffic with foreigners carried on in the English language, has, by the length of time, gradually undermined our mother tongue." This change affected the upper classes, especially, they said, those involved in trade and commerce. Although the consistory recognized its powerlessness "to stop the current of the prevalency of the English language," they nevertheless sought someone "qualified not only to edify ourselves, but by his piety, learning and eloquence to draw others."[5]

Having failed to retain its membership by a retreat to high-church piety, the Dutch Reformed Church resorted to English preaching tinged with evangelicalism. In a poignant testimony to the desuetude of the Dutch language and the affinity of a growing number of the Dutch with the Presbyterians, the New York consistory hired the Reverend Archibald Laidlie, graduate of the University of Edinburgh, to preach in English. The same year, 1763, Dominie Lambertus De Ronde of New York, who fancied himself fluent in English, undertook a translation of the Heidelberg Catechism which, he announced to the Classis, "is also very acceptable to the Professors in the Presbyterian College and to the members of those churches."[6] And in 1767, this same Dutch church that had sought earlier to reestablish instruction in the Dutch tongue published its church psalter, catechism, and liturgy in English. In his preface to the new volume, Dominie Johannes Ritzema, Du Bois's successor, solemnly offered reasons for the translation. "The Consistory of the Reformed Protestant Dutch Church of the City of *New-York*," he wrote, "by Reason of the Declension of the Dutch Language, found it necessary to have Divine Service performed in their Church in English."[7]

Despite insistent opposition from a party of Dutch traditionalists, the English language took hold in the Dutch churches; even the Classis of Amsterdam professed indifference to the language of worship, so long as the churches preserved sound doctrine. In anticipation of Laidlie's arrival, the New York consistory had authorized the construction of a gallery at the new church, and they appointed a catechist to teach the tenets of Dutch Calvinism in the English language.[8] Even though the church raised Laidlie's salary by subscription rather than through the endowment (reserved to the Dutch ministers), English worship in the Dutch church more than paid for itself; subscriptions for Laidlie's salary raised one hundred and twenty-five pounds per year more than budgeted, and from his inauguration in 1764 through 1772, the English services took in nearly three thousand pounds, one thousand more than expenses. Dutch became unfashionable. In 1765, just a year after Laidlie's arrival, he drew larger audiences than the Dutch dominies, who complained that they "have been made the butt of ridicule throughout the whole land." By 1767, he outdrew them three to one. The consistory soon called a second English-speaking minister and constructed another church to accommodate the English services.[9]

II

Although the Great Awakening had ebbed by midcentury, its effects lingered in the Middle Colonies. George Whitefield's sorties continued to bedevil the Anglicans. "I am sorry to say he has had more influence than formerly & I fear he has done a great deal of mischief," Samuel Seabury wrote in 1764 on the heels of Whitefield's tour. "The wildest notions are propagated here," Samuel Johnson, president of King's College, wrote to London, "both on the side of Enthusiasm and Infidelity."[10]

Dutch traditionalists continued to look askance at the revival. In 1763, Dominie De Ronde of New York City commented that "there are many errorists among us, such as Moravians, Anabaptists, Arminians and others," and he later worried about the religious innovations brought on by the revivalists. "There is much clamor about sudden conversions," he wrote, "but I fail to see any fruits." In his preface to *The True Spiritual Religion,* published in 1767, De Ronde wondered if his style of writing might "give offense to some, because it is not in that species of the evangelical strain, with such soothing expressions as tend to please the ear, without awakening the conscience." Dominie Ritzema, De Ronde's Dutch colleague, noted in 1769 that "the spirit of fanaticism and independence makes fearful progress" and that "people run from one church to another."[11]

The newly hired English-speaking ministers, however, evinced a sympathy for evangelicalism. Like Frelinghuysen on the Raritan, Laidlie organized conventicles and refused "to preach from Passiontexts, or holiday sermons, as he ought to have done," De Ronde reported, "nor is he willing to be subordinate." John Henry Livingston, the second English-speaking minister, hired in 1769, preached a sermon the next year during which he urged his auditors "to make up for the time we have lost by continuing so long in an unconverted state."[12]

The differences between revivalist and antirevivalist, evangelical and nonevangelical, also took institutional form within the Dutch Reformed Church. Although the Classis of Amsterdam had encouraged the formation of an American Coetus, they suddenly changed course when it became apparent that the Coetus ministers advocated far more independence than Amsterdam had envisioned. In 1760, Johannes Leydt, minister at New Brunswick, published *True Liberty the Way to Peace,* a kind of declaration of independence from Holland, in which he claimed for the Coetus various ecclesiastical powers, including the right of ordination.[13] Dominie Ritzema of New York, who complained about the "confusions and divisions which prevail, and of the altogether different conception of Church Government which obtains among the brethren of the Coetus," issued *A Short Refutation of Leydt's Book,* which argued that the sole right of promotion lay with the Classis. Amsterdam, indignant at Leydt's treatise, approved Ritzema's rejoinder and insisted on continued deference and subordination "in order to avoid a perfect Babel of confusion."[14]

The divisions persisted. Coetus ministers "are given up to fanaticism, and are, at bottom, Independents," Ritzema charged; "many simple souls in their congregations are enticed, caught and carried away" by the "so-called 'preaching the spirit' of these fanatics."[15] In 1763, the Coetus delegated one of their number, Jacob Hardenbergh of Raritan, New Jersey, to the Netherlands to press their agenda before the Classis of Amsterdam. Summoned before the Classis on July 18, 1763, Hardenbergh presented his case for forming an American classis and appointing a professor of theology in America. The Classis emphatically denied Hardenbergh's request and then regaled him with a history of the New Netherland churches. They listed the pages from Leydt's book that they had found particularly insulting, made clear to Hardenbergh the impertinence of his request, and warned him against trying to raise money in Holland for an American academy.[16] Undeterred, Hardenbergh appealed directly to the Synod of North Holland, which upheld the rulings of the Classis. The Synod also began to discern the intentions of the Coetus ministers in America. Their aim, the Synod decided, was to withdraw themselves "gradually from time to time, from the subordinate relation in which they stand, both to this Synod, in general and to the Classis of Amsterdam in particular," with a view toward "becoming wholly independent in the end." In affirming the Classis of Amsterdam, the Synod also expressed its outrage over Leydt's tract and the "detestable ingratitude" of the Coetus. "All of this," the synodical minutes read, "was by the president made known to Rev. Hardenberg [sic] in emphatic terms." Thus chastened, Hardenbergh returned to America, whereupon he resolved "that I would never again take part in any attempt to promote further relationship of our churches with those of Holland."[17]

The Coetus ministers proceeded with their designs. They continued to act independently of Amsterdam and in 1766 won from William Franklin, the British governor, a charter for Queen's College. On June 20, 1764, Dutch traditionalists organized the Conferentie, a party opposed to the Coetus. Again the factions traded charges, and the nature of these charges offers a glimpse into the inclinations of each side. Samuel Verbryck, a Coetus minister at Tappan, delivered

"some silly speeches" from the pulpit, his opponents charged, in
which he insisted that "the forms of prayer must be cast away, and we
must pray by the Spirit." Like Koelman in the Old World and Freeman, Frelinghuysen, and Goetschius in the New, Verbryck excommunicated his opponents and flouted religious holidays. Although bound
by the terms of his contract to preach on such occasions, "he does not
refrain from deriding the custom"; one Easter, his detractors alleged,
Verbryck preached on the crucifixion. On the other side, Johannes
Leydt asserted that Dominie Reinhardt Erickzon "never had the internal call, nor a commission from God" for the ministry.[18]

The evangelical and pietistic impulses of a Samuel Verbryck and a
Johannes Leydt coincided with a demand for ecclesiastical independence. The Conferentie, on the other hand, uncomfortable with the
vagaries of revivalism, branded their opponents schismatics and chose
to remain loyal to the Netherlands. The Coetus charged that the polity
of the Conferentie, with its avowed subordination to the Classis of
Amsterdam, violated not only the Scriptures but English freedoms
also.[19]

Indeed, in the politically charged atmosphere of the mid-eighteenth
century, ideas such as subordination, whether political or ecclesiastical, began to attract scrutiny. After his arrival in New York, Dominie
Hermanus Meyer of Kingston had taken a civil oath of allegiance; he
then argued that because he had abjured "all foreign power and authority" he could "consent no further to the subordination to the Classis of
Amsterdam." Meyer claimed that subordination "savored much of the
spirit of Popery" and "that the Pope pretended that his power, in
Ecclesiastical matters, extended over the whole world; and just so the
Classis of Amsterdam, not content with her jurisdiction in Holland,
labored to extend it further." After the consistories at Poughkeepsie
and Fishkill had cast their lot with the Coetus, "they bragged and
boasted, that now they were delivered from the Papal yoke of subordination to the Classis."[20] In New York City, Archibald Laidlie "does not
want to hear of 'Subordination,' " De Ronde reported; not long thereafter, in the throes of the Stamp Act crisis, Laidlie preached what at
least one auditor considered a "sed[i]t[iou]s sermon" for the purpose
of "exciting people to Reb[e]ll[io]n."[21]

For its part, the Classis maintained that it required nothing inconsis-
tent with a civil oath and that any "objection about such a matter,
with all the alarm excited in connection therewith, is indeed far-

fetched." Amsterdam chided the Coetus for propagating such notions. On the persistent issue of American ordinations and the need
for ministers, the Classis wondered if "the party desiring Independence" had not exaggerated this need in order to win ecclesiastical
autonomy from the Netherlands: "This, however unpleasant to hear,
is the one thing in your mind—Independence!"[22]

Dominies Ritzema and De Ronde led the traditionalist resistance to
the Coetus. Ritzema especially, who maintained close ties with the
Anglicans and served as a trustee for King's College, recognized that
the Coetus-Conferentie dispute represented more than an ecclesiastical squabble, that it had larger implications. He feared that if the
Dutch churches in America asserted their independence from the Netherlands church, they would thereby surrender the legal perquisites
granted them by the Articles of Capitulation in 1664: "If, then, we
withdraw ourselves from Holland, which we certainly do by refusing to
be in becoming subordination, I suspect that in time we shall be considered dissenters, and lose our privileges as an established Church,
and perhaps incur the danger of forfeiting our charters." Ritzema
feared alienating the English and regretted that Hermanus Meyer's
party in the Kingston church advocated something like democratic
rule. "For they have set up, and mean still further to carry, the rule of
the majority," Ritzema said, "by which they will be able to manage
everything their own way."[23]

III

Ritzema, De Ronde, and the entire Conferentie party, however, advocated positions very much at odds with the prevailing ecclesiastical and
political winds. In the fall of 1765, just as the colonists erupted in
rebellion against the Stamp Act, the Conferentie wrote the Classis of
Amsterdam to ask if the Netherlands ambassador to Britain might
intercede for them aginst the Coetus ministers. "We see no other resort
than to request the protection of our King," they wrote. While the
Livingston party in New York worried that the Church of England
might establish an American bishopric, Ritzema cavorted openly with
the Anglicans, served as a trustee for King's College, and maneuvered
for his own appointment as professor of theology in the Anglican
school. The Dutch, particularly those who sat under the preaching of
the English-speaking ministers, held contrary views. "We are con-

sumed by quarrels," Ritzema observed, referring to both the political
and the ecclesiastical situation.[24]

For its part, the Classis manifested a growing impatience—if not
outright contempt—for the American churches and their contentiousness. "All that we have ever derived from the New York Church has
been trouble," they wrote in 1765. "Its discords and oppositions have
grieved us much, and if no improvement is possible, we would be very
willing to be relieved of the care." Amsterdam, nevertheless, afraid
to see a "daughter departing from the ancient purity of doctrine,
divided and torn into several factions, and that in a land where there
is already a multitude of all kinds of sects," drafted a plan of union
and asked the Synod of North Holland for a free hand in dealing with
the American situation. The Classis even conceded that its relationship to the new American body would take the form of a "Close
Alliance" rather than subordination, "which is most hateful in that
land."[25]

Others recognized the need for some sort of compromise, lest the
American church become moribund. The consistory at New York City
had sought to maintain its neutrality throughout the disputes, in part
because its clergy had divided: Ritzema and De Ronde, the Dutch
preachers, supported the Conferentie; Laidlie and Livingston, the
English-speaking ministers, favored the Coetus. If some sort of agreement were not reached soon, the consistory argued, "the Coetus, think-
ing itself pushed aside, might easily go over to the Presbyterians" and
take with them "not less than ten thousand people of the Dutch
churches," while "those belonging to the Conferentie would, upon the
death of their present ministers; be in danger of dropping off to the
Church of England."[26]

Although Ritzema had stalked out of the early negotiations, the
Coetus and Conferentie finally settled their differences in June 1772,
but the terms of their reconciliation overwhelmingly favored the
Coetus. The new ecclesiastical body, called a General Assembly,
recognized the hitherto contested ordinations of the Coetus, assumed
responsibility for future ordinations, and agreed only to maintain a
correspondence with ecclesiastical authorities in Holland.[27]

As the American Revolution approached, political changes again
weighed on the Dutch Reformed Church. The prevalence of evangelical sentiment in the newly formed General Assembly roughly
paralleled the preponderance of Dutch clergy favorable to the Revolution.[28] Among those ministers with discernible political inclina-

TABLE 7.1.   Political Sympathies of Dutch Clergy, 1776

	Location	Faction	Party
Boelen, Hermanus	Jamaica	Conferentie	Tory
Cock, Gerhard	Germantown	Conferentie	
De Ronde, Lambertus	New York	Conferentie	
Froeligh, Solomon	Long Island		Whig
Fryenmoet, Johannes	Kinderhook	Conferentie	
Goetschius, Stephen	New Paltz	Coetus	
Haeghoort, Gerardus	Belleville	Conferentie	
Hardenbergh, Jacob	Raritan	Coetus	Whig
Jackson, William	Bergen	Coetus	Whig
Kern, Johannes	Montgomery	Conferentie	Tory
Kuypers, Warmoldus	Hackensack	Conferentie	Tory
Laidlie, Archibald	New York	Coetus	Whig
Leydt, Johannes	New Brunswick	Coetus	Whig
Livingston, John H.	New York	Coetus	Whig
Lydekker, Gerrit	Ridgefield	Conferentie	Tory
Marinus, David	Kakiat	Coetus	
Meyer, Hermanus	Kingston	Coetus	
Ritzema, Johannes	New York	Conferentie	Tory
Romeyn, Dirck	Hackensack	Coetus	Whig
Romeyn, Thomas	Fonda		
Rubel, Johannes	Long Island	Conferentie	Tory
Rysdyck, Isaac	Fishkill	Conferentie	
Schoonmaker, Henricus	Passaic	Coetus	Whig
Schuneman, Johannes	Catskill	Coetus	Whig
Schuyler, Johannes	Schoharie	Conferentie	
Vanderlinde, Benjamin	Paramus	Conferentie	
Van Harlingen, Johannes	Sourland		
Van Sinderen, Ulpianus	Long Island	Conferentie	Whig
Verbryck, Samuel	Tappan	Coetus	Whig
Vrooman, Barent	Schenectady	Coetus	
Westerlo, Eilardus	Albany	Coetus	Whig

tions (see Table 7.1), all but one of the Conferentie sympathizers remained loyal to Britain, and the lone exception, Dominie Van Sinderen of Long Island, had earlier supported the Coetus. All of the Whig clergy, on the other hand, had affiliated with the Coetus and acceded in its demands for ecclesiastical independence from the Netherlands.[29]

The ardor of the clergy's political convictions varied greatly. The few Tories among them generally kept a rather low profile, whereas several of the patriots exerted more forceful leadership—and sometimes suffered for it. Jacob Hardenbergh, who had traveled to Holland to argue for ecclesiastical autonomy, occupied a seat in the New Jersey constitutional convention and later served several terms in the state's General Assembly. His stance, however, offended the loyalists in the area, and he often slept with a loaded musket next to his bed. After the Battle of Long Island, Solomon Froeligh feared reprisals from the British and his Tory congregation, so he hid in the cellar of a friendly elder until he could flee to Fishkill. When the British occupied New York City during the Revolution, the Classis learned in 1778, Dutch church members "were for the most part scattered hither and thither" and "obliged to seek safety in the interior of this state." Both English-speaking ministers quit the city: John Livingston, whose public prayers endorsed patriotism, retreated to the upper Hudson; and in 1779, Archibald Laidlie died of consumption while in exile at Red Hook. In New Jersey, Dirck Romeyn, known as the "Rebel Parson," suffered the wrath of British and Hessian soldiers, who "plundered me of all my furniture, Cloathing, Books, Papers &c to the amount of £500 York currency at the Parsonage House at Schralenburgh."[30]

Toryism and its solicitude toward the English also found favor among the Dutch. Dominie Gerrit Lydekker's loyalist sentiments cost him his homestead and four hundred acres of land near Ridgefield, New Jersey; the advance of Continental soldiers in November 1776 forced him to leave his church and retire to New York, where he found a remnant of loyalist Dutch. When British troops appropriated the New York Dutch church for a hospital during their occupation of the city, Trinity Church allowed Lydekker and his Dutch congregation the use of St. George's Chapel. "The Christian-like behaviour and kind attention shown in our distress by members of the Church of England, will make a lasting impression on the minds of the Ancient Reformed Dutch Congregation," Lydekker promised in a note of appreciation, "who have always considered the interest of the two Churches inseparable, and hope that this instance of brotherly love, will evince to posterity the cordial and happy Union subsisting between us."[31]

Like their ministers, the Dutch laity also divided on their posture toward the Revolution. On Long Island, "the members of the Dutch Church are very numerous," Charles Inglis, an Anglican, wrote in 1776, "and many of them joined in opposing the rebellion." The

Dutch in the Hudson Valley largely favored the patriots.[32] In New Jersey, the Coetus-Conferentie affiliations provided the most reliable predictor of alignments during the Revolution. At Hackensack, for instance, the followers of Warmoldus Kuypers, a Conferentie minister, became Tories; the evangelically inclined party of Dirck Romeyn supported independence. Generally, those disposed to the Conferentie remained loyal to Britain, and the Coetus party joined the patriots.[33]

IV

With the conclusion of political independence from the British, the Dutch churches speedily effected their ecclesiastical independence from the Netherlands. Meeting in October 1784, the General Assembly discussed ways to forge a closer alliance with the Presbyterians, thus solemnizing a relationship begun by Theodorus Jacobus Frelinghuysen half a century earlier. The General Assembly also resolved to change its name to "The Synod of the Reformed Dutch Churches of New York and New Jersey" and thereby remove the last guise of subordination. Livingston, writing to Amsterdam, simply informed the Classis of this change and added a rather cryptic note: "The recognition of this by the Very Rev. Synod of North Holland and the Rev. Classis of Amsterdam, we will receive with great satisfaction."[34]

By the late 1780s, the American Synod recognized that most of the churches now conducted their worship in English rather than Dutch. In 1787, they authorized another, expanded translation of the psalm book, and the next year they called for the translation of the *Articles of the Synod of Dort,* "since the English language is our national tongue, and is making progress, and has already been adopted wholly or in part in worship in most of our congregations, and the rising generation seem to be little acquainted with the Dutch tongue."[35]

The dominies also had to adapt. On March 12, 1782, Albany's Eilardus Westerlo approached the pulpit and in a few prefatory remarks apologized for his halting English. "The present state & situation of this City & this Congregation," he said, impelled him "to try, (if it should please the Lord to strengthen & enable me) to proclaim unto you O my dear Hearers the great tidings of the Glorious Gospel—in a Language in which I am not used to preach."[36] Those clergy who refused to learn English faced expulsion. On February 10,

1785, deacons and elders from the New York City church informed Domine Ritzema that they deemed his services unnecessary. "There are not more than twenty or thirty people who are any longer in favor of Dutch," they explained. "The welfare of the Church demands English services." The consistory also relieved Lambertus De Ronde, Ritzema's Dutch colleague, and Ritzema recalled his visit to Long Island when Ulpianus Van Sinderen burst into tears as he told of his dismissal from the Dutch churches there. "It seems to me to indicate," the seventy-seven-year-old Ritzema observed, "that they are inclined to bear with no one, unless he is an American."[37]

As the trials of the Revolution settled into the background, the eclipse of Dutch culture became apparent. On the streets of New York City in 1794, William Strickland from Yorkshire, England, heard no language but English, even among children of Dutch or German descent. "The houses are in the stile we are accustomed to," he wrote; "within doors the furniture is all English or made after English fashions." Even in the Hudson Valley, one of the bastions of Dutch influence, Batavian culture had receded. At Fishkill, Strickland commented on the disrepair of the Dutch church and observed that the Dutch language "is rapidly declining, and the people are assimilating themselves to the English or American manners and language and with them to their religion also." During a visit near Poughkeepsie later the same year, Strickland found that "the Dutch, as Dutch in opposition to English, were fast wearing out in this country which a generation or two back might be said to have been entirely inhabited by such, and that they were assimilating themselves to the English or Americans." The Dutch language, he continued, "was no longer any where taught, and little used, except among some old people chiefly residing in retired and unfrequented places." Dutch culture's hold on the church also had slackened. Strickland learned that "the service of Religion was now performed here to the Dutch congregation in English, and that, more for form's sake that any thing else, a Sermon was preached once in four or five weeks in Dutch but that this would probably be soon discontinued, and that now service was performed in English in most of the Dutch churches."[38]

In a little more than a century, the Dutch of New Netherland, once the colony's dominant and ruling ethnic group, had assimilated and lost much of their distinctiveness. They had failed to sustain their ethnic identity in an increasingly English world. Many of those who claimed a Dutch lineage could no longer speak its language.

V

How did the Dutch experience in the Middle Colonies compare with other non-English groups? The Huguenots had succumbed most readily to the dominant English culture, because of such factors as a lack of English prejudice against them, exogamous marriages, and the desire for economic success. Huguenot assimilation late in the seventeenth century approximated the ready Anglicization of Dutch merchants after the English Conquest of 1664; their involvement in the colonial economy swept aside ethnic barriers in the quest for pecuniary gain.[39]

The Swedes, whose initial settlements along the Delaware had been the most precarious, surrendered their ethnic identity almost completely by the middle of the eighteenth century. Like Guiliam Bertholf, Bernardus Freeman, and, later, Theodorus Jacobus Frelinghuysen among the Dutch, Lars Tollstadius had exploited resentments within Swedish churches, siphoned off communicants into schismatic congregations, and contributed to the instability of the churches. Without the support of sympathetic magistrates and political institutions, Swedish Lutheran churches became Anglican. On May 27, 1742, the congregation of St. George's in Salem County, New Jersey, decided thereafter to conduct their services in English, "with Prayers and Ceremonies according to the Church of England." Considering their theological affinities with the Church of England, many Swedes thought it better simply to become Anglicans and thereby avoid unruly spirits such as Tollstadius.[40]

Many German settlers in the Middle Colonies, lacking strong ecclesiastical organizations in the New World, had found the pietism of Dunkers, Moravians, Heinrich Melchior Mühlenberg, and even Conrad Beissel to their liking. Anticlericalism among them gradually gave way to the Great Awakening, which in turn prompted an orthodox retrenchment and a strengthening of both religious institutions and ethnic distinctives.[41] The Dutch of New Jersey shared with their German neighbors a predilection to revivalism that grew out of spiritual neglect on the frontier, but, unlike that of the Germans, Dutch pietism in the Middle Colonies represented an active rebellion against Reformed orthodoxy, a rebellion engendered, at least in part, by class antagonisms and the long shadow of Leisler's Rebellion. Among the Dutch, pietism provided the language of dissent, a protest against traditional Reformed worship, the urban elite, and the Anglicizing tendencies of the dominies.

Loyalty to Old World cultures among immigrants to the Middle Colonies also determined both religious and ethnic cohesiveness. The lack of internal unity almost certainly contributed to the erosion of Huguenot identity; indeed, having left behind a homeland that had persecuted and expelled them, Huguenots found precious few reasons to retain French customs. For the Scots of New Jersey, however, the Great Awakening served further to unite them and emphasize their particularity, their connectedness with Scottish religious traditions, even though the revival brought them into contact with other ethnic groups. Scottish revivalism on both sides of the Atlantic was a communal exercise that reinforced ties of confession and kinship. Unlike the Scots, however, who came to the New World with a strong nationalistic identity forged in repeated skirmishes with England, the Dutch of New York, actually an amalgam of immigrants and descendants from all of the United Provinces, could draw on no such tradition, and by the time of the American Revolution, the majority had made their peace with English and American culture.[42]

Even ethnic suspicions between the Dutch and the English did not retard this process. England and the Netherlands had battled fiercely for maritime supremacy in the mid-seventeenth century, and those antagonisms carried over into the New World; boundary disputes with New England had flared for decades before English ships, a restive populace, and chronically inadequate defenses had convinced Pieter Stuyvesant to surrender. The English Conquest in 1664, the culmination of long-simmering tensions on both sides of the Atlantic, came just at a time when the Dutch colony had begun to show signs—however tentative—of permanence and even prosperity, a circumstance that lent a tinge of tragedy to New Netherland's demise. For Dutch artisans and small traders, however, the Conquest represented a personal tragedy as well, one that transcended mere sentiment or nationalism; the incursion of the English had frustrated their own economic aspirations, and the willingness of Dutch merchants and clergy to cooperate with English officials eventually sundered the Dutch community. With the seeds of internal division already sown as early as the 1660s, the English stepped up their pressures to make the Dutch into English, or at least to make them quiescent. That strategy met with rebellion in 1689, but after the turn of the century, when the Dutch had become a minority in New York, the English intensified their efforts and found that the Society for the Propagation of the Gospel, with its schools and aggressive proselytization, abetted by sympathetic governors, served as an effective tool for making the colony English.

The Dutch in New Jersey, however, like many of the Germans of Pennsylvania, gravitated toward a pietism articulated by preachers alienated from the religious establishment. Whereas the urbane Dutch clergy in New York had made their peace with English rule and Anglican religion by the early eighteenth century, the pietistic Dutch across the Hudson found the enthusiasm of the Great Awakening more palatable, and that fervor led quite comfortably into demands for ecclesiastical independence from Holland and, eventually, political independence from Britain.

For the Dutch, unlike other ethnic groups in the Middle Colonies, the inexorable process of assimilation was rather more complex and often tortuous, playing upon both internal divisions and external pressures. By the close of the American Revolution, however, the Dutch Reformed Church, a perpetual battleground for issues such as Anglicization, Leisler's Rebellion, pietism, and patriotism, faced a new century with an evangelical, assimilated clergy firmly in command; the War for Independence and the war of attrition had thinned the ranks of the traditionalists. The Church of England, the Presbyterians, and other English-speaking churches had claimed Dutch congregants through intermarriage and assimilation, and those Dutch who remained within the ambit of Dutch Calvinism preferred an evangelical religion with pietistic overtones, one that transcended ethnic boundaries.

After more than a century of English rule, the Dutch finally succumbed to the twin pressures of Anglicization, after the manner of the Church of England, on the one hand, and assimilation to the broader, heterogeneous culture of the Middle Colonies on the other. The orthodox clergy had struggled valiantly—they Anglicized in the seventeenth century, then resisted the English government after 1700, and then embraced it fully by the middle of the eighteenth century—but shifting political currents, cultural disintegration, and the enticements of the mainstream culture depleted their ranks. With so few reasons for remaining Dutch in eighteenth-century New York and New Jersey, the Dutch Reformed Church, the only Netherlands institution to survive the English Conquest of 1664, languished as a fiduciary of Batavian traditions and culture.

As William Strickland continued his tour of the Hudson Valley in the 1790s, he encountered delapidated and neglected Dutch church buildings, churchyard fences in disrepair. The Dutch, he concluded, "having forsaken their language," also forsook their religion, "having been led away by other more prevailing sects."[43]

APPENDIX A

Chronology of Dutch Reformed Churches

	Location*	First Settled Minister
1628	New Amsterdam (New York)	Michaëlius
1642	Fort Orange (Albany)	Megapolensis
1654	New Amstel, Del. (New Castle)	Welius
	Amersfoort (Flatlands)	Polhemus
	Bushwick	Polhemus
	Midwout (Flatbush)	Polhemus
1655	Gravesend	Polhemus
1659	Esopus (Kingston)	Blom
1660	Bergen, N.J.	(New York ministers)
	Brooklyn	Polhemus
	Harlem	(New York ministers)
	Stuyvesant's Chapel	Selyns
1662	Schenectady	Schaats
1680	Port Richmond (Staten Island)	Van Zuuren
1686	Hackensack, N.J.	Tesschenmaeker
1693	Acquackanonk, N.J. (Passaic)	Bertholf
1694	Tappan	Bertholf
1697	Tarrytown	Bertholf
	Middletown, N.J. (Holmdel)	Lupardus
1699	Marlboro, N.J. (Freehold)	Lupardus
	Raritan, N.J. (Somerville)	Bertholf
1700	Second River, N.J. (Belleville)	Bertholf
1701	Rochester (Accord)	(Kingston ministers)
1702	Jamaica	Antonides
1703	Three Mile Run, N.J.	Frelinghuysen
1707	Schaghticoke (Reynolds)	(Supply ministers)
1710	Ponds, N.J. (Oakland)	Bertholf
	Six Mile Run, N.J. (Franklin Park)	Van Vlecq

	Location*	First Settled Minister
1711	Stone Arabia (originally German)	(Supply ministers)
1712	Kinderhook	P. Van Driessen
1713	Pompton Plains, N.J.	Bertholf
1716	Claverack	J. Van Driessen
	Fishkill	J. Van Driessen
	Poughkeepsie	J. Van Driessen
1717	New Brunswick, N.J.	Frelinghuysen
1719	North Branch, N.J. (Readington)	Frelinghuysen
1720	Horseneck, N.J. (Fairfield)	(Supply ministers)
	Schoharie (Huntersfield)	(Supply ministers)
1722	Linlithgo (Livingston Manor)	J. Van Driessen
1724	Schraalenburg, N.J.	Erickzon
1727	Sourland, N.J. (Harlingen)	Frelinghuysen
	New Paltz (formerly Huguenot)	(Supply ministers)
1728	Germantown	J. Van Driessen
1729	Courtlandtown (Montrose)	Ritzema
1730	Katsbaan (originally German)	Mancius
1731	Newton	J. H. Goetschius
	Rhinebeck	Vas
	Success (North Hempstead)	J. H. Goetschius
1732	Oyster Bay	J. H. Goetschius
	Catskill (originally German)	Weiss
	Coxsackie (originally German)	Weiss
	Wallkill (Montgomery)	(Supply ministers)
1737	Marbletown	(Kingston ministers)
	Mahackemack (Port Jervis)	Mancius
	Shawangunck	(Kingston ministers)
	Minisink, N.J. (Montague)	Mancius
	Walpack, Pa.	Mancius
1745	Wawarasing (Naponoch)	Fryenmoet
1746	Gallatin (Mt. Ross)	Fryenmoet
	Ancram	(Supply ministers)
1749	New Hempstead (Clarkstown)	Verbryck
1755	Totowa, N.J. (Patterson)	Marinus
1756	Schodack	Fryenmoet
	Parsippany, N.J. (Montvale)	Marinus
1757	Hopewell	Rysdyck
1758	Bedminster, N.J.	Hardenbergh
	Neshanic, N.J.	Hardenbergh
	Caughnawaga (Fonda)	(Supply ministers)
	New Hackensack	(Supply ministers)

	Location*	First Settled Minister
1763	Beaverdam	Schuyler
1766	Hillsborough, N.J. (Millstone)	(Supply ministers)
	Red Hook Landing (Madalin)	(Supply ministers)
1767	Helderbergh	(Supply ministers)
1769	Clove	(Supply ministers)
	Dover	(Supply ministers)
	Hillsdale	(Supply ministers)
1770	English Neighborhood (Ridgefield)	Lydekker
	Manheim	(Supply ministers)
	New Hurley	S. Goetschius
	Schuylerville (Saratoga)	(Supply ministers)
1773	Kakiat (West New Hempstead)	Marinus

*Unless noted otherwise, locations are in New York.

APPENDIX B

Prosopography of Colonial Dutch Clergy
(alphabetical listing)

	Church Served	Tenure
Antonides, Vincentius (1670–1744)	Long Island	1705–44
Arondeus, Johannes	Long Island	1742–47
	Raritan	1747–54
Backerus, Johannes Cornelissen	New York	1647–49
Bertholf, Guiliam* (1656–c.1726)	Hackensack	1694–1724
Beys, Henricus (b. 1675)	Kingston	1705–8
University of Leiden		
Blauw, Cornelius	Fairfield	1762–68
University of Groningen	Hackensack	1768–71
Blom, Hermanus (b. 1628)	Kingston	1660–67
University of Utrecht		
Boel, Henricus (1692–1754)	New York	1713–54
University of Leiden		
Boelen, Hermanus	Jamaica	1766–72
	Newtown	1772–80
Bogardus, Everardus (1607–47)	New York	1633–47
University of Leiden		
Cock, Gerhard Daniel (d. 1791)	Germantown	1764–91
Coens, Henricus (d. 1735)	Passaic	1726–35
Curtenius, Antonius (1698–1756)	Hackensack	1730–55
University of Groningen	Long Island	1775–56
Dellius, Godfridus (1652–1714?)	Albany	1683–99
University of Leiden		
De Ronde, Lambertus (1720–95)	New York	1750–84
	Schagiticoke	1784–95
Drisius, Samuel (1600–1673)	New York	1652–73
University of Leiden		
Du Bois, Gualtherus (1671–1751)	New York	1699–1751

	Church Served	Tenure
Erickzon, Reinhardt (1695?–1771)	Hackensack	1725–28
University of Groningen	Schenectady	1728–36
	Freehold	1736–64
Freeman, Bernardus* (1662?–1743)	Schenectady	1700–1705
	Long Island	1705–41
Frelinghuysen, Henricus (d. 1757)	Warwarsing	1754–57
Dorsius, Goetschius		
Frelinghuysen, John (1727–54)	Raritan	1750–54
Frelinghuysen, Theodorus* (1691–1747)	Raritan	1720–47
University of Lingen		
Frelinghuysen, Theodore, Jr. (1723–61)	Albany	1749–59
Goetschius		
Froeligh, Solomon (1750–1827)	Jamaica	1775–76
Goetschius	Fishkill	1776–80
	Millstone	1780–86
	Hackensack	1786–1822
Fryenmoet, Johannes* (1720–78)	Minisink	1741–56
	Kinderhook	1756–78
Goetschius, John H. (1717–74)	Long Island	1741–48
Dorsius	Hackensack	1748–74
Goetschius, John M. (1724–71)	Schoharie	1757–60
Goetschius	New Paltz	1760–71
Goetschius, Stephen (c.1752–1837)	New Paltz	1775–96
Goetschius	Marbletown	1796–1814
	Saddle River	1814–35
Grasmeer, Wilhelmus	Rensselaer	1651–52
Haeghoort, Gerardus (d. 1783?)	Freehold	1731–35
	Belleville	1735–76
Hardenbergh, Jacob (1736–90)	Raritan	1758–81
J. Frelinghuysen	Marbletown	1781–86
	New Brunswick	1785–90
Jackson, William (1732–1813)	Bergen	1757–89
Goetschius, J. Frelinghuysen		
Kern, John Michael*	New York	1763–71
	Montgomery	1771–78
Keteltas, Abraham* (1733–98)	Jamaica	1760–62
Kuypers, Warmoldus (1732–97)	Rhinebeck	1769–71
University of Groningen	Hackensack	1771–97
Laidlie, Archibald* (1727–79)	New York	1764–79
University of Edinburgh		

	Church Served	Tenure
Leydt, Johannes* (1718–83)	New Brunswick	1748–83
Frelinghuysen, Goetschius		
Livingston, John H. (1746–1825)	New York	1770–1810
University of Utrecht	Queen's College	1810–25
Lupardus, Wilhelmus (d. 1702?)	Long Island	1695–1702
Luyck, Aegidius	New York	1671
Lydekker, Gerrit (1729–94)	Ridgefield	1770–76
Goetschius, Ritzema	New York	1776–83
Lydius, Johannes (d. 1709)	Albany	1700–1709
University of Leiden		
Mancius, George* (1706–62)	Schraalenburg	1731–32
	Kingston	1732–62
Marinus, David*	Passaic	1752–73
	Kakiat	1773–78
Megapolensis, Johannes (1601–70)	Albany	1642–49
	New York	1649–70
Megapolensis, Samuel (1634–1706)	New York	1664–68
University of Utrecht		
Meinema, Benjamin (d. 1761)	Poughkeepsie	1745–56
Meyer, Hermanus (c.1720–91)	Kingston	1763–72
University of Groningen	Fairfield	1772–85
	Totowa	1785–91
Michaëlius, Jonas* (b. 1577)	New York	1628–32
University of Leiden		
Morgan, Joseph* (1671–1740)	Freehold	1709–29
Muzelius, Frederick (1704–82)	Tappan	1726–49
Nucella, Johannes (d. 1722)	Kingston	1695–1704
Polhemus, Johannes (1598–1676)	Long Island	1655–76
Ritzema, Johannes (1710–96)	New York	1744–84
	Kinderhook	1778–88
Romeyn, Dirck* (1744–1804)	Marbletown	1766–75
Goetschius	Hackensack	1775–84
	Schenectady	1784–1804
Romeyn, Thomas (1729–94)	Long Island	1753–60
Frelinghuysen, Goetschius	Port Jervis	1760–72
	Caughnawaga	1772–94
Rosenkrantz, Abraham* (d. 1796)	New York	1758–59
Rubel, Johannes* (1719–97)	Long Island	1759–83
Rysdyck, Isaac (d. 1790)	Hopewell	1765–72
University of Groningen	Fishkill	1772–89

	Church Served	Tenure
Schaats, Gideon (1607–94)	Albany	1652–94
Schoonmaker, Henricus* (1739–1820)	Poughkeepsie	1763–64
Goetschius	Passaic	1774–99
	Totowa	1799–1816
Schuneman, Johannes (1712–94)	Catskill	1753–94
Frelinghuysen, Goetschius		
Schuyler, Johannes (d. 1779)	Schoharie	1736–55
	Hackensack	1755–66
	Beaverdam	1766–79
Selyns, Henricus (1636–1701)	Long Island	1660–64
University of Leiden	New York	1682–1701
Tesschenmaeker, Petrus (d. 1691)	New Castle	1679–82
University of Utrecht	Schenectady	1682–91
Van den Bosch, Lawrentius* (d. 1696)	Kingston	1686–89
Vanderlinde, Benjamin* (1719–89)	Paramus	1748–89
Dorsius, Goetschius		
Van Driessen, Johannes* (b. 1697)	Kinderhook	1727–35
University of Groningen		
Van Driessen, Petrus (d. 1738)	Albany	1712–38
University of Groningen		
Van Gaasbeck, Lawrentius (d. 1680)	Kingston	1678–80
University of Leiden		
Van Harlingen, Johannes (1724–95)	Sourland	1762–95
Van Harlingen, John M. (1761–1813)	Millstone	1787–95
	Seminary	1795–1812
Van Hovenbergh, Eggo Tonkens	Claverack	1749–56
	Rhinebeck	1756–64
Van Nieuwenhuysen, Wm. (d. 1681)	New York	1671–81
Van Rensselaer, Nicholas* (1647–78)	Albany	1675–77
University of Leiden		
Van Santvoord, Corn. (1688–1752)	Staten Island	1718–42
University of Leiden	Schenectady	1742–52
Van Schie, Cornelius (1703–44)	Poughkeepsic	1731–33
University of Leiden	Albany	1733–44
Van Sinderen, Ulpianus (1708–96)	Long Island	1746–84
Van Zuuren, Casparus (b. 1648)	Long Island	1677–85
University of Leiden		
Varick, Rudolphus (d. 1694)	Long Island	1686–94
University of Utrecht		
Vas, Petrus (1658?–1752)	Kingston	1710–52

	Church Served	Tenure
Verbryck, Samuel* (1721–84)	Tappan	1750–84
Goetschius, Leydt		
Vrooman, Barent (1725–83)	New Paltz	1753–54
University of Utrecht	Schenectady	1754–83
Weeksteen, Johannes (1643?–87)	Kingston	1681–87
University of Leiden		
Welius, Everardus (d. 1659)	New Castle	1657–59
Westerlo, Eilardus (1738–90)	Albany	1760–90
University of Groningen		

*Indicates ordination known to be from some authority other than the Classis of Amsterdam. Source of education, where known, appears beneath the minister's name.

Sources: Frederick Lewis Weis, "The Colonial Clergy of the Middle Colonies: New York, New Jersey, and Pennsylvania, 1628–1776," *Proceedings of the American Antiquarian Society* 66 (1956): 167–351; Edward T. Corwin, *Manual of the Reformed Church in America,* 4th ed. (New York, 1902).

APPENDIX C

New York City
Property Valuations, 1674

Property Holder	Oath*	Value in Dutch Florins
Abramse, Jacob		2,500
Andriese, Luycas	Yes	1,500
Backer, Hendrick Willemse		2,000
Backer, Reynier Willemse	Yes	5,000
Bartelse, Jonas	Yes	3,000
Bayard, Balthazar		1,500
Bayard, Nicholas	Yes	10,000
Beeckman, William	Yes	3,000
Bordingh, Claes		1,500
Clopper, Cornelius		5,000
Coerton, Barent		3,500
Coly, Jan		1,200
Cregier, Martin	Yes	2,000
De Forest, Isaac	Yes	1,500
De Haert, Balthazar	Yes	2,000
De Haert, Jacob		6,000
De Haert, Matthys		12,000
De Meyer, Nicholas	Yes	50,000
De Peyster, Johannes	Yes	15,000
Duyckingh, Evert	Yes	1,600
Ebbingh, Jeronimus	Yes	30,000
Harberding, Jan		2,000
Hondecoutre, Daniel		5,000
Hooghlandt, Christopher	Yes	5,000
Joosten, Jan	Yes	1,500
Kay, Jacob Theunisse		8,000
Kiersteede, Hans	Yes	2,000
Kip, Jacob	Yes	4,000

Property Holder	Oath*	Value in Dutch Florins
Lawrence, Jan	Yes	10,000
Leisler, Jacob	Yes	15,000
Levy, Assur	Yes	2,500
Lewis, Thomas		6,000
Luersen, Carsten		5,000
Luyck, Aegidius	Yes	5,000
Marius, Peter Jacob		5,000
Minvielle, Gabriel		10,000
Philipse, Frederick	Yes	80,000
Pietersen, Adolph		1,100
Pietersen, Evert		2,000
Richard, Poulis	Yes	5,000
Rombouts, Francois		5,000
Romyn, Simon Janse	Yes	1,200
Shakerly, Jan		1,400
Siecken, Dirck	Yes	2,000
Smit, Dirck		2,000
Smit, Hendrick Wesselse		1,200
Steenwyck, Cornelius	Yes	50,000
Ten Eyck, Coenraet	Yes	5,000
Van Bommel, Jan Hendrickse	Yes	1,500
Van Borsim, Cornelius		8,000
Van Brugh, Johannes	Yes	14,000
Van Clyff, Dirck	Yes	1,500
Van Cortlandt, Olof Stevens	Yes	45,000
Van Cortlandt, Stephanus		5,000
Vander Spiegel, Lourens		6,000
Van de Water, Jacob		2,500
Van Ruyven, Cornelius	Yes	18,000
Van Tright, Isaac		2,000
Van Vlecq, Isaac		1,500
Van Westveen, Cornelius D.		1,200
Varravanger, Jacob		8,000
Verplanck, Gelyn		5,000

*Signer of 1664 Oath of Allegiance to England.

Sources: Documents relative to the Colonial History of the State of New-York, 15 vols., ed. by E. B. O'Callaghan (Albany, 1856–87), II, 699–700; III, 74–77. For exchange rates, see John J. McCusker, *Money and Exchange in Europe and America, 1600–1775: A Handbook* (Chapel Hill, N.C., 1978), 42–60.

APPENDIX D

Consistory Members
of New York City Church,
1689–1701

1689 Consistory	Office	Politics
De Key, Jacobus	Elder	Anti-Leislerian
Marius, Pieter Jacobszen	Elder	Anti-Leislerian
Roelofsen, Boelen	Elder	Unknown
Van Brug, Johannes	Elder	Leislerian
De Forest, Isaac	Deacon	Anti-Leislerian
Kip, Johannes	Deacon	Anti-Leislerian
Schuyler, Brandt	Deacon	Anti-Leislerian
Spratt, John	Deacon	Leislerian
Ratio for 1689:		2 Leislerians/5 Anti-Leislerians

1690 Consistory	Office	Politics
Beekman, Wilhelmus	Elder	Leislerian
De Key, Jacobus	Elder	Anti-Leislerian
Van Brug, Johannes	Elder	Leislerian
Van Vleck, Isaac	Elder	Unknown
De Forest, Isaac	Deacon	Anti-Leislerian
Harberding, Jan	Deacon	Anti-Leislerian
Kip, Johannes	Deacon	Anti-Leislerian
Pietersen, Adolph	Deacon	Unknown
Ratio for 1690:		2 Leislerians/4 Anti-Leislerians

167

1691 Consistory	Office	Politics
Beekman, Wilhelmus	Elder	Leislerian
Kerfbyl, Johannes	Elder	Anti-Leislerian
Van Cortlandt, Stephanus	Elder	Anti-Leislerian
Van Vleck, Isaac	Elder	Unknown
Boelen, Jacob	Deacon	Leislerian
Harberding, Jan	Deacon	Anti-Leislerian
Kip, Jacobus	Deacon	Unknown
Pietersen, Adolph	Deacon	Unknown

Ratio for 1692: 2 Leislerians/3 Anti-Leislerians

1692 Consistory	Office	Politics
Kerfbyl, Johannes	Elder	Anti-Leislerian
Kip, Johannes	Elder	Anti-Leislerian
Marius, Pieter Jacobszen	Elder	Anti-Leislerian
Van Cortlandt, Stephanus	Elder	Anti-Leislerian
Boelen, Jacob	Deacon	Leislerian
De Key, Theunis	Deacon	Anti-Leislerian
Kip, Jacobus	Deacon	Unknown
Schuyler, Brandt	Deacon	Anti-Leislerian

Ratio for 1691: 1 Leislerian/6 Anti-Leislerians

1693 Consistory	Office	Politics
Harberding, Jan	Elder	Anti-Leislerian
Kip, Johannes	Elder	Anti-Leislerian
Marius, Pieter Jacobszen	Elder	Anti-Leislerian
Roelofsen, Boelen	Elder	Unknown
De Key, Theunis	Deacon	Anti-Leislerian
Schuyler, Brandt	Deacon	Anti-Leislerian
Spratt, Jan	Deacon	Leislerian
Van Cortlandt, Jacobus	Deacon	Anti-Leislerian

Ratio for 1693: 1 Leislerian/6 Anti-Leislerians

1694 Consistory	Office	Politics
Bayard, Nicholas	Elder	Anti-Leislerian
Harberding, Jan	Elder	Anti-Leislerian
Roelofsen, Boelen	Elder	Unknown
Van Vleck, Isaac	Elder	Unknown
De Forest, Isaac	Deacon	Anti-Leislerian
De Peyster, Johannes	Deacon	Leislerian
Spratt, Jan	Deacon	Leislerian
Van Cortlandt, Jacobus	Deacon	Anti-Leislerian

Ratio for 1694: 2 Leislerians/4 Anti-Leislerians

1695 Consistory	Office	Politics
Bayard, Nicholas	Elder	Anti-Leislerian
Beekman, Wilhelmus	Elder	Leislerian
Kerbfyl, Johannes	Elder	Anti-Leislerian
Van Cortlandt, Stephanus	Elder	Anti-Leislerian
Van Vleck, Isaac*	Elder	Unknown
De Forest, Isaac	Deacon	Anti-Leislerian
De Peyster, Johannes	Deacon	Leislerian
De Reimer, Isaac	Deacon	Leislerian
Kip, Jacobus	Deacon	Unknown

Ratio for 1695: 3 Leislerians/4 Anti-Leislerians

1696 Consistory	Office	Politics
Boelen, Jacob	Elder	Leislerian
Kerfbyl, Johannes	Elder	Anti-Leislerian
Marius, Pieter Jacobszen	Elder	Anti-Leislerian
Van Cortlandt, Stephanus	Elder	Anti-Leislerian
De Peyster, Isaac	Deacon	Leislerian
De Reimer, Isaac	Deacon	Leislerian
Kip, Jacobus	Deacon	Unknown
Ten Eyck, Dirck	Deacon	Leislerian

Ratio for 1696: 4 Leislerians/3 Anti-Leislerians

1697 Consistory	Office	Politics
Boelen, Jacob	Elder	Leislerian
Douw, Gerard	Elder	Unknown
Harberding, Jan	Elder	Anti-Leislerian
Marius, Pieter Jacobszen	Elder	Anti-Leislerian
De Peyster, Isaac	Deacon	Leislerian
Kip, Isaac	Deacon	Unknown
Roosevelt, Nicholas	Deacon	Leislerian
Ten Eyck, Dirck	Deacon	Leislerian

Ratio for 1697:   4 Leislerians/2 Anti-Leislerians

1698 Consistory	Office	Politics
Douw, Gerard*	Elder	Unknown
Harberding, Jan	Elder	Anti-Leislerian
Kip, Johannes	Elder	Anti-Leislerian
Roelofsen, Boelen	Elder	Unknown
Van Cortlandt, Jacobus	Elder	Anti-Leislerian
Kip, Isaac	Deacon	Unknown
Provoost, David, Jr.	Deacon	Leislerian
Roosevelt, Nicholas	Deacon	Leislerian
Van Giesen, Johannes	Deacon	Leislerian

Ratio for 1698:   3 Leislerians/3 Anti-Leislerians

1699 Consistory	Office	Politics
Beekman, Wilhelmus	Elder	Leislerian
De Peyster, Johannes	Elder	Leislerian
Roelofsen, Boelen	Elder	Unknown
Van Cortlandt, Jacobus	Elder	Anti-Leislerian
Goulet, Jacobus	Deacon	Leislerian
Provoost, David, Jr.	Deacon	Leislerian
Ringo, Albartus	Deacon	Leislerian
Van Giesen, Johannes	Deacon	Leislerian

Ratio for 1699:   6 Leislerians/1 Anti-Leislerian

1700 Consistory	Office	Politics
Beekman, Wilhelmus	Elder	Leislerian
Boelen, Jacobus	Elder	Leislerian
De Peyster, Johannes	Elder	Leislerian
De Reimer, Isaac	Elder	Leislerian
Goulet, Jacobus	Deacon	Leislerian
Ringo, Albartus	Deacon	Leislerian
Staats, Samuel	Deacon	Leislerian
Ratio for 1700:	7 Leislerians/0 Anti-Leislerians	

1701 Consistory	Office	Politics
Boelen, Jacobus	Elder	Leislerian
De Peyster, Isaac	Elder	Leislerian
De Reimer, Isaac	Elder	Leislerian
Roosevelt, Nicholas	Elder	Leislerian
Duiken, Gerritt	Deacon	Leislerian
Huigen, Lendert	Deacon	Leislerian
Kip, Isaac	Deacon	Unknown
Staats, Samuel	Deacon	Leislerian
Ratio for 1701:	7 Leislerians/0 Anti-Leislerians	

*Died in office.

Sources: "First Book of List of the Ministers, Elders and Deacons of the Low Dutch Church, New York," ms. at Collegiate Church, New York City; *Minutes of the Common Council of the City of New York,* 8 vols. (New York, 1905), II, 163–78; *Documents relative to the Colonial History of the State of New-York,* 15 vols., ed. by E. B. O'Callaghan (Albany, 1856–87), III, 588, 716–17, 749; *Ecclesiastical Records: State of New York,* 7 vols., ed. by Edward T. Corwin (Albany, 1901–16), II, 1246–61; John M. Murrin, "English Rights as Ethnic Aggression: The English Conquest, the Charter of Liberties of 1683, and Leisler's Rebellion in New York," in *Authority and Resistance in Early New York,* ed. by William Pencak and Conrad Edick Wright (New York, 1988), 56–94. Johannes De Peyster initially supported Leisler, later abandoned him, but he appears in the 1701 voting lists as the Leislerian candidate for alderman in the East Ward.

APPENDIX E

Dutch Reformed Polity

National Synod

Highest authority in Dutch Calvinism. The most famous meeting of a Dutch Synod occurred at Dort in 1618–19, when the Dutch Reformed Church repudiated Arminianism.

Synod

Two Synods in the Netherlands: North Holland and South Holland. The Synod of North Holland supervised the churches in New York and New Jersey.

Classis

The Classis of Amsterdam assumed direct responsibility for churches in North America. Other Classes in the Synod of North Holland: Hoorn, Edam, Haarlem, Alkmarr, Enkhuizen.

Coetus

A provisional ecclesiastical body in colonial areas. The Coetus at Suriname provided direct precedent for the Coetus in America, which was opposed by the Conferentie, who maintained their subordination to Holland.

Consistory

Ministers and elders of a particular congregation or collegiate churches.

Congregation

Members of the church, admitted either by baptism, confession of faith, or letter of transfer from another congregation.

NOTES

PREFACE

1. J. Franklin Jameson, ed., *Narratives of New Netherland, 1609–1664* (New York, 1909), 122–33, 391–415, quotes from 392, 396.
2. Ibid., 124–25.
3. See, for example, Benjamin C. Taylor, *Annals of the Classis of Bergen, of the Reformed Dutch Church, and the Churches under Its Care: Including, the Civil History of the Ancient Township of Bergen, in New Jersey,* 3d ed. (New York, 1857); Abraham Messler, *Forty Years at Raritan: Eight Memorial Sermons, with Notes for a History of the Reformed Dutch Churches in Somerset, N.J.* (New York, 1873); Edward T. Corwin, "The Character and Development of the Reformed Church in the Colonial Period," in *Centennial Discourses: A Series of Sermons Delivered in the Year 1876 by the Order of the General Synod of the Reformed (Dutch) Church in America,* 2d ed. (New York, 1877), 41–66.
4. John M. Murrin suggests that this process of Anglicization, which he demonstrates for Massachusetts, was common to all of the Atlantic colonies, that over the course of the eighteenth century colonial instituions—legal, religious, military—increasingly resembled their British counterparts. See "Anglicizing an American Colony: The Transformation of Provincial Massachusetts" (Ph.D. diss., Yale University, 1966).

CHAPTER 1

1. J. Franklin Jameson, ed., *Narratives of New Netherland, 1609–1664* (New York, 1909), 123–25, 131. On the life and career of Michaëlius, see A. Eekhof, *Jonas Michaëlius: Founder of the Church in New Netherland* (Leiden, 1926); Charles E. Corwin, "The First Dutch Minister in America," *Journal of the Presbyterian Historical Society* 12 (1925): 144–51.
2. *Colonial Records: General Entries, 1664–65,* New York State Library, *History Bulletin,* no. 2 (1899): 81, 82, 95–98.
3. William Smith, Jr., *The History of the Province of New-York* (London, 1757), 2 vols., ed. by Michael Kammen (Cambridge, Mass., 1972), I, 34. For other secondary treatments of the Conquest, see Mrs. Schuyler [Mariana Griswold] Van Rensclaer, *History of the City of New York in the Seventeenth Century,* 2 vols. (New York, 1090), I, chap. 15; John Romeyn Brodhead,

History of the State of New York, 2 vols. (New York, 1853–71), II, chap. 1; David T. Valentine, *History of the City of New York* (New York, 1853), chap. 12.

4. *Documents Relative to the Colonial History of the State of New-York,* 15 vols., ed. by E. B. O'Callaghan (Albany, 1856–87), II, 251; cf. *Ecclesiastical Records: State of New York,* 7 vols., ed. by Edward T. Corwin (Albany, 1901–16), I, 558. Although pagination in these volumes is continuous, I shall note the volume number as well as the page number for each citation.

5. *Eccl. Recs. N.Y.,* I, 560, 562.

6. Ibid., I, 548–50. For another translation of this letter, see A. P. G. van der Linde, ed. and trans., *Old First Dutch Reformed Church of Brooklyn, New York: First Book of Records, 1660–1752* (Baltimore, 1983), 229–33.

7. *Eccls. Recs. N.Y.,* I, 597. John M. Murrin comments: "No institution suffered more from the conquest than the Dutch Reformed church, which had just begun to flourish under Stuyvesant." "English Rights as Ethnic Aggression: The English Conquest, the Charter of Liberties of 1683, and Leisler's Rebellion in New York," in *Authority and Resistance in Early New York,* ed. by William Pencak and Conrad Edick Wright (New York, 1988), 61.

8. Quoted in E. B. O'Callaghan, *History of New Netherland; or, New York under the Dutch,* 2 vols. (New York, 1846–48), II, 531.

9. Ibid., II, 525–27; *N.-Y. Col. Docs.,* II, 444–45, 248–50. See also Henry H. Kessler and Eugene Rachlis, *Peter Stuyvesant and His New York* (New York, 1959), 268; For a full account of Stuyvesant's surrender, see chap. 15.

10. *N.-Y. Col. Docs.,* II, 509.

11. Ibid., II, 499–500.

12. *Eccl. Recs. N.Y.,* I, 593, 687; *N.-Y. Col. Docs.,* XIII, 416; cf. II, 722. Regarding Megapolensis's plight, see Gerald Francis De Jong, "Dominie Johannes Megapolensis: Minister to New Netherland," *New-York Historical Society Quarterly* 52 (1968): 39–45.

13. On February 6, 1665, pursuant to a petition from the directors of the West India Company, the States-General of the Netherlands "resolved and concluded to authorize said Directors hereby to attack, conquer and ruin the English everywhere, both in and out of Europe, on land and water, with whatever force, through God's blessing . . ." (*N.-Y. Col. Docs.,* II, 307).

14. David S. Lovejoy writes: "For some time New Netherlands had been a thorn in the side of good mercantilists in England and hungry colonists in America. Both saw their trade threatened, furs siphoned off to Holland, and the expansion of New England blocked by foreigners at New Amsterdam and Fort Orange (Albany)." *The Glorious Revolution in America* (New York, 1972), 98. Robert Brenner places the first Anglo-Dutch war within the broader context of English politics in the mid-seventeenth century. The merchants with interests in North America, he argues, gained ascendency over

the Levant–East India establishment in large measure because the political upheaval of the 1640s broke the power of the royalist-leaning merchant elite. The Independent victory of 1648, then, gave American traders access to the portals of power previously reserved only to the Levant–East India group. The Act of 1650, the Navigation Act of 1651, and the first Dutch war, therefore, should be seen as a flexing of the new merchants' political and commercial strength. "The Social Basis of English Commercial Expansion, 1550–1650," *Journal of Economic History* 32 (1972): 361–84.

15. *Col. Recs.: Gen. Entries,* 104. Robert C. Ritchie points out that the duke of York also expected a tidy profit from New York and that he and his advisers were chagrined when immediate profitability proved elusive. "The Duke of York's Commission of Revenue," *New-York Historical Society Quarterly* 58 (1974): 177–87; cf. idem, "London Merchants, the New York Market, and the Recall of Sir Edmund Andros," *New York History* 57 (1976): 5–29. For the larger context of Anglo-Dutch economic rivalries in the seventeenth century, see Charles Wilson, *Profit and Power: A Study of England and the Dutch Wars* (London, 1957).

16. George Masselman, "Dutch Colonial Policy in the Seventeenth Century," *Journal of Economic Hisotry,* 21 (1961): 455; *N.-Y. Col. Docs.,* III, 74–77.

17. Edward T. Corwin, *A Manual of the Reformed Church in America, 1628–1902,* 4th ed. (New York, 1902), s.v. "Bogardus, Everardus."

18. "Abstracts of Wills, Vol. II, 1708–1728," New-York Historical Society, *Collections,* Publication Fund Series, XXVI (New York, 1894), 167.

19. See the probate will of Margaret Van Varick (Rudolphus's widow), "Abstracts of Wills, Vol. I, 1665–1707," N.-Y. Hist. Soc., *Colls.,* Publication Fund Series XXV (New York, 1892), 260–61, 271–72.

20. Ibid., 450, 68; David McQueen, "Kings County, N.Y., Wills," *New York Genealogical and Biographical Register* 47 (1916): 168–69; cf. D. T. Valentine, *Manual of the Corporation of the City of New-York* (New York, 1858), 502. Regarding colonial exchange rates, see John J. McCusker, *Money and Exchange in Europe and America, 1600–1775: A Handbook* (Chapel Hill, N.C., 1978), esp. 42–60. Both English and Dutch currencies remained strong throughout the colonial period, and therefore the rate of exchange varied little, about nine or ten guilders (florins) to the pound. The Albany minister's estate, therefore, would be worth about four hundred pounds sterling.

21. Koert Burnham, "Godfrey Dellius: An Historical Obituary by a Protagonist," *De Halve Maen* 54 (Summer 1979): 14.

22. "Abstracts of Wills," N.-Y. Hist. Soc., *Colls.,* XXV, 211; on Steenwyck's wealth, see Appendix C. Selyns and his wife also owned "One fourth Parte of the Shipp Beavor." "Admiralty Court Document, Sept. 19, 1687," ms. in Emmet Collection (no. 10578), New York Public Library.

23. Lynn Haims, "Wills of Two Early New York Poets: Henricus Selyns and Richard Steer," *New York Genealogical and Biographical Record* 108 (1977): 5–6. When Selyns, senior minister in the New York City church, solicited funds for a new church building, his own pledge (out of 194 contributors) was by far the largest. See Kenneth Scott, "Contributors to Building of a Dutch Church in New York City, 1688," *De Halve Maen* 55 (Spring 1980): 10–12.

24. William J. Hoffman, "The Ancestry of Rev. Gualtherus du Bois and Two Generations of His Descendants," *New York Genealogical and Biographical Record* 82 (1951): 134–39.

25. Berthold Fernow, ed., *The Records of New Amsterdam from 1653–1674 Anno Dominie,* 7 vols. (New York, 1897), VII, 104; Appendix C lists Van Ruyven's tax assessment. In 1714, another wealthy Dutchman, A. D. Philipse, intervened on behalf of Godfridus Dellius, Dutch minister at Albany from 1683 to 1699. See Joel Munsell, ed., *The Annals of Albany,* 10 vols. (Albany, 1849–59), X, 223–24.

26. Josephine C. Frost, "Baptisms from the Records of the Reformed Protestant Dutch Church of the Town of Flatbush, Kings Co., New York," 2 vols., typescript at the Brooklyn Historical Society.

27. "Abstracts of Wills," N.-Y. Hist. Soc., *Colls.,* XXV, 68, 103, 150. The wife of an eighteenth-century clergyman "was a lady of gentle birth." See Henry Melchior Mühlenberg, *The Journals of Henry Melchior Mühlenberg,* 3 vols., trans. by Theodore G. Tappert and John W. Doberstein (Philadelphia, 1942–53), I, 283.

28. This sentiment resurfaced after the restoration of Dutch rule in the colony in 1673. See *N.-Y. Col. Docs.,* II, 752–53.

29. This understanding of *Anglicizers* and *Anglicization* I have appropriated from John M. Murrin; see "English Rights as Ethnic Aggression"; "Anglicizing an American Colony: The Transformation of Provincial Massachusetts" (Ph.D. diss., Yale University, 1966).

30. Jacob Judd, "Frederick Philipse and the Madagascar Trade," *New-York Historical Society Quarterly* 55 (1971): 354–74, Appendix C.

31. *Col. Recs.: Gen. Entries,* 137–38; Nicolls granted trading privileges to Jeremias Van Rensselaer in Rensselaerswyck (p. 119). Cf. A. J. F. van Laer, ed., *Correspondence of Jeremias van Rensselaer, 1651–1674* (Albany, 1932), 375, 391, 465; ms. copy, in Robert Livingston's hand, of letter from Jan Baptiste Van Rensselaer to Nicholas Van Rensselaer, January 10/20, 1678 (no. 10141), New York State Archives, Albany.

32. Ritchie, "London Merchants," 5–29. On colonial monopolies in this period, see Patricia U. Bonomi, *A Factious People: Politics and Society in Colonial New York* (New York, 1971), 52–53.

33. Luyck's name appears on the 1674 list of the city's wealthiest men (see Appendix C). Luyck was called to assist Samuel Drisius, who had become

senile. *Recs. of New Amsterdam,* VI, 292. In 1670, elders of New York City's Lutheran church described Drisius, the Dutch Reformed minister, as "not much good, his head being in a muddle." *The Lutheran Church in New York, 1649–1672: Records in the Lutheran Church Archives at Amsterdam, Holland,* trans. by Arnold J. F. van Laer (New York, 1946), 77.

34. Jan Kupp, "Aspects of New York–Dutch Trade under the English, 1670–1674," *New-York Historical Society Quarterly* 58 (1974): 139–47.

35. See Appendix C; "Abstracts of Wills," N.-Y. Hist. Soc., *Colls.,* XXV, 272.

36. Regarding the Dutch aversion to agriculture in the New World, see Oliver A. Rink, *Holland on the Hudson: An Economic and Social History of Dutch New York* (Ithaca, N.Y., 1986); Albert Cook Myers, ed., *Narratives of Early Pennsylvania, West New Jersey, and Delaware, 1630–1707* (New York, 1912), 316. On colonial apprenticeships, see Ronald W. Howard, "Apprenticeship and Economic Education in New Netherland and Seventeenth-century New York," in *Education in New Netherland and the Middle Colonies: Papers of the 7th Rensselaerswyck Seminar of the New Netherland Project,* ed. by Charles T. Gehring and Nancy Anne McClure Zeller (Albany, 1985), 17–33.

37. David Steven Cohen, "How Dutch Were the Dutch of New Netherland?" *New York History* 62 (1981): 43–60. On the economic history of New Netherland, see Rink, *Holland on the Hudson;* chap. 6 provides a profile of immigrants to New Netherland; cf. idem, "The People of New Netherland: Notes on Non-English Immigration to New York in the Seventeenth Century," *New York History* 62 (1981): 5–42. On Dutch affluence in the Netherlands, see Simon Schama, *The Embarrassment of Riches: An Interpretation of Dutch Culture in the Golden Age* (Berkeley and Los Angeles, 1988).

38. See Morton Wagman, "The Rise of Pieter Claessen Wyckoff: Social Mobility on the Colonial Frontier," *New York History* 53 (1972): 5–24; Judd, "Frederick Philipse," 354–55.

39. *N.-Y. Col. Docs.,* XIII, 405. The 1672 entry in "The First Book of the Lists of the Ministers, Elders and Deacons of the Low Dutch Church, New York" reads in part: "The number of Elders is increased from three to four, for the best interests of the church, as also for the better collecting of the ministers salary which comes from the congregation and is paid by the same" (ms. at Collegiate Church, New York City).

40. *Eccl. Recs. N.Y.,* I, 587, 595.

41. Ibid., I, 587.

42. Peter Christoph, Kenneth Scott, and Kenn Strycker-Rodda, eds., *New York Historical Manuscripts: Dutch: Kingston Papers,* 2 vols., trans. by Dingman Versteeg (Baltimore, 1976), II, 404. Even before the Conquest, Blom had hauled various Kingston church members into court to force payment of his salary. See Samuel Oppenheim, ed., *Dutch Records of Kingston,*

Ulster County, New York (Esopus, Wildwyck, Swanenburgh, Kingston), 1658–1684, with Some Later Dates (Cooperstown, N.Y., 1912), 117–20.

43. *Recs. of New Amsterdam*, VI, 58–59.

44. Peter R. Christoph and Florence A. Christoph, eds., *New York Historical Manuscripts: English: Books of General Entries of the Colony of New York, 1664–1673* (Baltimore, 1982), 447.

45. *Recs. of New Amsterdam*, VI, 240. Lovelace guaranteed a salary of one thousand guilders, firewood, and rent-free accommodations. The New York consistory later conveyed this guarantee to the Classis. *Eccl. Recs. N.Y.*, I, 620.

46. *Minutes of the Executive Council of the Province of New York: Administration of Francis Lovelace, 1668–1673*, 2 vols. (Albany, 1910), II, 617–18.

47. *Recs. of New Amsterdam*, VI, 300, 309–11.

48. Schaats himself requested a recall to Holland. Ibid., VI, 79; *Eccl. Recs. N.Y.*, I, 587–88. On Blom's complaints and judicial interventions, see *Dutch N.Y. Hist. Mss.: Kingston*, II, 290, 306, 320; the Dutch government of New Netherland had also intervened in the Blom case; see I, 209. For the Albany proceedings, see A. J. F. van Laer, ed., *Minutes of the Court of Albany, Rensselaerwyck and Schenectady, 1668–1685*, 3 vols. (Albany, 1926–32), I, 162, 322.

49. *N.-Y. Col. Docs.*, XIV, 652–53; *Recs. of New Amsterdam*, VI, 367–68.

50. *Documentary History of the State of New-York* [quarto ed.], 4 vols., ed. by E. B. O'Callaghan, (Albany, 1850–51), III, 530; unless noted otherwise, references to this set of documents will be from the quarto or large-paper edition published in 1850–51, rather than the small-paper octavo edition published in 1850.

51. *Eccl. Recs. N.Y.*, I, 601–3; cf. *N.-Y. Col. Docs.*, XIII, 423–24.

52. *Eccl. Recs. N.Y.*, I, 595–96.

53. Smith, *History of New-York*, I, 39. When English rule was restored, Manning was court-martialed, convicted of neglecting his duty, and dismissed from the crown's employ. Van Rensselaer, *City of New York*, II, 174–75. For documents pertaining to Manning's trial, see *Doc. Hist. N.-Y.*, III, 53–65.

54. *N.-Y. Col. Docs.*, II, 658, 578; Colve's commission is reprinted in II, 609–10. On the brief interval of Dutch rule, particularly its effect on New England interests, see Ronald D. Cohen, "The New England Colonies and the Dutch Recapture of New York, 1673–1674," *New-York Historical Society Quarterly*, 56 (1972): 54–78.

55. *N.-Y. Col. Docs.*, II, 572–73, 622–24, 666. The council also refused a request from Englishmen on Long Island to procure whaling tools from New England; II, 583–84.

56. *Recs. of New Amsterdam*, VI, 405–6.

57. *N.-Y. Col. Docs.*, II, 622, 574–75. The phrase "or at least well affected thereunto" may have been a caveat aimed at the English Puritans on Long

Island. In New Orange (New York City), for example, of the nine magistrates chosen in the brief interval of Dutch rule, eight of the names appear also on the 1674 list of property valuations (cf. II, 532, and Appendix C). Except for the explicit provision that magistrates belong to the Dutch Reformed Church, the restored Dutch rulers essentially reverted to the system of authority used in New Netherland. See Albert E. McKinley, "The English and Dutch Towns of New Netherland," *American Historical Review* 6 (1900–01): 1–18.

58. *Eccl. Recs. N.Y.*, I, 636–37; William A. Whitehead, ed., *Archives of the State of New Jersey: Documents Relating to the Colonial History of the State of New Jersey*, 1st Series, 42 vols. (Newark, 1880–1949), I, 135; *N.-Y. Col. Docs.*, II, 620–22. At the top of the list of instructions for Peter Alrich, "Schout Commander of the Southriver," was the following charge: "To see that sincere, true Christian religion in conformity with the Synod of Dordrecht be taught and to maintain it by all proper means"; XII, 510.

59. Quoted in Jerome R. Reich, *Leisler's Rebellion: A Study of Democracy in New York, 1664–1720* (Chicago, 1953), 30, 31–32.

60. Permission, however, was denied; *N.-Y. Col. Docs.*, III, 233, 236.

61. See Appendix C.

62. "Miscellaneous Documents," New-York Historical Society, *Collections*, Publication Fund Series, XLVI (New York, 1914), 83–84. The proclamation bore Nicholas Bayard's name as secretary; Bayard later opposed Leisler's Rebellion.

63. A. J. F. van Laer, ed., *Correspondence of Jeremias van Rensselaer, 1651–1674* (Albany, 1932), 116–17, 375.

64. On Van Rensselaer's insanity, see [James I. Wyer, Jr.] "Report on the Director, 1909," *New York State Library Annual Report* 92 (1909): 21. For a secondary treatment of the Van Rensselaer affair, see Lawrence H. Leder, "The Unorthodox Dominie: Nicholas Van Rensselaer," *New York History* 35 (1954): 166–76. The case is also reviewed in Charles H. McCormick, "Leisler's Rebellion (Ph.D. diss., American University, 1971), 60–66.

65. A. J. F. van Laer, ed., *Correspondence of Maria van Rensselaer, 1669–1689* (Albany, 1935), 43, 63, 65. The claim to Rensselaerswyck ultimately did not stand up in the courts, although his name does appear in the Albany county records as "director of colony Renselaerswyck." Jonathan Pearson, ed., *Early Records of the City and County of Rensselaerswyck* (Albany, 18769), 165, cf. 171. The Albany court did indeed appoint Van Rensselaer director of Rensselaerswyck, albeit on a provisional basis. A. J. F. van Laer, ed., *Minutes of the Court of Albany, Rensselaerswyck and Schenectady, 1668–1685*, 3 vols. (Albany, 1926–32), II, 87.

66. Joel Munsell, ed., *The Annals of Albany*, 10 vols. (Albany, 1849–59), VII, 265.

67. "Abstracts of Wills, Vol. I," 68.

68. *Eccl. Recs. N.Y.,* I, 677.

69. As a deacon, Van Rensselaer, in fact, could not legally administer Communion in an Anglican church, either.

70. *Doc. Hist. N.-Y.,* III, 526–27.

71. *Eccl. Recs. N.Y.,* I, 680–82.

72. Cuyler Reynolds, comp., *Albany Chronicles: A History of the City Arranged Chronologically, From the Earliest Settlement to the Present Time* (Albany, 1907), 75–77; cf. notarized document of the court appearance in Albany, September 8, 1676, Livingston Family Papers, 8. Miscellaneous Livingston Family Papers, C. Livingston Papers Relating to Albany and Albany County, 1673–1788, ms. at Franklin D. Roosevelt Presidential Library, Hyde Park, N.Y.; van Laer, *Albany Court Minutes,* II, 147, 150. In a later deposition, Leisler and Milborne refuted Van Rensselaer's charges and deflated his pretensions, arguing that blasphemy "is of a higher order than a dominie can pretend to. Van Laer, ed., *Albany Court Minutes,* II, 153.

73. Van Laer, ed., *Albany Court Minutes,* II, 162–63.

74. See Appendix C. Leisler's warrant appears in *Doc. Hist. N.-Y.,* III, 528.

75. Ibid., III, 529.

76. For the consistory's declaration, see *Early Records of the City and County of Albany and Colony of Rensselaerswyck,* Vol. 3, trans. by Jonathan Pearson, ed. by A. J. F. van Laer, *New York State Library History Bulletin* 10 (1918): 347–48.

77. *Doc. Hist. N.-Y.,* III, 530. For documents concerning the Van Rensselaer affair, see also *Annals of Albany,* VI, 67–74; and for a quite different interpretation of the case, which views Van Rensselaer with considerably more sympathy, see Dunkin V. R. Johnston, "Dominie Nicholas Van Rensselaer: An Historical Enigma," typescript (no. SC5490) at New York State Archives, Albany.

78. *Eccl. Recs. N.Y.,* I, 702; cf. Edward T. Corwin, *A Manual of the Reformed Church in American, 1628–1902,* 4th ed. (New York, 1902), s.v. "Van Rensselaer, Nicholas"; Van Rensselaer, *City of New York,* II, 183.

79. I have appropriated the phrase "alien standards of English justice" from John Murrin.

80. See Douglas Nobbs, *Theocracy and Toleration: A Study of the Disputes in Dutch Calvinism from 1600 to 1650* (Cambridge, Eng., 1938).

81. *A Platform of Church Discipline Gathered Out of the Word of God: and Agreed upon by the Elders: and Messengers of the Churches Assembled in the Synod at Cambridge in New England* (Cambridge, Mass., 1649), 28. For Calvin's view, see [John] Calvin, *Institutes of the Christian Religion,* 2 vols., ed. by John T. NcNeill, trans. by Ford Lewis Battles (Philadelphia, 1960), II, 1485–87. St. Augustine asked: "For what doth it matter in respect of this short and transitory life, under whose dominion a mortal man doth live, as

long as he be not compelled to acts of impiety or injustice" *The City of God,* 2 vols. trans. by John Healy (London, 1945), I, 164.

82. *Eccl. Recs. N.Y.,* I, 55.

83. For a treatment of Bogardus's dispute with Kieft, see Quirinus Breen, "Dominie Everhardus Bogardus," *Church History* 2 (1933): 78–90.

84. Richard Hooker, *Of the Laws of Ecclesiastical Polity: An Abridged Edition,* ed. by A. S. McGrade and Brian Vickers (New York, 1975), 352.

85. *The Colonial Laws of New York: From the Year 1664 to the Revolution,* 5 vols. (Albany, 1894–96), I, 25.

86. Keith to S.P.G., September 4, 1703, Records for the Society for the Propagation of the Gospel (microfilm), Letterbook Series A, Vol. 1, no. 121.

87. See Smith, *History of New-York,* I, 43, on James's intentions.

88. *Eccl. Recs. N.Y.,* I, 686; Smith, *History of New-York,* I, 44. Of the Van Rensselaer affair, Lawrence Leder writes: "It was this schism which largely determined the character and complexion of a later development—the Leisler Rebellion of 1689–1691." "Unorthodox Dominie," *New York History* 35 (1954): 173. Milborne absented himself from the colony from 1677 to 1678. On his return Andros had him incarcerated for a day on the charge that he had " 'presumed to clamor' and to write 'scurrilously' against the government of the province and magistracy of the city." When Milborne and Andros (now relieved of his post) found themselves in London in 1681, Milborne sued Andros for false arrest and was awarded forty-five pounds in damages. *N.-Y. Col. Docs.,* III, 300–301; Van Rensselaer, *City of New York,* II, 185.

89. "Calendar of Council Minutes," *New York State Library History Bulletin* 6 (1902): 27. Jacob Milborne, though English, already had identified himself with the Dutch. He had joined the Dutch Reformed Church, spent time in Holland before 1689, and eventually married Leisler's daughter.

90. Andros's order appears in *Eccl. Recs. N.Y.,* I, 724–26; cf. *N.-Y. Col. Docs.,* XXI, 633.

91. *Eccl. Recs. N.Y.,* I, 730–33. Interestingly, the Labadist Jasper Danckaerts was in New York on September 24, 1679, when Dominie Schaats came down from Albany to assist in the examination of Tesschenmaeker. Danckaerts identified both Schaats and Tesschenmaeker as Voetians and the other ministers (Van Nieuwenhuysen, Van Gaesbeck, and Van Zuuren) as Coccians, referring to Dutch theologians Gysbertus Voetius (1589–1676), a pietist, and his less pietistic countryman Johannes Coccejus (1603–69). *Journal of Jasper Danckaerts, 1679–1680,* ed. by Bartlett Burleigh James and J. Franklin Jameson (New York, 1913), 44–45.

92. *Eccl. Recs. N.Y.,* I, 726–39.

93. Ibid., I, 675. Though flawed in several particulars, "The Labadist Colony in Maryland," by Bartlett Burleigh James, offers a brief summary of this group's doctrine, communal life, and early settlement in the New World.

Papers of the American Society of Church History 8 (1897): 149–60. A more reliable account is James Tanis, "Reformed Pietism in Colonial America," in *Continental Pietism and Early American Christianity,* ed. by F. Ernest Stoeffler (Grand Rapids, Mich. 1976), 34–73.

94. For a brief treatment of Labadism, see F. Ernest Stoeffler, *The Rise of Evangelical Pietism* (Leiden, 1965), 162–69.

95. *Eccl. Recs. N.Y.,* I, 656–58.

96. Ibid., I, 724; II, 785; cf. II, 746–47, 876. For a summary of Koelman's perambulations around the Netherlands, see II, 874–75.

97. Ibid., II, 823–24.

98. Tesschenmaeker, offering reasons for his leaving, complained of "the worn out condition of my clothes" and that he was "destitute and disheartened" (ibid., II, 835). Indeed, the documents attest that he was in considerable financial difficulty. See *N.-Y. Col. Docs.,* XXI, 641, 643.

99. *Eccl. Recs. N.Y.,* II, 831; on New Castle's membership at the time, see II, 833. In their separate accounts, Tesschenmaeker and Van Zuuren imply that Koelman himself had initiated the contact (II, 835, 839). This seems plausible in light of Jasper Danckaerts's earlier visit to New Castle and his disparaging comments about Tesschenmaeker (see note 100). Danckaerts, a Labadist, might well have returned to the Netherlands and informed Koelman of a possible opening on the Delaware.

100. It is quite possible that the New Castle congregation was happy to be rid of Tesschenmaeker. Jasper Danckaerts had heard Tesschenmaeker preach on December 17, 1679, and reported that he had "never heard worse preaching." Though certainly not an unbiased observer, he described the dominie as a man of "no grace" and "a perfect worldling." Danckaerts continued: "It seems that in these spiritually, as well as physically, waste places, there is nevertheless a craving of the people to accept anything that bears even the name of food, in order to content rather than to satisfy themselves therewith." *Journal of Jasper Danckaerts,* 138.

101. *Eccl. Recs. N.Y.,* II, 830, 832. Selyns thought Koelman so perfidious that he might try to leave Amsterdam under an assumed name, thereby eluding the Netherlands ecclesiastical authorities. He was perhaps especially aware of the Labadist threat because he had only recently left the Netherlands. At any rate, he urged that Koelman's "coming over ought to be anticipated and prevented" (II, 833).

102. Ibid., II, 876.

103. Ibid., II, 849–50. Tesschenmaeker took over the church at Staten Island and eventually went on to Schenectady, where he died at the hands of the French and the Indians in 1690.

104. Although his conclusions have been contested, Thomas J. Archdeacon calculates that by 1703, seventy-eight percent of the inhabitants of the poorest area in New York were Dutch. He also observes: "By 1703 dispropor-

tionately large numbers of Englishmen and Huguenots made their residences on the wealthiest streets of the island. Dutch grandees lived side by side with the new elite, but the ordinary Dutch inhabitants who formed so large a part of the port's population filled the more modest streets and the poorer districts." *New York City, 1664–1710: Conquest and Change* (Ithaca, N.Y., 1976), 92, 86. In her study of Albany, Donna Merwick contends that the English takeover engendered considerable resentment and divisions within Albany society. "Becoming English: Anglo-Dutch Conflict in the 1670's in Albany, New York," *New York History* 62 (1981): 389–414. Cf. *Eccl. Recs. N.Y.*, I, 686.

105. Of the nine Dutchmen chosen to form the municipal government of New York City (now, briefly, Fort Orange) after the Dutch Reconquest in 1673, only one name does not appear on the 1674 list of property valuations in New York City. Cf. Appendix C and *N.-Y. Col Docs.*, II, 575.

106. *Eccl. Recs. N.Y.*, I, 717. Van Zuuren clearly was out of step with the other dominies, for in later correspondence he identifies three kinds of communicants: the first, very few, take the side of the English; the second "try to serve two masters"; and the third is the very small number of "faithful adherents of God." He continued: "Here it is the English Party [lit. the Anglicized people] who destroy our New Netherland" (II, 792–93; brackets in quoted source).

107. Ibid., I, 733. Even Andros had reported to London in 1678: "Ministers have been soe scarce & Religions many that noe acct cann be giuen of the number married." *Doc. Hist. N.-Y.*, I, 61.

108. As early as September 1665, the Classis of Amsterdam received a letter from Dominie Drisius expressing his desire to return to Holland following the English Conquest. The Classis, however, resolved that he be encouraged "to remain there, and to oppose the introduction of the English Liturgy into our Church, as much as possible." *Eccl. Recs. N.Y.*, I, 575.

109. Ibid., I, 648. Regarding Van Ruyven's wealth, see Appendix C.

Chapter 2

1. The only real exception to this was Dominie Gideon Schaats's brief disagreement with his congregation at Albany, a result of family problems. See *Documentary History of the State of New-York* [quarto ed.] 4 vols., ed. by E. B. O'Callaghan (Albany, 1850–51), III, 533–34.

2. *Ecclesiastical Records: State of New York*, 7 vols., ed. by Edward T. Corwin (Albany, 1901–16), II, 755, 838, 861–62), 886–87; *Doc. Hist. N.-Y.*, I, 117.

3. *Eccl. Recs. N.Y.*, II, 829, 866.

4. Ibid., II, 842–43, 872–73, 891–92, 949–50. The calls for fast days were

renewed on the two succeeding years and observed again early in January 1688; the latter two proclamations sound much more like jeremiads than the first two, calling the people to repentance for their sins.

5. Ibid., II, 867. On the politics in New York during these years, see Robert C. Ritchie, *The Duke's Province: A Study of New York Politics and Society, 1664–1691* (Chapel Hill, N.C., 1971). Thomas F. O'Connor's "Religious Toleration in New York, 1664–1700," *New York History* 17 (1936): 391–410 attributes the relative toleration on the part of the English in the early years after the Conquest to their magnanimity and liberality. O'Connor, however, fails to account for the fact that the English were badly outnumbered by other ethnic groups, especially the Dutch. On this issue, Milton M. Klein's assessment is more accurate. Klein argues that religious toleration in New York, from the Flushing Remonstrance of 1657 under the Dutch to the Articles of Capitulation to the abortive Charter of Libertyes under the English, was a pragmatic response to the colony's rampant diversity. "New York in the American Colonies: A New Look," *New York History* 53 (1972): 132–56.

6. *Documents Relative to the Colonial History of the State of New-York,* 15 vols., ed. by E. B. O'Callaghan (Albany, 1856–87), III, 331. New York was the last of the Restoration proprietaries to have a representative assembly. On the duke's reluctance to grant an assembly to New York, see David S. Lovejoy, *The Glorious Revolution in America* (New York, 1972), 106–21; cf. idem, "Equality and Empire: The New York Charter of Libertyes, 1683," *William and Mary Quarterly* (3d ser.) 21 (1964): 493–515. A fiscal crisis in the colony finally forced James's hand.

7. *The Colonial Laws of New York: From the Year 1664 to the Revolution,* 5 vols. (Albany, 1894–96), I, 115.

8. *N.-Y. Col. Docs.,* III, 357.

9. *Col. Laws N.Y.,* I, 123–24.

10. Albert E. McKinley, "The Transition from Dutch to English Rule in New York," *American Historical Review* 6 (1900–01): 693–724, esp. 703. On the process of Anglicization and New York's relation to New England in these years, see Dixon Ryan Fox, *Yankees and Yorkers* (New York, 1940), chap. 5. Regarding the Anglicization of Dutch institutions, see Michael Kammen, *Colonial New York—A History* (New York, 1975), chap. 6.

11. Herbert Alan Johnson, "English Statutes in Colonial New York," *New York History* 58 (1977): 277–96; idem, "The Prerogative Court of New York, 1868–1776," *American Journal of Legal History* 17 (1973): 95–144; idem, *Essays on New York Colonial Legal History* (Westport, Conn., 1981), 37–54; T. Raymond Naughton, "Criminal Law in Colonial New York," *New York History* 14 (1933): 235–40; Jessica Kross Ehrlich, " 'To Hear and Try All Causes betwixt Man and Man': The Town Court of Newton, 1659–1690," *New York History* 59 (1978): 277–305, esp. 279–80. By 1691, justices of the peace, a peculiarly English institution, were firmly entrenched in New York. See Douglas Greenberg, *Crime and Law Enforcement in the Colony of New*

York, 1691–1776 (Ithaca, N.Y., 1976), chap. 1; "Law in Colonial New York: The Legal System of 1691," *Harvard Law Review* 80 (1967): 1757–72; Julius Goebel, Jr., and T. Raymond Naughton, *Law Enforcement in Colonial New York: A Study in Criminal Procedure, 1664–1776* (New York, 1944).

12. William Heard Kilpatrick, *The Dutch Schools of New Netherland and Colonial New York,* U.S. Bureau of Education Bulletin, 1912, no. 12, chaps. 9–13.

13. Robert C. Ritchie, "London Merchants, the New York Market, and the Recall of Sir Edmund Andros," *New York History* 57 (1976): 5–29. Although he overstates the Dutch elite's resistance to Anglicization, Steve J. Stern offers a detailed account of Anglo-Dutch relations in New York after the English Conquest in "Knickerbockers Who Asserted and Insisted: The Dutch Interest in New York Politics, 1664–1691," *New-York Historical Society Quarterly* 58 (1974): 113–38.

14. *N.-Y. Col. Docs.* III, 372. James subsequently turned over the management of ecclesiastical affairs to the Lords of Trade (III, 388).

15. *Eccl. Recs. N.Y.,* II, 956, 958; in Selyns's letter, Andros's benevolence was at least implied.

16. The tax strike of 1681 and the intense agitation in New York for a colonial assembly apparently had little impact on the Dutch community.

17. The best secondary treatment of the American responses to the Glorious Revolution is Lovejoy, *Glorious Revolution in America.*

18. See "Nicholson Keeps the News Secret, March 1, 1689," in *The Glorious Revolution in America: Documents on the Colonial Crisis of 1689,* ed. by Michael G. Hall, *et al.* (Chapel Hill, N.C., 1964), 102. For Van Cortlandt's account of the rebellion, see *N.-Y. Col. Docs.,* III, 590–97.

19. "Documents Relating to the Administration of Leisler," New-York Historical Society, *Collections,* Publication Fund Series, I (New York, 1686), 324; *Eccl. Recs. N.Y.,* II, 1027. On the composition of the militia, see Kenneth Scott, "Jacob Leisler's Fifty Militiamen," *New York Genealogical and Biographical Record* 94 (1963): 65–72. For a brief profile of Leisler, see Thomas J. Archdeacon, *New York City, 1664–1710: Conquest and Change* (Ithaca, N.Y., 1976), 108–12. Leisler earlier had served on a grand jury, hearing charges of witchcraft against a man and his wife. *Doc. Hist. N.-Y.,* IV, 133–38.

20. *N.-Y. Col. Docs.* III, 615–16, 738.

21. *Calendar of State Papers, Colonial Series: America and West Indies,* 44 vols. (London, 1860–1969), VIII, 202. Leisler had dropped out of the Dutch church several years earlier. See John M. Murrin, "English Rights as Ethnic Aggression: The English Conquest, the Charter of Liberties of 1683, and Leisler's Rebellion in New York," in *Authority and Resistance in Early New York,* ed. by William Pencak and Conrad Edick Wright (New York, 1988), chap. 3.

22. *Cal. State Papers,* VIII, 117; "Leisler Documents," N.-Y. Hist. Soc., *Colls.,* I, 399, 380.

23. See *N.-Y. Col. Docs.*, IX, 411; Helen Broshar, "The First Push Westward of the Albany Traders," *Mississippi Valley Historical Review* 7 (1920–21): 228–41. Even the Catholic Thomas Dongan feared a French invasion (N.-Y. Col. Docs., III, 511). Bernard Mason writes: "Within the colony an exaggerated fear of Catholics and Catholicism gave credence to wild rumors of papist plots to seize control of the colony." "Aspects of the New York Revolt of 1689," *New York History* 30 (1949): 165–66. After news of the Glorious Revolution reached New York, but before the rebellion broke out, Jacob Leisler refused to pay duties on a shipment of wine because Matthew Plowman, Nicholson's collector, was Catholic (Lovejoy, *Glorious Revolution in America*, 255). Plowman, in fact, shortly after Leisler's takeover, wrote to the Marquis of Halifax with intelligence about how the colony might be taken from "these rebellious Dutchmen" ("Leisler Documents, " N.-Y. Hist. Soc., *Colls.*, I, 290–91). Halifax, apparently unbeknownst to Plowman at the time, supported William.

24. "Leisler Documents," N.-Y. Hist. Soc., *Colls.* I, 306; *Narratives of the Insurrections, 1675–1690,* ed. by Charles M. Andrews (New York, 1915), 375–76.

25. *N.-Y. Col. Docs.* III, 614–15. In 1691, Leisler refused to surrender the fort to Major Richard Ingoldesby, convinced that the "officers & Soldiers were King James Men & Papists." Quoted in Lawrence H. Leder, "Captain Kidd and the Leisler Rebellion," *New-York Historical Society Quarterly* 38 (1954): 51. Leisler doubtless derived great pleasure from appropriating a French ship, rechristening it *Jacob,* and sending it out as a privateer in 1689. Jacob Judd, "Frederick Philipse and the Madagascar Trade," *New-York Historical Society Quarterly* 55 (1971): 356.

26. "Leisler Documents," N.-Y. Hist. Soc., *Colls.,* I, 398; Thomas F. O'Connor, "A Jesuit School in Seventeenth Century New York," *Mid-America* 3 (1932): 265–68.

27. *Doc. Hist. N.-Y.,* III, 73; Joel Munsell, ed., *The Annals of Albany,* 10 vols. (Albany, 1849–59), VII, 271.

28. *Glorious Rev. Docs.,* 98.

29. "Leisler Documents," N.-Y. Hist. Soc., *Colls.,* I, 399. Leislerians charged that "the heads of our church" participated in the celebrations honoring the prince of Wales.

30. "New York in 1692," New-York Historical Society, *Collections,* 2d series, II (New York, 1849), 243.

31. Selyns wrote: "I have had the pleasure of receiving a call from him, and I have the privilege of calling on him whenever I desire." *Eccl. Recs. N.Y.,* II, 867.

32. Ibid., II, 1000; *N.-Y. Col. Docs.,* III, 731–33.

33. "Leisler Documents," N.-Y. Hist. Soc., *Colls.,* I, 409.

34. *Doc. Hist. N.-Y.,* II, 213; *N.-Y. Col. Docs.,* III, 583.

35. *Glorious Rev. Docs.*, 132; *Narratives of Insurrections*, 364; *Doc. Hist. N.-Y.* [octavo ed.], II, 391. The characterization "Boors and butterboxes," from a poem by Robert Livingston, may have been a play on words; the Dutch term for "farmer" is *boer*. The *Oxford English Dictionary* defines butterbox as a "Contemptuous designation for a Dutchman." Another anti-Leislerian characterized Leisler and Milborne as "base villains" who had "gathered together a rabble of the worse men." *Cal. State Papers*, VIII, 344. Lawrence H. Leder writes that "Leisler's government was composed of members of the middle and lower economic classes." "Captain Kidd and the Leisler Rebellion," *New York Historical Society Quarterly* 38 (1954): 50. Albany, too, was divided by the Leisler troubles. See Alice P. Kenney, *The Gansevoorts of Albany: Dutch Partricians in the Upper Hudson Valley* (Syracuse, N.Y., 1969), 16–20.

36. *N.-Y. Col. Docs.*, III, 595–96.

37. "Leisler Documents," N.-Y. Hist. Soc., *Colls.*, I, 402. One Leislerian characterized Bayard thus: "as inveterate as any Papist against the Revolution" (376). For a membership list of the Dutch church, recording the names of the three councilors, see Henricus Selyns, *Records of Dominie Henricus Selyns of New York, 1686–7*, Holland Society of New York, *Collections* (New York, 1916), V. Two of Nicholson's three council members had just recently served as elders in the New York City Dutch church. Bayard was last chosen elder in 1688 (one year before the rebellion) and Van Cortlandt in 1686. See "The First Book on the List of the Ministers, Elders and Deacons of the Low Dutch Church, New York," ms. at Collegiate Church, New York City. Regarding the composition of the consistory, see Appendix D.

38. *N.-Y. Col. Docs.*, III, 738–47; Lawrence H. Leder, " '. . . Like Madmen through the Streets': The New York City Riot of June 1690," *New-York Historical Society Quarterly* 39 (1955): 405–15; quote regarding Leisler's son on 410. Another account put the number of rioters at "thirty odd" and attributed the uprising to "news that King James's party in Ireland hold power." *Cal. State Papers*, VIII, 286.

39. *N.-Y. Col. Docs.* III, 739; Leder, " 'Like Madmen through the Streets' " 412.

40. Leder, " 'Like Madmen through the Streets,' " 414. Recounting the incident some years later, a prominent anti-Leislerian recalled that Selyns "was most grosly abused by Leysler himself in the Church at the time of Divine Service, and threatened to be silenced." *Narratives of Insurrections*, 367. Personality conflict cannot be discounted as the source of acrimony between Leisler and Selyns. Although he served as deacon at the time, Leisler did not participate in the call of Selyns, suggesting, as John Murrin points out, that his disaffection may have arisen in part from the church's hiring of Selyns ("English Rights as Ethnic Aggression").

41. *Ecc. Recs. N.Y.*, II, 1048–49.

42. Lovejoy, *Glorious Revolution in America,* 104. On the economic divisions during this period, see Patricia U. Bonomi, *A Factious People: Politics and Society in Colonial New York* (New York, 1971), 56–81.

43. Bernard Mason, "Aspects of New York Revolt," *New York History* 30 (1949): 168. New York City's three councilors at the time of the rebellion were Nicholas Bayard, Stephanus Van Cortlandt, and Frederick Philipse, all of whom appear prominently on the 1674 "wealthy list" (see Appendix C).

44. Archdeacon, *New York City,* 98. See Appendix C for a correlation between the city's wealthiest inhabitants in 1674 and those who had signed the 1664 Oath of Allegiance to England.

45. "NYK—1664—Notes," fol. 5, in "Papers Relating to New York 1608–1792," Chalmers Collection, New York Public Library.

46. *N.-Y. Col. Docs.,* III, 739; affidavit of Michael Hanse before John Lawrence, Mayor, April 22, 1691, ms. in Emmet Collection (no. 10579), New York Public Library; *Doc. Hist. N.-Y.* [octavo ed.], II, 390.

47. *N.-Y. Col. Docs.,* IV, 1111; on Beekman, see Philip L. White, *The Beekmans of New York in Politics and Commerce, 1647–1877* (New York, 1956), chap. 4.

48. *N.-Y. Col. Docs.,* III, 585, 738–39.

49. Ibid., III, 748–49; *Doc. Hist. N.-Y.,* [octavo ed.], II, 386. I have counted Jan Harberding among the Dutch church deacons, although he was not elected until later that year. See "First Book of Lists," ms. at Collegiate Church.

50. Although he fails to take religious motivations sufficiently into account, Thomas Archdeacon's research suggests that Leisler's Rebellion was a movement comprised of displaced Dutch who had grown weary of the pressures of Anglicization. As such, it was an ethnic movement, and few of its followers were English or French. "The Age of Leisler——New York City, 1689–1710: A Social and Demographic Interpretation," in *Aspects of Early New York Society and Politics,* ed. by Jacob Judd and Irwin H. Polishook (Tarrytown, N.Y., 1974), 63–82; idem, " 'Distinguished for Nation Sake': The Age of Leisler in New York City," in *Colonial America: Essays in Politics and Social Development,* ed. by Stanley N. Katz, 2d ed. (Boston, 1976), 143–54. On the Dutch ruling elite against which the Leislerians revolted, Charles H. McCormick comments: "The aristocracy prior to Leisler's Rebellion is virtually synonymous with government placemen and one broad alliance, which might awkwardly be termed the Van Courtland-Schuyler-Bayard-Teller-De Lavall-Van Rensselaer connection." "Leisler's Rebellion" (Ph.D. diss., American University, 1971), 42.

51. *Cal. State Papers,* VIII, 117. When Jacob Milborne marched to Albany to secure the town's submission, he spoke directly to the "Common People" to enlist their support. Quoted in Lawrence H. Leder, *Robert Livingston, 1654–1728, and the Politics of Colonial New York* (Chapel Hill, N.C., 1961), 62.

52. For a discussion of clerical wealth, see Chapter 1. In accounting for the clergy's sympathies during the rebellion, Gerald F. De Jong writes that "the ministers were perhaps influenced by social considerations. They tended to consider themselves on the social level of the 'aristocrats' and people of influence, such as Nicholas Bayard, Stephanus Van Cortlandt, and Frederick Philipse of New York and Peter Schuyler of Albany, all of whom were opponents of Leisler and had been councillors of Lieutenant-governor Nicholson." *The Dutch Reformed Church in the American Colonies* (Grand Rapids, Mich., 1978), 55.

53. *Eccl. Recs. N.Y.*, II, 754–55. Robert C. Ritchie writes: "The new clergy who emigrated during the 1680s accepted English domination. Henricus Selyns, Rudolphus Varick, and Godfridius Dellius cooperated with the English rather than fight them." *The Duke's Province: A Study of New York Politics and Society, 1664–1691* (Chapel Hill, N.C., 1977), 148.

54. *N.-Y. Col. Docs.*, XIV, 650; *Eccl. Recs. N.Y.*, II, 884. Gerald De Jong writes: "Except for a few isolated incidents, the English governors for many years after the conquest made no determined effort to establish the Anglican Church among the Dutch colonists." *The Dutch in America, 1609–1974* (Boston, 1975), 91. A notable exception to this was Andros's forcing of Nicholas Van Rensselaer onto the Albany congregation.

55. *Eccl. Recs. N.Y.*, II, 952–53. No action was taken on this request.

56. John Calvin had taught that the magistrates—both godly and ungodly—were ordained of God and must be obeyed. See [John] Calvin, *Institutes of the Christian Religion*, 2 vols., ed. by John T. McNeill, trans. by Ford Lewis Battles (Philadelphia, 1960), II, 1151–52, 1183–84. Calvin had written that "if the correction of unbridled despotism is the Lord's to avenge, let us not at once think that it is entrusted to us, to whom no command has been given except to obey and suffer" (II, 1518). Given the generally amicable relations between the Dutch clergy and the English magistrates, it is unlikely that they regarded the English colonial government as despotic; nor were the ministers convinced that Leisler and Milborne comprised a "constituted magistracy" which had risen "to protect the liberties of the people" (II, 1518, n. 54).

57. Varick to Selyns, November 30, 1689, "Translations of Letters about Dominie Van den Bosch, 1689," Frederick Ashton De Peyster mss., New-York Historical Society; *Eccl. Recs. N.Y.*, II, 1007–8.

58. Charles H. McCormick believes that the delay in reestablishing English rule in the colony exacerbated the pro- and anti-Leislerian tensions. "Governor Sloughter's Delay and Leisler's Rebellion, 1689–1691," *New-York Historical Society Quarterly* 62 (1978): 238–52.

59. *Narratives of Insurrections*, 331–32. See John Pershing Luidens, "The Americanization of the Dutch Reformed Church" (Ph.D. diss., University of Oklahoma, 1969). Luidens writes of Leisler's Rebellion that "the result for the Dutch Church was a cleavage between clergy and members as great as

that dividing the social classes" (p. 75). Moreover, "By siding with the wealthy parishioners (merchants and landownders) and the English authority, the clergymen had caused many members to drop out of the Dutch churches" (p. 78).

60. *N.-Y. Col. Docs.*, IV, 219, 533; *Narratives of Insurrections*, 367; *Eccl. Recs. N.Y.*, II, 1050.

61. *Eccl. Recs. N.Y.*, II, 1052, 922, 1007–8; *N.-Y. Col. Docs.*, III, 748–49 (punctuation added).

62. "Leisler Documents," N.-Y. Hist. Soc., *Colls.*, I, 404.

63. Ibid., 334; cf. *Cal. State Papers*, X, 150.

64. Lawrence H. Leder, ed., "Records of the Trials of Jacob Leisler and His Associates," *New-York Historical Society Quarterly* 36 (1952): 452; "Leisler Documents," N.-Y. Hist. Soc., *Colls.*, I, 311–14; *Journal of the Legislative Council of the Colony of New York: Began the 9th Day of April, 1691, and Ended the 27 of September, 1743*, ed. by E. B. O'Callaghan (Albany, 1861), 3. Nicholas Bayard, Stephanus Van Cortlandt, and William Pinhorne, all bitter enemies of Leisler, were appointed "to collect evidence" against the Leislerians (*Cal. State Papers*, VIII, 402). The Leislerian defendant was probably either Leisler himself or Milborne, the only two who refused to enter pleas. On April 1, 1691, Leisler, after refusing a second time to plead, "was ordered to be tyed up and put in irons." "Copy of the Trial of Jacob Leisler and His Accomplices," Public Record Office, London, typescript (no. 10239) in New York State Archives, Albany. Cf. *Narratives of Insurrections*, 369, 392–93.

65. *Journal of Legislative Council*, 5, 20.

66. Kingston Consistory to [New York Ministers], August 30, 1690, "Translations of Letters about Dominie Van den Bosch, 1689," Frederick Ashton De Peyster mss., New-York Historical Society.

67. *Narratives of Insurrections*, 390.

68. Henry C. Murphy, *Anthology of New Netherland; or, Translations from the Early Dutch Poets of New York with Memoirs of Their Lives* (New York, 1865), 114.

69. *Eccl. Recs. N.Y.*, II, 1250–51, 1255–57; "Leisler Documents," N.-Y. Hist. Soc., *Colls.*, I, 406–8. This source says: "The joy of those who tried to kill him [Leisler] was inexpressible" (p. 408). For a documentary account of Leisler's trial, see Leder, ed., "Records of the Trials," 431–57.

70. For details of the execution, see *Doc. Hist. N.-Y.* [octavo ed.], II, 376–80, 382. One account claims that Leisler was laid in a vault he had built himself. *Cal. State Papers*, XII, 100.

71. I have quoted verses 1–3, 6–7, 11–12 (King James Version).

72. "Leisler Documents," N.-Y. Hist. Soc., *Colls.*, I, 406–7, 426.

73. Ibid., 409. This figure roughly corresponds to the Leislerians' claim that "those who were in favor of the Revolution were certainly ten to one" (p. 400).

74. The Long Island reference appears in *Eccl. Recs. N.Y.*, II, 1051; Albany in II, 1065.

75. On November 20, 1693, Selyns and Varick wrote to the Classis: "The arrearages of our salaries have become very large, and are paid in equally large promises. We are trying, however, to get our salaries on a better footing by the help of their Royal Majesties [William and Mary]" (ibid., II, 1089). In 1694, Selyns reported that his "salary is better paid; but the arrearages remain unpaid, and I see no prospect of their ever being paid" (ibid., II, 1108).

76. Varick's letter to the Classis could hardly have encouraged prospective clergy. He lamented: "I have received but little of my salary in four years, and that only from a few special friends in my congregation: I do not yet see how I am able to obtain my back pay. Ministers who serve here will have to live on their own fat" (ibid., II, 1051).

77. Ibid., II, 1048; *Cal. State Papers,* VIII, 534.

78. See Appendix D.

79. "Records of the Reformed Dutch Church in the City of New York—Church Members' List," *New York Genealogical and Biographical Record* 59 (1928): 69–76, 158–65, 259–66, 372–79. I am grateful to Joyce Diane Goodfriend for insights into Dutch church membership in the 1690s and for permission to cite her evidence; "The Social Dimensions of Congregational Life in New York City, 1664–1730," paper read at the Organization of American Historians Annual Convention, New York, April 1986.

80. See Appendix D.

81. *Eccl. Recs. N.Y.*, II, 1211, 1212; cf. II, 1273.

82. *Eccl. Recs. N.Y.*, II, 1042–43, 1258; "Leisler Documents," N.-Y. Hist. Soc., *Colls.,* I, 408. The dominies obviously believed that English law was on their side, because later in this letter they refer to "everything that was illegally done" against them during the Rebellion (*Eccl. Recs. N.Y.*, II, 1042–43). Even the venerable Increase Mather from Boston weighed in against the executions, writing that their "innocent blood is still crying in the ears of the Lord." *Doc. Hist. N.-Y.,* [octavo ed.], II, 437.

83. Roswell Randall Hoes, comp., *Baptismal and Marriage Registers of the Old Dutch Church of Kingston, Ulster County, New York* (New York, 1891), 53.

84. "Leisler Documents," N.-Y. Hist. Soc., *Colls.,* I, 398.

85. *Eccl. Recs. N.Y.*, III, 1490. The resolution was dated May 24, 1702. No doubt the interment of Leisler in the Dutch church rankled Selyns because Selyns himself planned to be buried there. Lynn Haims "Wills of Two Early New York Poets: Henricus Selyns and Richard Steer," *New York Genealogical and Biographical Register,* 108 (1977): 5.

86. Consistory elections were scheduled for that day, October 20, 1698, but church records indicate cryptically that the election was postponed for a week "for necessary and important reasons." "First Book of Lists," ms. at Collegiate Church.

87. *N.-Y. Col. Docs.,* IV, 620 621, 401; "Leisler Documents," N.-Y. Hist. Soc., *Colls.,* I, 411. The drumbeat itself may have been reminiscent of Leisler's rule, because Leislerians in the fort often used drums for communication, as a signal of danger, or to call the militia to assembly (*ibid.,* 268, 292, 305–306).

88. On New York's population, see "Garrett Abeel's Records," *Year Book of the Holland Society of New York* (New York, 1916), 70.

89. *N.-Y. Col. Docs.,* IV, 401, 620–21; *Cal. State Papers,* XII, 100. Another account reads: "Most of the principal inhabitants who had before suffered so severely withdrew in terror and secured their affects as well as they could during the time this mob was so up." (*Cal. State Papers, xii,* 100). On Leisler and Milborne's hangings and beheadings, see the deposition of Thomas Jeffers, "Leisler Documents," N.-Y. Hist. Soc., Colls., I, 321; cf. 425–26. This latter account, ostensibly on the authority of an eyewitness, says that Leisler's "head was sewd to his neck" after the executions and that the reburials took place amidst "a very great Snow Storm." Also: "Stories were propagated of Leisler's apparition in a Coach at the place he was buried."

90. Murrin, "English Rights as Ethnic Aggression," esp. Table 3.2.

91. *Eccl. Recs. N.Y.,* II, 1274–77.

92. Ibid., II, 1108, 1051–52.

93. *Cal. State Papers,* XII, 100; *N.-Y. Col. Docs.,* IV, 523, 400. Bellomont's arrival inspired conservative reactions from the anti-Leislerians. In 1699, Thomas and Parmyter testified that they had heard James Spencer "railing in a scurrilous manner against Leisler's party, saying that they were all rogues and my Lord Bellomont was no better for taking their parts." *Cal. State Papers,* XII, 72. Regarding Bellomont and the effect of English politics on colonial government in New York during these years, see John D. Runcie, "The Problem of Anglo-American Politics in Bellomont's New York," *William and Mary Quarterly* (3d ser.) 26 (1969): 191–217.

94. *Narratives of Insurrections,* 396.

95. *Eccl. Recs. N.Y.,* II, 1108.

96. Wayne Andrews, ed., "A Glance at New York in 1697: The Travel Diary of Dr. Benjamin Bullivant," *New-York Historical Society Quarterly* 40 (1956): 66. Bullivant saw some "shelling peas at theyr doors children playing at theyr usuall games in the streets & ye taverns filled."

97. *Eccl. Recs. N.Y.,* II, 1313–14; Koert Burnham, "Godfrey Dellius: An Historical Obituary by a Protagonist," *De Halve Maen* 54 (Summer 1979): 14.

98. Dellius to S.P.G., May 29, 1702, and May 7, 1705, Records of the Society for the Propagation of the Gospel, 1702–37 (microfilm), Letterbook Series A, Vol. 1, nos. VII and LXX.

99. Dellius to S.P.G., April 16, 1704, ibid., no. CLXIX: Dellius to Secretary of S.P.G., October 11, 1703, Lambeth Palace, Fulham Papers (microfilm), Vol. 6, fols. 178–79.

100. As an example of the Leislerian attempts to restore Dutch culture to the colony, the mayor and aldermen of New York City during the rebellion, "not being able to express Themselfs in ye English Tongue," had to secure the services of an Englishman in order to communicate with Connecticut authorities. See letter dated May 9, 1690, Livingston Family Papers, 1. Papers of Robert Livingston (1654–1728), B. Indian Affairs, 1666–1727, 1768, ms. at Franklin D. Roosevelt Presidential Library, Hyde Park, N.Y.

101. *Doc. Hist. N.-Y.,* II, 214. Thomas Archdeacon outlines the calamitous political infighting between Leislerian and anti-Leislerian Dutch in the years following the rebellion. See *New York City,* chap. 6. Patricia Bonomi writes that "the political history of New York from 1692 until 1710 is a rapid series of policy and party reversals which pitted 'ins' against 'outs' and interest against interest, making factional strife an almost endemic condition of the colony's public life." *A Factious People,* 78. Lawrence Leder contends that it was not until the end of the first decade of the eighteenth century that Leisler's Rebellion ceased to be the touchstone of New York politics. *Robert Livingston,* 200. Jerome R. Reich argues that Leisler's partisans were democrats protesting the arbitrary rule of James II, and that the Rebellion of 1689 prefigures the American Revolution a century later. See *Leisler's Rebellion: A Study of Democracy in New York, 1664–1720* (Chicago, 1953).

102. *Eccl. Recs. N.-Y.,* II, 1052. ;

103. On Bellomont's league with the Leislerians, see *N.-Y. Col. Docs.,* IV, 523.

104. Burnham, "Godfrey Dellius," 4–6, 14–15. Cf. John C. Rainbolt, "A 'Great and Usefull Designe': Bellomont's Proposal for New York, 1698–1701," *New-York Historical Society Quarterly* 53 (1969): 336–39. For documentary sources, see *Eccl. Recs. N.Y.,* II, 1313–35; and *N.-Y. Col. Docs.,* IV, 487–90, 510, 581–82. Dellius's defense against Bellomont's charges appears in *Eccl. Recs. N.Y.,* II, 1394–1422. Dellius later spoke bitterly about Bellomont's "ill administration" of New York. Godfrey Dellius to Paul Dudley, September 16, 1701, "The Winthrop Papers," Massachusetts Historical Society, *Collections* (6th ser.) 3 (Boston, 1889): 520–24.

105. *Cal. State Papers,* VIII, 698; *Eccl Recs. N.Y.,* II, 1231.

CHAPTER 3

1. This appears as one of the prefatory poems in Cotton Mather, *Magnalia Christi Americana, Books I and II,* ed. by Kenneth B. Murdock with Elizabeth W. Miller (Cambridge, Mass., 1977), 88.

2. Quoted in Henry C. Murphy, *Anthology of New Netherland: or, Translations from the Early Dutch Poets of New York with Memoirs of Their Lives* (New York, 1865), 96.

3. The Test Act, originally passed under Charles II, appears in George Burton Adams and H. Morse Stephens, eds., *Select Documents of English Constitutional History* (New York, 1929), 436–39.

4. *Ecclesiastical Records: State of New York,* 7 vols., ed. by Edward T. Corwin (Albany, 1901–16), II, 1016. The 1683 Charter had extended toleration to Catholics.

5. Ibid., II, 1045, 1075–76. Regarding the checkered history of the Ministry Act and its ultimate failure (by English standards), see Cynthia A. Kierner, "A Concept Rejected: New York's Anglican 'Establishment,' 1693–1715," *Essays in History* 26 (1982): 71–100. Kierner points out that the zealotry of successive English governors toward the establishment of Anglicanism had much to do with their political affiliations back in England. See also Edward T. Corwin, "The Ecclesiastical Condition of New York at the Opening of the Eighteenth Century," *Papers of the American Society of Church History* (2d ser.) 3 (1912): 81–115; R. Townsend Henshaw, "The New York Ministry Act of 1693," *Historical Magazine of the Protestant Episcopal Church* 2 (1933): 199–204; E. Clowes Chorley, "The Beginnings of the Church in the Province of New York," *Historical Magazine of the Protestant Episcopal Church* 13 (1944): 15–19; Jean Paul Jordan, "The Anglican Establishment in Colonial New York, 1693–1783" (Ph.D. diss., Columbia University, 1971), 71–83.

6. The Ministry Act appears in *The Colonial Laws of New York: From the Year 1664 to the Revolution,* 5 vols. (Albany, 1894–96), I, 328–31.

7. *Eccl. Recs. N.Y.,* II, 1084.

8. *Col. Laws N.Y.,* I, 576–79. Regarding Fletcher's difficulties implementing the legislation, see Borden W. Painter, "The Vestry in the Middle Colonies," *Historical Magazine of the Protestant Episcopal Church* 47 (1978): 9–10. Painter writes that the Ministry Act of 1693 "proved to be of dubious value for the Anglicans." He notes "the vagueness and ambiguity of the act, for it did not mention the Church of England, only saying that each clergyman should be 'a good and sufficient Protestant Minister.' All freeholders, regardless of religious affiliation, had the franchise to elect the wardens and vestrymen. As a result, chaos, confusion, and contention reigned in several of the parishes set up by the act."

9. *Eccl. Recs. N.Y.,* II, 1095; members of the 1694 vestry are listed on *ibid.*

10. Ibid., II, 1097 n.

11. Ibid., II, 1114–15.

12. Ibid., II, 1116; for a juxtaposition of the two charters, see II, 1136–65.

13. Ibid., II, 1142.

14. Ibid., II, 1171–72, 1168–69. Lord Bellomont, Fletcher's successor, insisted that the Dutch church had bribed Fletcher for the charter. See *Calendar of State Papers, Colonial Series: America and West Indies,* 44 vols. ed. by

W. N. Sainsbury, J. W. Fortescne, and Cecil Headlam (London, 1860–1969), XI, 539, 545.

15. *Eccl. Recs. N. Y.*, II, 1134–35, 1178; Morgan Dix and Charles Thorley Bridgeman, *A History of the Parish of Trinity Church in the City of New York,* 6 vols. (New York, 1901–62), I, 90, 110–11. The town vestry continued as a civil body until the American Revolution.

16. Lewis Morris to S.P.G., May 30, 1709, Records of the Society for the Propagation of the Gospel (microfilm), Letterbook Series C, I. Sixty years after the passage of the Ministry Act, William Livingston argued passionately in the *Independent Reflector* that the Church of England had indeed never been established in the province. See William Livingston, *The Independent Reflector; or, Weekly Essays on Sundry Important Subjects More Particularly Adapted to the Province of New-York,* ed. by Milton M. Klein (Cambridge, Mass., 1963), 367–77.

17. Bayard Still, *Mirror for Gotham: New York as Seen by Contemporaries from Dutch Days to the Present* (New York, 1956), 21; John Miller, *New York Considered and Improved, 1695,* ed. by Victor Hugo Paltsits (Cleveland, 1903), 40; William Warren Sweet, *Religion in Colonial America* (New York, 1942), 206; and Marcus L. Hansen, "The Minor Stocks in the American Population of 1790," *American Historical Association Proceedings* (Washington, D.C., 1932), 363–79, csp. 363–65.

18. Hansen writes: "The Dutch migration to New Jersey did not begin in full force until after 1700." "Minor Stocks," 366. He adds: "But the original habitat to which the greatest number of the now widely spread descendants of colonial Dutch trace their ancestry lies midway between New York and Albany, the region known as 'the Esopus,' now Ulster County, or more generally the hinterland of Kingston and Newburgh. Sound strategy and agricultural possibilities combined to encourage the settlement of this area" (368). On Dutch settlement in the Hudson Valley, see Sophia Gruys Hinshalwood, "The Dutch Culture Area of the Mid-Hudson Valley" (Ph.D. diss., Rutgers University, 1981); Beverly McAnear, "Politics in Provincial New York, 1689–1761" (Ph.D. diss., Stanford University, 1935), chap. 2. Wesley Frank Craven places the beginning of Dutch migration to New Jersey at 1664. *The English Colonization of North America* (Princeton, N.J., 1964), 14. Peter O. Wacker finds a movement of Hollanders into the Raritan as early as the 1680s. *Land and People: A Cultural Geography of Preindustrial New Jersey: Origins and Settlement Patterns* (New Brunswick, N.J., 1975), 133.

19. "Letters respecting New Jersey in 1681," *New Jersey Historical Society Proceedings* (n.s.) 15 (1930): 523, 530–31.

20. *Archives of the State of New Jersey: Documents Relating to the Colonial History of the State of New Jersey,* 1st Series, 42 vols. ed. by William A. Whitehead (Newark, 1880–1949), III, 333.

21. *Documents Relative to the Colonial History of the State of New-York,*

15 vols., ed. by E. B. O'Callaghan (Albany, 1856–87), IV, 37; Charles Maar, "Causes of the Dutch Migrations into and out of New Jersey," *Somerset County Historical Quarterly* 7 (1918): 168–71. Wacker notes that "Dutch settlers from Long Island were streaming into the area [Middlesex, Somerset, and Monmouth counties] in the 1680's and 90's." *Land and People*, 168.

22. Christopher Bridge to S.P.G., March 20, 1715, S.P.G. Records, Letterbook Series A, Vol. 11, New-York Letters. In New Rochelle in 1733, another Anglican complained that his parishioners "being crowded upon one another they have but little land." C. Stouppe to S.P.G., August 10, 1733, S.P.G. Records, Letterbook Series B, Vol. 1, no. 23.

23. Quoted in Carl Bridenbaugh, *Cities in the Wilderness: The First Century of Urban Life in America, 1625–1742* (New York, 1938), 148. According to one account, New York City had 343 houses in 1678; by 1696, there were 594 houses and a population of 6000. "NYK—1664—Notes," fol. 5, in "Papers Relating to New York 1608–1792," Chalmers Collection, New York Public Library.

24. Kingston baptismal records appear in Roswell Randall Hoes, comp., *Baptismal and Marriage Registers of the Old Dutch Church of Kingston, Ulster County, New York* (New York, 1891).

25. *Documentary History of the State of New-York* [quarto ed.], 4 vols. ed. by E. B. O'Callaghan, (Albany, 1850–51), III, 77; William Andrews to S.P.G., March 9, 1712/13, S.P.G. Records, Letterbook Series A, vol. 8, New-York Letters, No. 24.

26. *Cal. State Papers*, XIII, 678; *N.-Y. Col. Docs.*, IV, 334–35. Cornbury's observations in 1708 confirm this trend (V, 56). On the earliest Dutch settlement in New Jersey, see Reginald McMahon, "The Achter Col Colony on the Hackensack," *New Jersey History* 89 (1971): 221–40. Hansen writes: "When these original Dutch farming communities could no longer provide for their natural increase a distinct migration was necessary and their descendants in 1790 are to be found in northern New Jersey and in remoter settlements in the West." "Minor Stocks," 367.

27. A. Van Doren Honeyman, "An Early DeReimer Dutch Bible," *New Jersey Historical Society Proceedings* (n.s.) 12 (1927): 454.

28. Sources for these statistics are Hansen, "Minor Stocks," 365; *N.-Y. Col. Docs.*, V, 339; cf. Evarts B. Greene and Virginia D. Harrington, *American Population before the Federal Census of 1790* (New York, 1932), 94–96.

29. See Joyce Diane Goodfriend, " 'Too Great a Mixture of Nations': The Development of New York City Society in the Seventeenth Century" (Ph.D. diss., University of California at Los Angeles, 1975), 164–65.

30. *Archives N.J.*, II, 179, 132; cf. 218–21. This issue had long been festering. In 1690, Daniel Coxe referred to "the Governour of New Yorks Instructions who is ordered to bee carefull yt ye Government of New East Jersey do not incroach upon ye Trade of New York." Quoted in Eugene R. Sheridan,

"Daniel Coxe and the Restoration of Proprietary Government in East Jersey, 1690—A Letter," *New Jersey History* 92 (1974): 108. See also James H. Levitt, *For Want of Trade: Shipping and the New Jersey Ports, 1680–1783,* New Jersey Historical Society, *Collections* (Newark, 1981), XVII, esp. chaps. 1–2.

31. G. M. Waller, "New York's Role in Queen Anne's War, 1702–1713," *New York History* 33 (1952): 40–53. In 1694, four years after the massacre in Schenectady, Fletcher wrote: "I have latlie seen with a heavie hart, forescore fine farms all deserted about Albany, after the great expence of the owners in building and improving." Quoted in Hansen, "Minor Stocks," 371 n.

32. George Keith to S.P.G., November 29, 1702, S.P.G. Records, Letterbook Series A, vol. 1, no. L; John Bartow to S.P.G., December 1, 1707, S.P.G. Records, Letterbook Series A, vol. 3, no. CLXXXIV; *Minutes of the Common Council of the City of New York, 1674–1776,* 8 vols. ed. by Herbert L. Osgood (New York, 1905), II, 203. On the 1702 epidemic, see John Duffy, *A History of Public Health in New York City 1625–1866* (New York, 1968), 35–36.

33. Miller, *New York Considered and Improved,* 69.

34. *Cal. State Papers,* VIII, 201, 242.

35. "Documents Relating to the Administration of Leisler," New-York Historical Society, *Collections,* Publication Fund Series (New York, 1868), I, 330, 323–24.

36. *Narratives of the Insurrections, 1675–90,* ed. by Charles M. Andrews (New York, 1915), 396; *N.-Y. Col. Docs.,* IV, 213, 861. One Leislerian characterized Fletcher's administration as "a perfect sink of Corruption." *Narratives of Insurrections,* 396. Cornbury's administration also contributed to Dutch uneasiness with New York. Edward T. Corwin writes: "Meantime, the arbitrary acts and oppressions of Cornbury drove a large number of Dutch families into New Jersey (1702–10)." "Ecclesiastical Condition of New York at the Opening of the Eighteenth Century," American Society of Church History, *Papers,* 2d ser. (New York, 1912), III, 104.

37. *Eccl. Recs. N.Y.,* II, 1428. On the Dutch elite's domination of the Reformed church, see Goodfriend, " 'Too Great a Mixture of Nations,' " 195–96. Garret C. Schenck observes that "nearly all the first settlers in [northern New Jersey] came from the city of New York, and the larger part of them were memebers of the Reformed Church there." "Early Settlements and Settlers of Pompton, Pequannoc and Pompton Plains," *New Jersey Historical Society Proceedings* (n.s.) 4 (1919): 68.

38. "Leisler Documents," N.-Y. Hist. Soc., *Colls.,* I, 397.

39. Miller, *New York Considered and Improved,* 54–56.

40. In 1702, a traveling Quaker wrote of being billeted in "a small house of a poor Dutchman" on Long Island. The home had only one bed, but the host "laid me down a coat on the floor" amid "fleas and mosquitos a-plenty."

Quoted in Jacqueline Overton, "The Quakers on Long Island," *New York History* 21 (1940): 157. The visitor received "good water to drink, but little victuals."

41. I arrived at this conclusion reluctantly, but only after countless hours of searching through what church records remain, especially for New Jersey. I felt somewhat vindicated later (though no less disappointed) when I came across Abraham Messler's aside regarding early-eighteenth-century Dutch church records for New Jersey. Messler, a nineteenth-century Reformed church historian, commented that "the materials have nearly all perished." *Forty Years at Raritan: Eight Memorial Sermons, with Notes for a History of the Reformed Dutch Churches in Somerset County, N.J.* (New York, 1873), 168.

42. *N.-Y. Col. Docs.,* IV, 401.

43. Ibid., IV, 620.

44. Francis L. Hawks, ed., "The Memorial of Col. Morris concerning the State of Religion in the Jerseys," *New Jersey Historical Society Proceedings* 4 (1849–50): 118.

45. Sources for this conclusion are Joseph Anthony Loux, Jr., trans. and ed., *Boel's Complaint against Frelinghuisen* (Rensselaer, N.Y., 1979); Teunis G. Bergen, *Register in Alphabetical Order, of the Early Settlers of Kings County, Long Island, N.Y., from Its First Settlement by Europeans to 1700* (New York, 1881). This latter source shows a large number of Dutch family names that originated in Kings County and then moved west to New Jersey.

46. Morris to Lord Bishop of London, June 1704, Fulham Papers, Vol. 6, fols. 126–28; *Eccl. Recs. N.Y.,* IV, 2506; Peter Kalm, *The America of 1750: Peter Kalm's Travels in North America,* rev. ed., 2 vols., ed. by Adolph B. Benson (New York, 1937), I, 119. Cf. Peter O. Wacker, "The Dutch Culture Area in the Northeast, 1609–1800," *New Jersey History* 104 (1986): 1–21.

47. Hansen, "Minor Stocks," 372; cf. Bertus Harry Wabeke, *Dutch Emigration to North America, 1624–1860: A Short History,* Booklets of the Netherlands Information Bureau, no. 10 (New York, 1944), chap. 2; Nelson R. Burr, "The Religious History of New Jersey before 1702," *New Jersey Historical Society Proceedings* 56 (1938): 176–77. On the rapid rise of population in New Jersey, see William L. Tucker, "New Jersey—Her People," *New Jersey Historical Society Proceedings* 57 (1939): 174. William Huddleston in 1708 identified Kings and Ulster counties as being generally Dutch. Huddleston to S.P.G., July 15, 1708, S.P.G. Records, Letterbook Series A, Vol. 4, no. LVIII. On the Dutch incursion into Pennsylvania, see Warren S. Ely, "Dutch Settlement in Bucks County," *Bucks County Historical Society Papers* 5 (1926): 1–13. Ely shows that the Dutch who came to Bucks County were generally third-generation settlers who "took a prominent part in the revolutionary war" on the patriot side (p. 4).

48. By 1790, Hansen argues, "the northeastern part of the State [New

Jersey] was as completely Dutch as any region in New York." "Minor Stocks," 370. This area—particularly its northern reaches—was later memorialized in Washington Irving's writings. On the persistence of Dutch culture in northern New Jersey, see Peter O. Wacker, "Dutch Material Culture in New Jersey," *Journal of Popular Culture* 11 (1977–78): 948–58; John D. Prince, "Netherland Settlers in New Jersey," *New Jersey Historical Society Proceedings* (3d ser.) 9 (1914): 1–7; Schenck, "Early Settlements," 58–71; Burton H. Allbee, "Ancient Dutch Architecture," *Bergen County Historical Society Papers and Proceedings* 5–6 (1908–10): 19–22; Adrian C. Leiby, *The Early Dutch and Swedish Settlers of New Jersey* (Princeton, N.J., 1964), chap. 9; Cornelius C. Vermeule, "Influence of the Netherlandish People in New Jersey," *Genealogical Magazine of New Jersey* 4 (1928): 49–56; W. W. Scott, "Dutch Buildings, Customs, Habits, etc.," *Americana* 16 (1922): 368–79; J. Dyneley Prince, "The Jersey Dutch Dialect," *Dialect Notes* 3 (1910): 459–84; Van Cleaf Bachman, Alice P. Kenney, and Lawrence G. Van Loon, " 'Het Poelmeisie': An Introduction to the Hudson Valley Dutch Dialect," *New York History* 61 (1980): 161–85; Richard H. Amerman, "Dutch Life in Pre-Revolutionary Bergen County," *New Jersey Historical Society Proceedings* 76 (1958): 161–81.

49. Wacker, *Land and People,* 162–64; Hansen, "Minor Stocks," 371–72; Thomas L. Purvis, "The European Origins of New Jersey's Eighteenth-Century Population," *New Jersey History* 100 (1982): 15–31. Burials in New York following the 1731 smallpox epidemic provide another indication of population trends. Interments in the Anglican cemetery totaled 229; those in the Dutch cememtery came to 212. James H. Cassedy, *Demography in Early America: Beginnings of the Statistical Mind, 1600–1800* (Cambridge , Mass., 1969), 122.

50. *Cal. State Papers,* XIV, 95; XV, 44; quoted in Charles Smith Lewis, "George Keith, the Missionary," *New Jersey Historical Society Proceedings* (n.s.) 13 (1928): 44; John D. Cushing, comp., *The Earliest Printed Laws of New Jersey, 1703–1722* (Wilmington, Del., 1978), 2–3.

51. For a detailed treatment, see Eugene R. Sheridan, *Lewis Morris, 1671–1746: A Study in Early American Politics* (Syracuse, N.Y., 1981), esp. chaps. 2–5. See also John R. McCreary, "Governors, Politicians, and the Sources of Instability in the Colonies: New Jersey as a Test Case," *Journal of the Alabama Academy of Science* 42 (1971): 215–27; Larry R. Gerlach, " 'Quaker' Politics in Eighteenth Century New Jersey: A Documentary Account," *Journal of the Rutgers University Library* 34 (1970): 1–12.

52. John E. Stillwell, ed., *Historical and Genealogical Miscellany: Early Settlers of New Jersey and Their Descendants,* 5 vols. (New York, 1903–32), IV, 29; Morris to S.P.G., May 30, 1709, S.P.G. Records, Letterbook Series A, Vol. 4, no. CXLIX; *N.-Y. Col. Docs.,* IV, 1044.

53. *Archives N.J.,* III, 9; cf. Robert Greenhalgh Albion, "New Jersey

and the Port of New York," *New Jersey Historical Society Proceedings* 58 (1940): 86.

54.*N.-Y. Col. Docs.*, V, 37.

55. Brooke to S.P.G., October 11, 1706, S.P.G. Records, Letterbook Series A, Vol. 3, no. VI.

56. *Archives N.J.*, V, 21. On New York's growing role in the Atlantic economy during this period, see Glen Gabert, "The New York Tobacco Trade, 1716–1742," *Essex Institute Historical Collections* 105 (1969): 103–27; Curtis P. Nettels, "England's Trade with New England and New York, 1685–1720," *Colonial Society of Massachusetts Publications* 28 (1935): 322–50; idem, "The Economic Relations of Boston, Philadelphia, and New York, 1680–1715," *Journal of Economic and Business History* 3 (1931): 185–215; William I. Davisson and Lawrence J. Bradley, "New York Maritime Trade: Ship Voyage Patterns, 1715–1765," *New-York Historical Society Quarterly* 55 (1971): 309–17.

57. Taken from a Dutch-English grammar, published in New York City in 1730; quoted in Edgar Franklin Romig, " 'The English and Low-Dutch School-master,' " *New-York Historical Society Quarterly* 43 (1959): 157–58. Even if this sentence is fictional, it doubtless reflected popular conceptions.

58. Andrew Burnaby, *Travels through the Middle Settlements in North America, in the Years 1759 and 1760; with Observations upon the State of the Colonies* (New York, 1904), 108, 114–15.

59. The sources for these population figures are *Archives N.J.*, V, 164; *Doc. Hist. N.-Y.*, [octavo ed.], I, 693–94; Vermeule, "Influence of Netherlandish People," 53; cf. Greene and Harrington, *American Population*, 96–98, 109–10.

60. Tucker, "New Jersey—Her People," 173–74; Hubert G. Schmidt, "Germans in Colonial New Jersey," *American-German Review* 24 (June–July 1958): 4–9; Walter Allen Knittle, *The Early Eighteenth Century Palatine Emigration: A British Government Redemptioner Project to Manufacture Naval Stores* (Philadelphia, 1936). Like other frontier settlers, the Palatines were poor. See Elias Neau to S.P.G., July 5, 1710, S.P.G. Records, Letterbook Series A, Vol. 5, no. CXXXIV.

61. *Archives N.J.*, V, 22. On New Jersey's ethnic diversity, see Purvis, "European Origins," 15–31; cf. George S. Pryde, "Scottish Colonization in the Province of New York," *New York History* 16 (1935): 138–57; idem, "The Scots in East New Jersey," *New Jersey Historical Society Proceedings* (n.s.) 15 (1930): 1–39. On the westward spread of population generally in this period, see Herman R. Friis, "A Series of Population Maps of the Colonies and the United States, 1625–1790," *Geographical Review* 30 (1940): 463–70, esp. plate between 464 and 465.

62. *Eccl. Recs. N.Y.*, II, 1043. Adrian C. Leiby characterizes Harlem as "the very hotbed of Leislerian sentiment." *The United Churches of Hacken-*

sack and Schraalenburgh, New Jersey, 1689–1822 (River Edge, N.J., 1976), 31.

63. This point is made rather effectively by Martin E. Lodge, "The Crisis of the Churches in the Middle Colonies," *Pennsylvania Magazine of History and Biography* 95 (1971): 195–220. Lodge contends that the attraction to pietism and, ultimately, the Great Awakening arose from this failure and that after the Awakening denominations set about the task of providing indigenous institutions adequate for their particular followings. Cf. idem, "The Great Awakening in the Middle Colonies" (Ph.D. diss., University of California at Berkeley, 1964).

64. Regarding the pietist incusions among the Germans, see John B. Frantz, "The Awakening of Religion among the German Settlers in the Middle Colonies," *William and Mary Quarterly* (3d ser.) 33 (1976): 266–88.

65. Suzanne B. Geissler, "A Step on the Swedish Lutheran Road to Anglicanism," *Historical Magazine of the Protestant Episcopal Church* 54 (1985): 43–45. Such was his influence that even after Tollstadius's untimely death in 1706, a Swedish minister complained that the Raccoon church "is more obstinate and spunky than ever." Quoted on p. 45. Cf. Donald Einar Bjarnson, "Swedish-Finnish Settlements in New Jersey in the Seventeenth Century," *Swedish Pioneer Historical Quarterly* 27 (1976): 239–40.

66. My account of Bertholf borrows from Howard G. Hageman, "William Bertholf: Pioneer Dominie of New Jersey," *Reformed Review* 29 (1976): 73–30. See also Leiby, *United Churches,* chap. 2.

67. See Howard G. Hageman, "Henricus Selyns," in *Cultural Mosaic of New Netherland* (Rensselaersville, N.Y., 1972). Hageman was among the first to hint at a connection between Leislerianism and Labadism. Wallace N. Jamison writes of Bertholf: "Not only was he the first resident minister of his church in New Jersey, but his evangelical zeal laid an important foundation for the Evangelical Awakening of the eighteenth century." *Religion in New Jersey: A Brief History* (Princeton, N.J, 1964), 23.

68. *Eccl. Recs. N.Y.,* II, 1051–52.

69. Bertholf was ordained by Middleburg on September 16, 1693. Regarding the ordination, see Benjamin C. Taylor, *Annals of the Classis of Bergen of the Reformed Dutch Church, and the Churches under Its Care* (New York, 1857), 172–74.

70. Sources for this information are George Olin Zabriskie, "Residents of North-Eastern New Jersey in 1694," *New York Genealogical and Biographical Record* 108 (1977): 157–58; *Archives N.J.,* XXIII, XXX.

71. For a detailed account of the grisly massacre, see "Massacre of Shinnectady, February 9, 1689/90," Livingston Family Papers, 1. Papers of Robert Livingston, B. Indian Affairs, 1666 1727, 1768, ms. at Franklin D. Roosevelt Presidential Library, Hyde Park, N.Y. The French apparently tried to spare Tesschenmaeker, hoping "to obtain information from him."

But he was killed "and his papers burnt before he could be recognized" (*N.-Y. Col. Docs.*, IX, 468).

72. *Eccl. Recs. N.Y.*, II, 1105–06.

73. Ibid., II, 1043.

74. Quoted in Thomas Jefferson Wertenbacker, *The Founding of American Civilization: The Middle Colonies* (New York, 1938), 92–93; *Eccl. Recs. N.Y.*, II, 1107.

75. *Eccl. Recs. N.Y.*, II, 1111. This was the culmination of an earlier bequest to the Dutch Reformed Church, made by John Archer in 1684. On the competing legal claims to Fordham Manor from 1684 to 1695, see Harry C. W. Melick, "The Fordham 'Ryott' of July 16, 1688," *New-York Historical Society Quarterly* 36 (1952): 210–20. Other bequests for ministerial salaries for the New York church were made by Peter Jacobs Marius in 1702 and by Jan Harberding in 1722. *Eccl. Recs. N.Y.*, III, 1518–19; "Abstracts of Wills, Vol. II, 1702–1728," New-York Historical Society, *Collections,* Publication Fund Series, XXVI (New York, 1893), 283–85.

76. *Eccl. Recs. N.Y.*, II, 1107.

77. *Cal. State Papers,* XII, 14.

78. *N.-Y., Col. Docs.,* IV, 533.

79. *Eccl. Recs. N.Y.*, II, 1259; on Bellomont's role, see *Cal. State Papers,* XII, 100.

80. *Eccl. Rec. N.Y.*, II, 868; William Stevens Perry, ed., *Historical Collections relating to the American Colonial Church,* 5 vols. (Hartford, Conn., 1878; reprint ed. New York, 1969), V, 44; *Memorial of St. Mark's Church in the Bowery* (New York, 1899), 106–11.

81. Thomas Archdeacon comments: "The failure of Leisler discredited the Dutch who opposed the new order, and in the aftermath of the rebellion the English were able to translate their growing numerical and economic strength into firm control of the city. While Leisler's disciples remained under restraint, the English leaders took from the government major economic benefits for themselves and their allies and made the Anglican Church the legal religious establishment." *New York City, 1664–1710: Conquest and Change* (Ithaca, N.Y., 1976), 123.

CHAPTER 4

1. William Vesey to S.P.G., May 11, 1714, Records of the Society for the Propagation of the Gospel, 1702–1737 (microfilm), Letterbook Series A, Vol. 9, New-York papers, no. 6.

2. For detailed treatments of this practice, see David E. Narrett, "Patterns of Inheritance in Colonial New York City, 1664–1775" (Ph.D. diss., Cornell University, 1981); William John McLaughlin, "Dutch Rural New

York: Community, Economy, and Family in Colonial Flatbush" (Ph.D. diss., Columbia University, 1981). Cf. Linda Briggs Biemer, *Women and Property in Colonial New York: The Transition from Dutch to English Law, 1643–1727* (Ann Arbor, Mich., 1983). For other perspectives on Dutch cultural modernity, see Jan deVries, "On the Modernity of the Dutch Republic," *Journal of Economic History* 33 (1973): 191–202; J. L. Price, *Culture and Society in the Dutch Republic during the 17th Century* (London, 1974).

    3. *Ecclesiastical Records: State of New York,* 7 vols., ed. by Edward T. Corwin, (Albany, 1901–16), II, 1316–17, 1348–49.

    4. Ibid., II, 1349, 1344. In its letter to the other churches, the Classis wrote: "Rev. Brethren, whither does this tend? Do you not perceive that by such conduct the ruin of the Church in those parts is assured? Will not the Church, under such conditions, soon fall under the government of others?" (II, 1349).

    5. Ibid., II, 1386–90, 1385; III, 1473. The New York dominies insisted that "we can recognize no one as belonging to this corporation, (this Body of Ministers in America) except such as also recognized the same Classis of Amsterdam, as that Body to which all our ecclesiastical disputes must be referred," because, they continued, "in case some dispute should arise, which may God forbid, between you and your pastor; and should you wish to choose us as arbitrators in the case; the Rev. Freerman would be able to say with the greatest justice,—I do not belong to that Classis of Amsterdam to which those ministers belong; but the Classis of Lingen is the one which can alone act on my case" (II, 1385).

    6. Ibid., II, 1373; III, 1475. There maybe some merit to the accusation about Freeman's avarice. Freeman quite transparently used Schenectady's refusal to issue a certificate of dismissal in order to exact higher wages from Long Island. See III, 1539–43. On Freeman's ministry at Schenectady and his spectacular success among the Indians, see John J. Birch, *The Pioneering Church of the Mohawk Valley* (Schenectady, N.Y., 1955), chap. 4.

    7. *Eccl. Recs. N.Y.,* III, 1639.

    8. *Documentary History of the State of New-York* [quarto ed.], 4 vols., ed. by E. B. O'Callaghan (Albany, 1850–51), III, 92; *Eccl. Recs. N.Y.,* III, 1641, 1544–48. Freeman's original call came to the attention of the Council of New York, which merely commented that Freeman would likely accept it. *Calendar of State Papers, Colonial Series: America and West Indies,* 44 vols., ed. by W. N. Sainsbury, J. W. Fortescue, and Cecil Headlam (London, 1860–1969), XV, 178.

    9. *Doc. Hist. N.-Y.,* III, 93. The two calls appear in juxtaposition to each other. *Eccl. Recs. N.Y.,* III, 1522–26; on Freeman's wife's refusal to remove to Schenectady, see III, 1983.

    10. *Eccl. Recs. N.Y.,* III, 1631–35, 1642, 1647. Repeatedly Du Bois referred to Freeman's "artful" (i.e., deceptive) dealings.

11. Ibid., III, 1577, 1644–45. Regarding the provision in the original call that Freeman should be subject to the Classis of Amsterdam, this, the Long Island consistories said, was treated cavalierly and contemptuously by Freeman, who maintained that his loyalties lay with the Classis of Lingen (III, 1644, 1535–38). Cornbury even issued an edict to the effect that the Long Island church property and records were under the jursidiction of Freeman rather than Antonides. Doc. Hist. N.-Y., III, 94.

12. Eccl. Recs. N.Y., III, 1942–43; Doc. Hist. N.-Y., III, 95.

13. Sources for Table 4.1 are: Bergen Papers and Long Island Town Records, James A. Kelly Institute, St. Francis College, Brooklyn; "Abstracts of Wills," 27 vols., New-York Historical Society, Collections, Publication Fund Series, XXV–XLI (New York, 1892–1909); Doc. Hist. N.-Y. [octavo ed.], II, 493–511, III, 133–38; Teunis G. Bergen, Register in Alphabetical Order, of the Early Settlers of Kings County, Long Island, N.Y., from Its First Settlement by Europeans to 1700 (New York, 1881).

14. Doc. Hist. N.-Y., III, 112; Eccl. Recs. N.Y., III, 1650–51.

15. [E. Clowes Chorley], "The Seal of the S.P.G," Historical Magazine of the Protestant Episcopal Church 12 (1943): 253; cf. S.P.G. Records, Journals, Vol. 1. On the founding and initial years of the S.P.G., see Samuel Clyde McCulloch, "The Foundation and Early Work of the Society for the Propagation of the Gospel in Foreign Parts," Huntington Library Quarterly 8 (1944–45): 241–58.

16. New York missionaries to S.P.G., November 12, 1705, S.P.G. Records, Letterbook Series A, Vol. 2, no. CXXII.

17. Eccl. Recs. N.Y., III, 1923, 1551, 1751; John Bartow to S.P.G., June 10, 1709, S.P.G. Records, Letterbook Series A, Vol. 5, no. IX; William A. Bultmann, "The S.P.G. and the French Hugeunots in Colonial America," Historical Magazine of the Protestant Episcopal Church 20 (1951): 156–72; Robert M. Kingdon, "Why Did the Huguenot Refugees in the American Colonies Become Episcopalian?" Historical Magazine of the Protestant Episcopal Church 49 (1980): 317–35; Jon Butler, The Huguenots in America: A Refugee People in New World Society (Cambridge, Mass., 1983). Regarding the Germans, see Eccl. Recs. N.Y., III, 1871–72, 2111–12; Glenn Weaver, "John Frederick Haeger: S.P.G. Missionary to the Palatines," Historical Magazine of the Protestant Episcopal Church 27 (1958): 112–25.

18. Doc. Hist. N.-Y., III, 139.

19. Eccl. Recs. N.Y., III, 1743; Muirson to S.P.G., January 9, 1707/8, S.P.G. Records, Letterbook Series A, Vol. 3, no. CLXVIII; C. Stouppe to S.P.G., December 11, 1727, S.P.G. Records Letterbook Series C, Vol. 1; Mackenzie to S.P.G., November 8, 1705, S.P.G. Records, Letterbook Series A, Vol. 2, no. CXVI; Mackenzie to S.P.G., May 4, 1711, S.P.G. Records, Vol. 6, no. LXXIV.

20. Bartow to S.P.G., June 9, 1712, S.P.G. Records, Vol. 7, New-York Letters, no. 31.

21. *Doc. Hist. N.-Y.*, III, 540–42, 77; Barclay to S.P.G., September 26, 1710, S.P.G. Records, Letterbook Series A, Vol. 5, no. CLXXVI.

22. Barclay to S.P.G., December 7, 1710, S.P.G. Records, Letterbook Series A, Vol. 6, no. L. For a survey of Dutch defections to the Church of England, see Nelson R. Burr, "The Episcopal Church and the Dutch in Colonial New York and New Jersey—1664–1784," *Historical Magazine of the Protestant Episcopal Church* 19 (1950): 90–111, esp. 100–109. Burr believes that much of the Society's success was the result of their establishment of schools that taught English to Dutch schoolchildren.

23. *Doc. Hist. N.-Y.*, III, 75. For a biographical sketch of Vesey, see Clifford K. Shipton, *New England Life in the 18th Century: Representative Biographies from "Sisbley's Harvard Graduates"* (Cambridge, Mass., 1963), 12–19.

24. *Eccl. Recs. N.Y.*, III, 1903, 1923; cf. Caleb Heathcote to S.P.G., February 4, 1711, S.P.G. Records, Letterbook Series A, Vol. 7, New-York Letters, no. 15 (punctuation added).

25. *Eccl. Recs. N.Y.*, III, 1743, 1833, 1880; Secretary of S.P.G. to Robert Hunter, July 26, 1712, S.P.G. Records, Letterbook Series A, Vol. 7, New-York Letters from the Society, no. 13. In what may be a signal of final resignation to the dominion of the English in New York, the consistory of the New York church on December 13, 1711, unanimously resolved "that henceforth the books of Elders, Deacons and Church Masters shall no longer be kept in guilders, but in pounds, shillings and pence." *Eccl. Recs. N.Y.*, III, 1897.

26. Haeger to S.P.G., August 15, 1711, S.P.G. Records, Letterbook Series A, Vol. 6, no. CXXXVI.

27. John Pershing Luidens comments: "The Society was unusually vigorous in Dutch areas where the pastorates were unfilled or poorly served or dissension produced indifference, both in New York and New Jersey." "The Americanization of the Dutch Reformed Church" (Ph.D. diss., University of Oklahoma, 1969), 92.

28. Arthur D. Pierce, "A Governor in Skirts," *New Jersey Historical Society Proceedings* 83 (1965): 1–9. Robert Livingston, a contemporary, described Cornbury thus: "Tis said he is wholly addicted to his pleasure, and enriching himself with strange and unheard of methods, having some few Creatures about him, whose Councils he pursues to the mischief of the Principal Inhabitants. His dressing himself in womens Cloths Commonly every morning is so unaccountable that if hundred[s] of Spectators did not dayly see him, it would be incredible." Michael G. Hall, Lawrence H. Leder, and Michael G. Kammen, eds., *The Glorious Revolution in America: Documents on the Colonial Crisis of 1689* (Chapel Hill, N.C., 1964), 139. Even after leaving office, Elias Neau recorded, Cornbury continued the practice, "but now 'tis after the Dutch manner." Neau to S.P.G., February 27, 1708/9, S.P.G. Records, Letterbook Series A, Vol. 4, no. CXXI. Regarding Corn-

bury's career before coming to New York, see Milton Rubincam, "The Formative Years of Lord Cornbury, the First Royal Governor of New York and New Jersey," *New York Genealogical and Biographical Register* 71 (1940): 106–16. A portrait of Cornbury in female attire (original at the New-York Historical Society) is reproduced in Jacob Judd and Irwin H. Polishook, eds., *Aspects of Early New York Society and Politics* (Tarrytown, N.Y., 1974), 53.

29. *Documents Relative to the Colonial History of the State of New-York*, 15 vols., ed. by E. B. O'Callaghan (Albany, 1856–87), V, 38; Charles Worthen Spencer, "The Cornbury Legend," *New York State Historical Association Proceedings* 13 (1914): 309–20, quotation on 310.

30. Talbot to S.P.G., January 10, 1707/8, S.P.G. Records, Letterbook Series A, Vol. 3, no. CLXXXVI.

31. John Thomas to S.P.G., March 1, 1705, S.P.G. Records, Letterbook Series A, Vol. 2, no. LXXI.

32. Cornbury to S.P.G., November 29, 1707, S.P.G. Records, Letterbook Series A, no. CLV. The missionary apparently found this punishment so odious that he later declared that "he had rather be taken into France than into the Fort of New York." John Talbot to S.P.G., August 24, 1708, S.P.G. Records, Letterbook Series A, Vol. 4, no. LII. On Cornbury's appeal for more S.P.G. missionaries, see, for example, Cornbury to S.P.G., July 15, 1705, and September 22, 1705, Vol. 2, nos. XCI, CXXXI.

33. *The Colonial Laws of New York: From the Year 1664 to the Revolution*, 5 vols. (Albany, 1894–96), I, 543–45. This figure contrasts sharply with the twenty pounds per annum allowed to the minister of the French church. *Doc. Hist. N.-Y.*, III, 263. Cornbury's resolve to place an Anglican ministrer in the Huguenot church (see below) may reflect his discomfort at being forced to allocate public money to a non-Anglican minister.

34. *Col. Laws N.Y.*, I, 564–69; *Doc. Hist. N.-Y.*, III, 74.

35. *Doc. Hist. N.-Y.*, III, 130; cf. William Urquhart and John Thomas to S.P.G., July 4, 1705, S.P.G. Records, Letterbook Series A, Vol. 2, no. CV.

36. Urquhart to S.P.G., November 1, 1704, S.P.G. Records, Letterbook Series A, Vol. 2, no. XXVII.

37. *Doc. Hist. N.-Y.*, III, 74–76, 128–29. Vesey had considerably less success in securing the cooperation of Robert Hunter, a later governor. See Alison Gilbert Olson, "Governor Robert Hunter and the Anglican Church in New York," in *Statesmen, Scholars and Merchants: Essays in Eighteenth-Century History Presented to Dame Lucy Sutherland*, ed. by Anne Whiteman, J. S. Bromley, and P. G. M. Dickson (Oxford, Eng., 1973), chap. 3.

38. Quary to S.P.G., January 20, 1707/8, S.P.G. Records, Letterbook Series A., Vol. 4, no. XXXVI. Although they met with mixed success, the Anglicans also sought, with Cornbury's help, to make legal inroads in New Jersey. See Edward J. Cody, "The Growth of Toleration and Church-State Relations in New Jersey, 1689–1763: From Holy Men to Holy War," in

Economic and Social History of Colonial New Jersey, ed. by William C. Wright (Trenton, N.J., 1974), 42–63; Gordon Turner, "Church-State Relationships in Early New Jersey," *New Jersey Historical Society Proceedings* 69 (1951): 212–23; Nelson R. Burr, "New Jersey: An Anglican Venture in Religious Freedom," *Historical Magazine of the Protestant Episcopal Church* 34 (1965): 3–34.

39. John Bartow to S.P.G., May 25, 1703, and August 8, 1706, S.P.G. Records, Letterbook Series A, Vols. 1 and 3, nos. CV and XLIII.

40. John Thomas to S.P.G., December 3, 1710, S.P.G. Records, Letterbook Series A, Vol. 6, no. IV.

41. Keith to S.P.G., February 24, 1702/3, S.P.G. Records, Letterbook Series A, Vol. 1, no. LXXXVII.

42. Bartow to S.P.G,, December 1, 1707, S.P.G. Records, Letterbook Series A, Vol. 3, no. CLXXXIV; cf. Elizabeth Davidson, *The Establishment of the English Church in Continental American Colonies* (Durham, N.C., 1936), 44–45. On the clerical configuration on Long Island, see Samuel Irenaeus Prime, "Early Ministers of Long Island," *Journal of the Presbyterian Historical Society* 23 (1945): 180–94.

43. *Eccl. Recs. N.Y.,* III, 1765; for Freeman's account of the entire affair, see III, 1762–67.

44. Eburne to S.P.G., October 25, 1705, and November 12, 1705, S.P.G. Records, Letterbook Series A., Vol. 2, nos. CXIII, CXIV; cf. *Eccl. Recs. N.Y.,* III, 1574, 1617, 1661; *Doc. Hist. N.-Y.,* III, 584.

45. *Eccl. Recs. N.Y.,* III, 1652, 1636, 1711; cf. 1657–62. Cornbury obstinately refused to grant Henricus Beys a license on the grounds that to do so violated his instructions from Queen Anne regarding the approval of ministers. Though informed that these instructions applied only to the Anglican church, he would not relent. The governor apparently was determined to exercise tighter control over the colony's religious situation; indeed, he had complained earlier about his predecessors' laxity in these matters (III, 1679–80, 1574).

46. Ibid., III, 1660–62, 1636–37, 1616.

47. "New York in 1692," New-York Historical Society, *Collections,* 2d Series, II (New York, 1849), 244; *Doc. Hist. N.-Y.,* II, 34; *N.-Y. Col. Docs.,* IX, 739. Regarding the Anglican designs on the colonies, John Frederick Woolverton comments that the S.P.G. pursued the following objectives: "to tie economically profitable colonies closer to the mother country; to secure Indian allies against the French and Spanich on the mainland of the continent; and to build a homogeneous society." *Colonial Anglicanism in North American* (Detroit, 1984), 86.

48. *N.-Y. Col. Docs.,* IV, 526.

49. Lord Bishop of London to S.P.G., January 29, 1706/7, S.P.G. Records, Letterbook Series A, Vol. 3, no. XXVII.

50. Moore to S.P.G., November 13, 1705, S.P.G. Records, Letterbook Series A, Vol. 2, no. CXXII.

51. Cornbury to S.P.G., September 22, 1705, S.P.G. Records, Letterbook Series A, Vol. 2, no. CXXXI.

52. Cornbury to S.P.G., November 29, 1707, S.P.G. Records, Letterbook Series A, Vol. 3, no. CLV.

53. Morris to S.P.G., March 25, 1711, S.P.G. Records, Letterbook Series A, Vol. 7, New-York Letters, no. 12. On the connection between "establishment" and "good order," see, for example, Caleb Heathcote to S.P.G., April 20, 1709, and October 6, 1708, Vol. 4, nos. CXLIV, CLXV. In this respect, the aims of religious proselytization among the Dutch were not dissimilar from those among the Indians. Christianization of the Indians around Albany, a former missionary observed, "contributed very much to the safety of [English] Lives & Estates." Godfridus Dellius to Secretary of S.P.G., October 11, 1703, Lambeth Palace, Fulham Papers (microfilm), Vol. 6, fols. 178–79. Regarding Anglicanism's role in buttressing the civil order, see Patricia U. Bonomi, *Under the Cope of Heaven: Religion, Society, and Politics in Colonial America* (New York, 1986), chap. 7.

54. Thomas Barclay to S.P.G., April 17, 1713, S.P.G. Records, Letterbook Series A, Vol. 8, New-York Letters, no. 36.

55. Gerald F. De Jong, *The Dutch Reformed Church in the American Colonies* (Grand Rapids, Mich., 1978), 60. The catechist for blacks was Elias Neau; see Sheldon S. Cohen, "Elias Neau, Instructor to New York's Slaves," *New-York Historical Society Quarterly* 55 (1971): 7–27; John H. Hewitt, "New York's Black Episcopalians: In the Beginning, 1704–1722," *Afro-Americans in New York Life and History* 3 (1979): 9–22. For a detailed treatment of Anglican missions to slaves, see Frank J. Klingberg, "The S.P.G. Program for Negroes in Colonial New York," *Historical Magazine of the Protestant Episcopal Church* 8 (1939): 306–71.

56. As early as 1697, Thomas Bray, later to be the Society's founder, wrote the following in regard to the Church of England's mission among the colonists: "It will be farther requisite to have free Schools erected, at leastwise one in every County, for the Education of their Children." Thomas Bray, *Rev. Thomas Bray: His Life and Selected Works Relating to Maryland,* ed. by Bernard C. Steiner, *Maryland Historical Society Fund Publication* no. 37 (Baltimore, 1901), 77. The resounding success of this strategy may even help to explain the intensity of New York's loyalism during the American Revolution.

57. *Col. Laws N.Y.,* I, 516–17.

58. Heathcote to S.P.G., December 7, 1707, S.P.G. Records, Letterbook Series A, Vol. 3, no. CLXI.

59. Mackenzie to S.P.G., March 18, 1712/13, S.P.G. Records, Letterbook Series A, Vol. 8, New-York Letters, no. 19.

60. Barclay to S.P.G., June 12, 1711, S.P.G. Records, Letterbook Series A, Vol. 6, no. CXXIX.

61. Barclay to S.P.G., April 17, 1713, S.P.G. Records, Letterbook Series A, Vol. 8, New-York Letters, no. 36.

62. Ibid.; Simon Brown to S.P.G., April 10, 1713, no. 32; John Bartow to S.P.G., April 10, 1714, Vol. 9, New-York Letters, no. 7. Ronald William Howard writes: "Between 1691 and 1720, education was utilized as a social and religious instrumentality to create Anglo-American unity out of the ethnic and religious diversity of New York." "Education and Ethnicity in Colonial New York, 1664–1763: A Study in the Transmission of Culture in Early America" (Ph.D. diss., University of Tennessee, 1978), 211. Howard argues throughout that Anglicanization in New York came about primarily through education. On the role of schools in S.P.G. missions, see William Webb Kemp, *The Support of Schools in Colonial New York by the Society for the Propogation of the Gospel in Foreign Parts* (New York, 1969). For a contrary view on the extent of Anglican influence on education in colonial New York, see Robert Francis Seybolt, "The S.P.G. Myth: A Note on Education in Colonial New York," *Journal of Educational Research* 13 (January–May 1926): 129–37.

63. They wrote: "If things are to proceed in this fashion, practically holding back the training schools of the Dutch, in which alone our children could be educated in our religion, is not the hope of expecting a rich harvest and fruitage destroyed? Will not the churches in the course of time decline, and our labors in many respects be found fruitless?" *Eccl. Recs. N.Y.*, III, 1654.

64. *N.-Y. Col. Docs.*, IV, 622; *The Lutheran Church in New York, 1649–1772: Records in the Lutheran Church Archives at Amsterdam, Holland*, trans. by Arnold J. F. van Laer (New York, 1946), 90, 203. During Cornbury's administration, Lutheran pastors asked Old World authorities for "a little booklet in which, by means of short questions and answers, the difference between the Lutheran and the so-called Reformed opinions were exposed, every point thus concluding 'Therefore the Lutheran opinion is the better one' " (pp. 99–100).

65. *Eccl. Recs. N.Y.*, III, 1659; George Keith, " 'An Account of the State of the Church in North America, by Mr. George Keith and Others,' " *Historical Magazine of the Protestant Episcopal Church* 20 (1951): 368.

66. *Eccl. Recs. N.Y.*, III, 1655, 1630.

67. *Cal. State Papers*, XXII, 20. Anne supported Poyer; cf. XXII, 102, 125.

68. Morris to S.P.G., May 30, 1709, S.P.G. Records, Letterbook Series C, Vol. 1. Morris acknowledged that his letter of criticism against Cornbury "is not perhaps a procedure of ye greatest prudence."

69. *Eccl. Recs. N.Y.*, III, 1978.

70. Theodorus Jacobus Frelinghuysen, *Sermons by Theodorus Jacobus Frelinghuysen*, trans. by William Demarest (New York, 1856), 353–54. For a

treatment of the political situation back in England during Hunter's administration, see James Edward Scanlon, "British Intrigue and the Governorship
of Robert Hunter," *New-York Historical Society Quarterly* 57 (1973): 199–
211. In 1715, Hunter warned: "If ye Society take not more care for ye future
then has been taken hitherto in ye choice of their missionaries, instead of
establishing Religion they'll destroy all Government and good manners."
Cal. State Papers, XXIII, 144. Hunter's early attempts to modulate the intense Anglicization and Anglicanization in New York were frustrated,
prompting him to write a farcical play, *Androboros*, satirizing his political
and ecclesiastical enemies. See Lawrence H. Leder, "Robert Hunter's
Androboros," *Bulletin of the New York Public Library* 68 (1964): 153–60.

71. *Eccl. Recs. N.Y.*, III, 1958. Elsewhere he wrote: "The people, thank
God, take good pleasure in the sacred services, and I have a large audience."
A later account noted that "Vreeman gets many more auditors than An-
tonides" (III, 1959, 2000).

72. *Lutheran Church Recs.*, 203; *Eccl. Recs. N.Y.*, III, 1986, 1654. Regarding Freeman's charisma, Nucella of Kingston wrote that when Freeman arrived in Albany, "I noticed that most of the congregation were not a little
taken with Rev. Freerman." *Eccl. Recs., N.Y.*, II, 1422.

73. *Eccl. Recs. N.Y.*, III, 1857. The Classis expressed its frustration "because we lack the power to do anything definitely against him in another
Kingdom." Nevertheless, the Classis firmly quashed the idea of forming an
American classis to deal with the matter: "The objection rose to this that such
a Classis would be the ruin of the churches of New York. This is so obvious
that it needs no proof" (III, 1857–58). To Antonides the Classis wrote: "You
and your good friends can also readily see that we have no power, in the
domains of another nation, to take special action against Freerman [*sic*],
especially since he has the government on his side" (III, 1719).

74. Legal depositions of this period appear in *Doc. Hist. N.-Y.*, III, 80–
115. For their part, the magistrates seemed none too pleased about having to
deal with the dispute. One of the governor's aides complained: "The works of
these Dutch ministers is the occasion of all our quarrels" (III, 110). For the
majority and minority reports of Ingoldesby's committee, see III, 101–2.

75. *Eccl. Recs. N.Y.*, III, 1859, 1929–31. Repeatedly the Classis requested
Freeman "to give assurances to the other brethren that you will adhere to the
Netherlands Church-Order, and will maintain all proper correspondence
with this classis. For on this subject they seem to have imbibed some misgivings about you. By an open declaration on your part, these can easily be
removed" (III, 2034).

76. Ibid., III, 1944, 1959. Freeman's party issued proposals for peace in
1712, prompting a protracted discussion. He proposed that both men's calls
"shall be regarded by each side, as good and lawful, by way of Christian
concession" (III, 1925–26; cf. 1927–28).

77. *Doc. Hist. N.-Y.*, III, 111; *Eccl. Recs. N.Y.*, III, 2066. Robert Hunter

actually succeeded in healing many of the colony's wounds. For a discussion of the chaotic conditions Hunter faced, see Lawrence H Leder, "The Politics of Upheaval in New York, 1689–1709," *New-York Historical Society Quarterly* 44 (1960): 413–27.

78. *Eccl. Recs. N.Y.*, III, 2085. For the formal agreement among the consistories, see "Certified Copy by Rutgert Van Brunt of a Declaration of the Authorized Representatives of the Six Churches . . .," ms. [no. 1973.106] at Brooklyn Historical Society. Signatories included Cornelius Sebring, Jeronimus Remsen, Pieter Stryker, Jan Vanderveer, Johannes Schenck, J. Van Zandt, Jan Terhuenen, Gerrit Hansen, Pieter Cortelyou, Theodorus Polhemus, Cornelius Van Brunt, and Theodorus Van Wyck. Some in the colony apparently still refused to acknowledge Freeman's ordination. As late as 1734, Lutheran ministers wrote of Freeman that he was "a good preacher, but he is a tailor and his ordination is no good." *Lutheran Church Recs.*, 203.

79. *Eccl. Recs. N.Y.*, III, 2090–91, 2085. For other accounts of the troubles on Long Island, see Thomas M. Strong, *The History of the Town of Flatbush, in Kings County, Long-Island* (New York, 1842), 84–87; Henry R. Stiles, *A History of the City of Brooklyn*, 3 vols. (Brooklyn, 1867–70), I, 169–82.

80. *Eccl. Recs. N.Y.*, III, 2085.

81. Ibid., III, 2182–84.

82. For a broad survey of disputes on the Raritan, see William Stockton Cranmer, "The Famous Frelinghuysen Controversy," *Somerset County Historical Quarterly* 5 (1916): 81–89; for a detailed treatment, see chap. 5 herein.

83. *Eccl. Recs. N.Y.*, III, 1667–68. Cornbury clearly manipulated the S.P.G. in New York in his own ends. The Society was not always, in all places, used as a tool of cultural aggression. See, for example, Eamon Duffy, "*Correspondence Fraternelle*; The SPCK, the SPG, and the Churches of Switzerland in the War of the Spanish Succession," in *Reform and Reformation: England and the Continent c1500–c1750*, ed. by Derek Baker (Oxford Eng., 1979), 251–80.

84. *Eccl. Recs. N.Y.*, III, 1975; II, 776.

85. Still later, with the accession of the House of Hanover, the fort bore yet another name: George.

86. *Eccl. Recs. N.Y.*, III, 1664.

87. *Waare Christelyke Religie Voorgestelt, by forme van Vragen en Antwoorden, Ten gebruyke van sulke, Die sich bereyden om tot de gemeynschop van de Gereformeerd Kerke, en 't gebruyk van 's Herren Heylig Avondmaal toegelaten te worden* (New York, 1700). Cf. Hendrik Edelman, *Dutch-American Bibliography, 1693–1794* (Nieuwkoop, Netherlands, 1974), 24.

88. *Eccl. Recs. N.Y.*, III, 1653. Du Bois's work appeared as *Kort-Begryp der waare Christelyke Leere, uit den Heidelbergischen Catechismus uitgetrokken, door ordre der Christelyke Synod te Dordrecht, Anno 1618 & 1619* (New York, 1706).

89. *Eccl. Recs. N.Y.*, III, 1883, 1903–05, 1916–17. On the altar rail, com-

pare Anglican procedure: John Bartow to S.P.G., December 1, 1707, S.P.G. Records, Letterbook Series A, Vol. 3, no. CLXXXIV. The orthodox clergy's "retreat" to sacramentalism in New York roughly coincided with a similar movement in New England; see E. Brooks Holifield, *The Covenant Sealed: The Development of Puritan Sacramental Theology in Old and New England, 1570–1720* (New Haven, Conn., 1974).

90. *Eccl. Recs. N.Y.*, III, 1663. Regarding Beys's conversion, see III, 1743; Lewis Morris to S.P.G., May 30, 1709, S.P.G. Records, Letterbook Series A, Vol. 4, no. CXLIX.

Chapter 5

1. I am building here on the findings of Joyce D. Goodfriend, "The Social Dimensions of Congregational Life in Colonial New York City, 1664–1730," paper given at the Organization of American Historians Annual Convention, New York, April 1986. Regarding the Huguenots, see Jon Butler, *The Huguenots in America: A Refugee People in New World Society* (Cambridge, Mass., 1983), 166.

2. Kenneth Scott, "Contributors to Building of a New Dutch Church in New York City, 1688," *De Halve Maen* 55 (Spring 1980): 10–12; "The First Book of the Lists of the Ministers, Elders and Deacons of the Low Dutch Church, New York," ms. at Collegiate Church, New York City; John M. Murrin, "English Rights as Ethnic Aggression: The English Conquest, the Charter of Liberties of 1683, and Leisler's Rebellion in New York," in *Authority and Resistance in Early New York,* ed. by William Pencak and Conrad Edick Wright (New York, 1988), chap. 3. Leisler does not appear as a subscriber to the church building in 1688, although Jacob Milborne provided a modest contribution, On Dutch-English intermarriages in the seventeenth century, see Charles B. Moore, "English and Dutch Intermarriages," *New York Genealogical and Biographical Register* 3 (1872): 153–64; 4 (1873): 13–20, 127–39.

3. See David E. Narrett, "Preparation for Death and Provision for the Living: Notes on New York Wills (1665–1760)," *New York History* 57 (1976): 417–37, esp. 425–26.

4. Linda Briggs Biemer, *Women and Property in Colonial New York: The Transition from Dutch to English Law, 1643–1727* (Ann Arbor, Mich., 1983). Biemer writes that "English common law, introduced gradually after England conquered Dutch New Netherland in 1664, limited the economic, political, and social roles women in New York could legally play (p. 75). Cf. Sherry Penney and Roberta Willenkin, "Dutch Women in Colonial Albany: Liberation and Retreat," *De Halve Maen* 52 (Spring 1977): 9–10, 14–15; 52 (Summer 1977): 7–8, 15.

5. Lewis Morris to S.P.G., July 5, 1710, and November 15, 1710, S.P.G. Records (microfilm), Letterbook Series A, Vols. 5 and 6, nos. CXLIII and III.

6. Morris to S.P.G., March 25, 1711, S.P.G. Records, Letterbook Series A, Vol. 7, New-York Letters, no. 12.

7. Barclay to S.P.G., July 5, 1709, and June 12, 1711, S.P.G. Records, Letterbook Series A, Vols. 5 and 6, nos. I and CXXIX.

8. Barclay to S.P.G., April 17, 1713, S.P.G. Records, Letterbook Series A, Vol. 8, New-York Letters, no. 36.

9. Elias Neau to S.P.G., June 21, 1709, S.P.G. Records, Letterbook Series A, Vol. 4, no. CLV; Patricia U. Bonomi and Peter R. Eisenstadt, "Church Adherence in the Eighteenth-Century British American Colonies," *William and Mary Quarterly* (3d ser.) 39 (1982): [284].

10. Andrews to S.P.G., May 25, 1714, S.P.G. Records, Letterbook Series A, Vol. 9, New-York Letters, no. 18.

11. Edward Vaughan to S.P.G., September 8, 1715, S.P.G. Records, Letterbook Series A, Vol. 11, New-York Letters.

12. Morris to Archdeacon Beveridge, September 3, 1702, S.P.G. Records, Letterbook Series A, Vol. 1, no. XLV; John Talbot to S.P.G., April 7, 1704, and August 20, 1708, Vols. 1 and 4, nos. CLXXXI and LI. On the lack of Anglican success in New Jersey, see Robert Wm. Duncan, Jr., "A Study of the Ministry of John Talbot in New Jersey, 1702–1727: On 'Great Ripeness,' Much Dedication, and Regrettable Failure," *Historical Magazine of the Protestant Episcopal Church* 42 (1973): 233–56.

13. *Ecclesiastical Records: State of New York,* 7 vols., ed. by Edward T. Corwin (Albany, 1901–16), IV, 2613.

14. See Bryan R. Wilson, "An Analysis of Sect Development," *Patterns and Sectarianism: Organisation and Ideology in Social and Religious Movements,* ed. by Bryan R. Wilson (London, 1967), chap. 1; H. Richard Niebuhr, *The Social Sources of Denominationalism* Hamden, Conn., 1929), chap. 2. I am using the term *charismatic* here and throughout in a rather narrow sense, referring to an individual's popular appeal; I am not referring to any claims of divine authority or inspiration, even though some of the pietists came quite close to making that claim.

15. Quote from Arnold J. F. van Laer, ed., "The Lutheran Church in New York, 1649–1772: Records in the Lutheran Church Archives at Amsterdam, Holland," *Bulletin of the New York Public Library* 49 (1945): 822. Regarding charismatic leadership, see Max Weber, *Max Weber: The Interpretation of Social Reality,* ed. by J. E. T. Eldridge (New York, 1975), 229–35. For Frelinghuysen's thoughts on religious "calling," see Theodorus Jacobus Frelinghuysen, *Sermons by Theodorus Jacobus Frelinghuysen,* trans. by William Demarest (New York, 1856), 374–83.

16. [John] Calvin, *Institutes of the Christian Religion,* 2 vols. ed. by John T.

McNeill (Philadelphia, 1960), II, 1021–22. The best treatment of seventeenth-century Puritan criteria for church membership is Edmund S. Morgan, *Visible Saints: The History of a Puritan Idea* (New York, 1963).

17. *Eccl. Recs. N.Y.*, IV, 2788; Wilson, "Analysis of Sect Development," 23–28.

18. *Documents Relative to the Colonial History of the State of New-York*, 15 vols., ed. by E. B. O'Callaghan (Albany, 1856–67), III, 588. Not all pietists looked askance at sacramentalism; Heinrich Melchior Mühlenberg, a Lutheran, combined a sacramental theology with a pietistic scorn for mere formalism.

19. *Eccl. Recs. N.Y.*, II, 732, 778. Wilhelmus Van Nieuwenhuysen wrote to Amsterdam about the dangers of "so many sheep without a shepherd" in 1676: "It is well known to you that trees grow miserably wild, if not trimmed and pruned in their season" (I, 688).

20. Ibid., II, 749–50.

21. Ibid., IV, 2937, 3075, 2609.

22. Edward T. Corwin, *Manual of the Reformed Church in America,* 4th ed. (New York, 1902), s.v. "Vrooman, Barent"; Alice P. Kenney, *Stubborn for Liberty: The Dutch in New York* (Syracuse, N.Y., 1975), 132–33. See also Douglas Jacobsen's observations on what he calls "peasant religion" in the Middle Colonies. "Johann Bernhard van Dieren: Peasant Preacher at Hackensack, New Jersey, 1724–40," *New Jersey History* 100 (1982): esp. 24–27.

23. Frelinghuysen, *Sermons,* 26, 369.

24. Ibid., 35; Henry Melchior Mühlenberg, *The Journals of Henry Melchior Mühlenberg,* 3 vols., trans by Theodore G. Tappert and John W. Doberstein (Philadelphia, 1942–53), I, 284. For an extended treatment of ritual expression as an index of social engagement, see Mary Douglas, *Natural Symbols: Explorations in Cosmology* (New York, 1970); Victor W. Turner, *The Ritual Process: Structure and Anti-Structure* (Chicago, 1969).

25. Douglas, *Natural Symbols,* 161–62.

26. Bertholf had preached at Raritan twice a year since 1699. Abraham Messler, *Forty Years at Raritan: Eight Memorial Sermons, with Notes for a History of the Reformed Churches in Somerset County, N.J.* (New York, 1873), 163.

27. On pietism in general, see F. Ernest Stoeffler, *The Rise of Evangelical Pietism* (Leiden, 1965). For a useful, brief treatment of pietism in the Netherlands, see Martin H. Prozesky, "The Emergence of Dutch Pietism," *Journal of Ecclesiastical History* 28 (1977): 29–37. On Frelinghuysen's pietistic roots in the Old World and his influence in the New, see M. Eugene Osterhaven, "The Experiential Theology of Early Dutch Calvinism," *Reformed Review* 27 (1974): 180–89; F. J. Schrag, "Theodorus Jacobus Frelinghuysen: The Father of American Pietism," *Church History* 14 (1945): 201–16.

28. The best secondary treatment of Frelinghuysen is James Tanis, *Dutch*

Calvinistic Pietism in the Middle Colonies: A Study in the Life and Theology of Theodorus Jacobus Frelinghuysen (The Hague, 1967). Other biographies include Peter H. B. Frelinghuysen, Jr., *Theodorus Jacobus Frelinghuysen* (Princeton, N.J., 1938). Herman Harmelink III takes issue with the hagiographical treatments of Frelinghuysen, but he then goes on to make the rather specious claim that Frelinghuysen played no role whatsoever in the Awakening. "Another Look at Frelinghuysen and his 'Awakening,' " *Church History* 37 (1968): 423–38. On Frelinghuysen's ordination, see *Eccl. Recs. N.Y.*, III, 2121. Bernardus Freeman of Long Island initiated Frelinghuysen's call; see Messler, *Forty Years at Raritan*, 166, 177–78.

29. *Eccl. Recs. N.Y.*, III, 2182–83. For Bertholf's charges, see II, 1107.

30. Tanis, *Dutch Calvinistic Pietism*, 43.

31. Quoted in ibid., 51.

32. *Eccl. Recs. N.Y.*, III, 2183.

33. Quoted in Tanis, *Dutch Calvinistic Pietism*, 54.

34. Frelinghuysen, *Sermons*, 88, 82.

35. For the identity of Teunissen's wife, see "Records of the Harlingen Reformed Dutch Church, Montgomery Township, Somerset County," *Genealogical Magazine of New Jersey* 15 (1940): 63. On Teunissen's (or Teunisse's) wealth, see "Tax Lists of the City of New York, December 1, 1695–July 15, 1699," 2 vols., New-York Historical Society, *Collections*, Publication Fund Series, XLIII–XLIV (New York, 1910–11).

36. *Boel's "Complaint" Against Frelinghuisen*, trans. and ed. by Joseph Anthony Loux, Jr. (Rensselaer, N.Y., 1979), 34–35.

37. Ibid., 49, 51, 56.

38. Ibid., 49, 53, 55.

39. Ibid., 90.

40. Frelinghuysen, *Sermons*, 21.

41. *Eccl. Recs. N.Y.*, III, 2119; *Boel's "Complaint,"* 33–36. Freeman's tract appeared as *Verdeedinging . . . wegens but . . . Klagte* (New York, 1726); Van Santvoord's, *Samenspraak over de Klaghte*.

42. *Eccl. Recs. N.Y.*, IV, 2309–12. For a survey of the dispute, see James J. Bergen, "The 'Rebellion' at Raritan in 1723," *Somerset County Historical Quarterly* 3 (1914): 173–84, 241–49.

43. *Boel's "Complaint,"* 23, 42, 65.

44. Ibid., 74. There is evidence (from church records) that Frelinghuysen later baptized infants. For a treatment of Frelinghuysen's sacramental theology, see Tanis, *Dutch Calvinistic Pietism*, 138–45.

45. *Boel's "Complaint,"* 33, 144–48, 156. Frelinghuysen and Schuurman married daughters of Albert Terhune of Flatbush; see Messler, *Forty Years at Raritan*, 180.

46. *Boel's "Complaint,"* 156, 89, 74–75, 107, 104; Tanis, *Dutch Calvinistic Pietism*, 143; Messler, *Forty Years at Raritan*, 181. Frelinghuysen's reputation

as a low-church zealot and an "errorist" had also reached German Reformed congregations in Pennsylvania. *Eccl. Recs. N.Y.,* IV, 2425–26.

47. *Eccl. Recs. N.Y.,* IV, 2351, 2352–54, 2401–2, 2421, 2422.

48. Frelinghuysen, *Sermons,* 354.

49. For the names of Frelinghuysen's opponents and supporters, see *Boel's "Complaint,"* 47, 51–52, 57. For the wills, see "Calendar of New Jersey Wills," 5 vols., in *Archives of the State of New Jersey, Documents Relating to the Colonial History of the State of New Jersey,* 1st Series, 42 vols., ed. by William A. Whitehead (Newark, 1880–1949), XXIII, XXX, XXXII–IV. Regarding Tobias Boel's estate, see "Inventory & Appraisament of the Goods & Chattles Rights & Credits of the Late Deceased Mr. Tobias Boel Gentleman Takin in New York ye 22d May 1728," ms. at New-York Historical Society.

50. A translation of this sermon appears as chap. 1 in Frelinghuysen, *Sermons.* James Tanis says that this sermon was preached "before 15 June 1721." *Dutch Calvinistic Pietism,* 183.

51. Frelinghuysen, *Sermons,* 30–31; Bernardus Freeman, "The Mirror of Self-Knowledge or a Collection of Learned Sayings by the Reverend Bernardus Freeman, Minister of the Prot. R. D. Churches in Kings County [1717]," trans. by Jeremiah Johnson (1831), ms. at New-York Historical Society.

52. *Boel's "Complaint,"* 65, 83, 117.

53. Ibid., 141.

54. *Eccl. Recs. N.Y.,* IV, 2459–60.

55. Ibid., IV, 2520, 2538–43, 2638–40; on Frelinghuysen's mental health at the time, see IV, 2640. Frelinghuysen himself preached that "we have often been severely afflicted and chastened by the hand of God, not only with bodily sickness, but also with spiritual desertions." *Sermons,* 355. In 1759, Mühlenberg referred obliquely to Frelinghuysen's "flourishing period, his downfall, and his rehabilitation before his departure." *Journals of Henry Melchior Mühlenberg,* I, 392.

56. *Eccl. Recs. N.Y.,* IV, 2659, 2593.

CHAPTER 6

1. *Ecclesiastical Records: State of New York,* 7 vols., ed. by Edward T. Corwin (Albany, 1901–16), IV, 2340–41.

2. Ibid., IV, 2337–39, 2614, 2619–21.

3. Ibid., IV, 2397–99.

4. Ibid., IV, 2341.

5. See Ronald William Howard, "Education and Ethncity in Colonial New York, 1664–1763: A Study in the Transmission of Culture in Early America" (Ph.D. diss., University of Tennessee, 1978), esp. chaps. 3–4.

Public schools were established in New York City in 1732. *Eccl. Recs. N.Y.,* IV, 2608. Jessica Kross shows that in Newton, where the Dutch took great pains to maintain their ethnic distinctiveness, Dutch schoolchildren still attended English schools and learned the English language. *The Evolution of an American Town: Newtown, New York, 1642–1775* (Philadelphia, 1983), 270–72.

6. Sherry Penney and Roberta Willenkin, "Dutch Women in Colonial Albany: Liberation and Retreat," *De Halve Maen* 52 (Spring 1977): 14.

7. Roderic H. Blackburn, "Dutch Material Culture: Architecture," *De Halve Maen* 57 (Fall 1982): 1–5; idem, "Dutch Material Culture: Silversmiths," *De Halve Maen* 55 (Fall 1980): 5–11.

8. *Eccl. Recs. N.Y.,* IV, 2376–78; on increases in attendance at New York, see IV, 2450–51. Cf. Alice P. Kenney, "Religious Artifacts on the Dutch Colonial Period," *De Halve Maen* 53 (Winter 1977–78): 1–2, 16, 19, 14. Kenney suggests that the octagonal style was popular in the rural Netherlands (p. 2).

9. Edgar Franklin Romig, " 'The English and Low-Dutch School-Master,' " *New-York Historical Soceity Quarterly* 43 (1959): 149–59, quoted on 149.

10. *Eccl. Recs. N.Y.,* III, 2667; IV, 2678. On Tennent, see Milton J Coalter, Jr., *Gilbert Tennent, Son of Thunder: A Case Study of Continental Pietism's Impact on the First Great Awakening in the Middle Colonies* (Westport, Conn., 1986), esp. 12–25.

11. *Eccl. Recs. N.Y.,* IV, 2587. James Tanis, Frelinghuysen's biographer, has suggested in personal correspondence that Frelinghuysen's lack of commitment to the Dutch language may have stemmed from the fact that German was his native tongue and that he learned Dutch only in his teens.

12. Theodorus Jacobus Frelinghuysen, *Sermons by Theodorus Jacobus Frelinghuysen,* trans. by William Demarest (New York, 1856), 358; *Eccl. Recs. N.Y.,* IV, 2465–66, 2587.

13. *Eccl. Recs. N.Y.,* IV, 2557, 2569.

14. Ibid., IV, 2659–60, 2587, 2582–83. In the early 1730s, German Lutherans had anticipated great success on the Raritan, except for the presence of "fanatics," the "followers of Frelinghuysen." *Lutheran Church in New York and New Jersey, 1722–1760: Lutheran Records in the Ministerial Archives of the Staatsarchiv, Hamburg, Germany,* trans. by Simon Hart and Harry J. Kreider (New York, 1962), 16–17. On the Great Awakening among the Dutch, see Charles Hartshorn Maxson, *The Great Awakening in the Middle Colonies* (Chicago, 1920), chap. 2. Maxson is quite sympathetic to Frelinghuysen and the revival.

15. *Documentary History of the State of New-York* [quarto ed.], 4 vols., ed. by E. B. O'Callaghan (Albany, 1850–51), III, 613–2; *Eccl. Recs. N.Y.,* IV, 2734, 2737, 2738, 2743.

16. George Whitefield, *George Whitefield's Journals (1737–1741)* (London, 1905; reprint ed. Gainsville, Fla., 1969), 405.

17. Ibid., 348. For biographies of Whitefield, see, among others, Stuart C. Henry, *George Whitefield: Wayfaring Witness* (New York, 1957); Arnold A. Dallimore, *George Whitefield: The Life and Times of the Great Evangelist of the Eighteenth-Century Revival* 2 vols. (Westchester, Ill,, 1979).

18. Jonathan Edwards, *The Great Awakening*, ed. by C. C. Goen, *The Works of Jonathan Edwards*, (New Haven, Conn., 1972), IV, 156; Henry Melchior Mühlenberg, *The Journals of Henry Melchior Mühlenberg*, 3 vols., trans. by Theodore G. Tappert and John W. Doberstein (Philadelphia, 1942–53), I, 392. Writing from his Stockbridge exile in 1751, Edwards linked the revival among the Dutch in the Middle Colonies with that back in the Netherlands. "The Dutch people in the provinces of New-York and New-Jersey, have been famed for being generally exceedingly ignorant, stupid and profane, little better than the savages of our American deserts," he wrote. "But it is remarkable, that things should now begin to appear more hopeful among them, about the same time that religion is reviving among the Dutch in their mother country." Quoted in Sereno E. Dwight, *The Life of President Edwards* (New York, 1830), 461.

19. Frelinghuysen, *Sermons*, 371; *New-York Weekly Journal*, November 26, 1739; *Archives of the State of New Jersey: Documents Relating to the Colonial History of the State of New Jersey*, 1st Series, 42 vols., ed. by William A. Whitehead (Newark, 1880–1949), XXI, 240; *Doc., Hist. N.-Y.*, III, 192–93. The Boston correspondent singled out Gilbert Tennent as "an *awkward Imitator* of Mr. *Whitefield.*" *Archives N.J.*, XII, 240.

20. *Eccl. Recs. N.Y.*, IV, 2964, 2756–57, 2798–99. For a contemporary account of this occasion, see an article in the *New England Weekly Journal*, December 4, 1739, reprinted in Richard L. Bushman, ed., *The Great Awakening: Documents on the Great Revival of Religion, 1740–1745* (New York, 1970), 22–23. Commenting on a similar outing, Whitefield claimed to have preached to "upwards of two thousand" and added: "I have not felt greater freedom in preaching, and more power in prayer, since I came to America, than I have here in New York. I find that little of the work of God has been seen in it for many years." *Whitefield's Journals*, 345–46.

21. *Whitefield's Journals*, 411; *Archives N.J.*, XII, 23.

22. James I. Good, *History of the Reformed Church in the United States, 1725–1792* (Reading, Pa., 1899), 171–89; "Minutes of the Presbytery of Philadelphia, 1733–1746," typescript at Presbyterian Historical Society, 59–60; *Eccl. Recs. N.Y.*, IV, 2684–85, 2741. Cf. William J. Hinke, *Ministers of the German Reformed Congregations in Pennsylvania and Other Colonies in the Eighteenth Century*, ed. by George W. Richards (Lancaster, Pa., 1951), s.v. "John Henry Goetschy (Goetschius)."

23. Howard G. Hageman, "The Dutch Battle for Higher Education in the Middle Colonies," in *Education in New Netherland and the Middle Colonies:*

Papers of the 7th Rensselaerswyck Seminar of the New Netherland Project, ed. by Charles T. Gehring and Nancy Anne McClure Zeller (Albany, 1985), 38–39; idem, *Two Centuries Plus: The Story of New Brunswick Seminary* (Grand Rapids, Mich., 1984), 1–7.

24. *Eccl. Recs. N.Y.,* IV, 2743–45, 2752–53; Edward T. Corwin, *A Manual of the Reformed Church in America,* 4th ed. (New York, 1902), s.v. "Goetschius, John Henry"; Benjamin C. Taylor, *Annals of the Classis of Bergen, of the Reformed Dutch Church, and the Churches under Its Care* (New York, 1857), 180. Frelinghuysen, *Sermons,* 361–83. For a sketch of the life and career of Peter Henry Dorsius, including documentary materials, see William J. Hinke, "Life and Work of the Rev. Peter Henry Dorsius," *Bucks County Historical Society Papers* 5 (1926): 44–67; Good, *History of the Reformed Church,* 190–99.

25. Typescript translation of *The Unknown God,* translated for the author by Liesbeth Fontijn.

26. *Eccl. Recs. N.Y.,* IV, 2787–88, 2829, 2889–91, 2841. The testimony regarding Anitje Onderdonk was disputed.

27. Ibid., IV, 2896, 2789, 2840, 2877, 2881.

28. Ibid., IV, 2944–46; V, 3622. Curtenius, according to Mühlenberg, "complained of his colleague, who, he said, was too impetuous and hasty and too ready to begin all sorts of innovations." *Mühlenberg's Journals,* I, 298.

29. *Eccl. Recs. N.Y.,* IV, 2949, 3072, 3074, 3080.

30. Ibid., IV, 2913, 2915, 3131; Joh. Hend., Goetschius, *De Onbekende God . . .* (New York, 1743), 3–8.

31. Even the New York consistory heard complaints in 1747 that sermons were too long. *Eccl. Recs. N.Y.,* IV, 2955–56.

32. Ibid., IV, 2840, 3131, 2837, 2841, 2891; *Mühlenberg's Journals,* I, 298. Goetschius's condemnation of the Dutch clergy was directed toward Vincentius Antonides and Bernardus Freeman; however, Goetschius at other points declared his admiration for Freeman. Cf. *Eccl. Recs. N.Y.,* IV, 2885. Tennent's tract was preached originally at Nottingham, Pa., March 8, 1740. Gilbert Tennent, *The Danger of an Unconverted Ministry* (Philadelphia, 1740).

33. Typescript translation of *The Unknown God.*

34. *Eccl. Recs. N.Y.,* V, 3627; IV, 2888, 2898–99, 2881, 2841.

35. Ibid., IV, 2719; *coetus* is pronounced "SEE-tus."

36. Ibid., IV, 2696, 2798–99, 2716.

37. Ibid., IV, 3052, 3075.

38. Ibid., V, 3493, 3494, 3541.

39. The perils of Atlantic voyages were, of course, quite real. For an account of an eighteenth-century crossing, see William U. Helfferich, "The Journal of Rev. Johann Heinrich Helfferich," *Pennsylvania Folklife* 28 (1979): 17–24.

40. *Archives N.J.,* XII, 550, 585. Cf. Gerald F. De Jong, "The Education

and Training of Dutch Ministers," in *Education in New Netherland and the Middle Colonies: Papers of the 7th Rensselaerswyck Seminar of the New Netherland Project,* ed. by Charles T. Gehring and Nancy Anne McClure Zeller (Albany, 1985), 9–16.

41. Hageman, "Dutch Battle for Higher Education," 36–37.

42. Quoted in Gerald F. De Jong, *The Dutch Reformed Church in the American Colonies* (Grand Rapids, Mich., 1978), 218.

43. *Eccl. Recs. N.Y.,* V, 3605.

44. Ibid., V, 3561, 3564.

45. Ibid., V. 3533. Elsewhere Curtenius wrote that he opposed American ordinations because "the door would be opened for the introduction into our Church of Arminians and Independent Presbyterians" (V, 3519).

46. Ibid., V, 3649.

47. Cf. ibid., V, 3425; "The Letters and Papers of Cadwallader Colden," Vol. VII, New-York Historical Society, *Collections,* Publication Fund Series, LVI (New York, 1923), 346.

48. See, for example, *Eccl. Recs. N.Y.,* V, 3680; in 1758, the Coetus appointed Johannes Barcolo, a graduate of the Presbyterian College of New Jersey, as a ministerial candidate (V, 3720).

49. Ibid., V, 3584. Clearly, the traditionalists saw the English as allies. Arondeus refused to become a member of the Coetus and stipulated "that whenever dissatisfied with their decisions, he might appeal to the English Church and the English law" (V, 3187). For a review of the circumstances and the opposition of non-Anglicans to the founding of King's College, see Milton M. Klein, "Church, State, and Education: Testing the Issue in Colonial New York," *New York History* 45 (1964): 291–303; David C. Humphrey, *From King's College to Columbia, 1746–1800* (New York, 1976), chaps. 3–5.

50. *Eccl. Recs. N.Y.,* V, 3609, 3610.

51. Ibid., V, 3637–38.

52. Ibid., V, 3708.

53. Ibid., V, 3762–92, 3585. The Coetus's five proposed classes were New York, New Brunswick, Hackensack, Kingston, and Albany.

54. At one count during the Old Light–New Light fracas of the 1750s, the Van Sinderen party claimed the backing of 158 families; Arondeus had the allegiance of 176 families. Ibid., V, 3190–93, 3214.

55. For a treatment of the social forces behind Dutch revivalism in New Jersey, see Randall H. Balmer, "The Social Roots of Dutch Pietism in the Middle Colonies," *Church History* 53 (1984): 187–99.

56. *Whitefield's Journals,* 405.

57. Regarding the Shepherd's Tent and the book-burning episode, see Richard Warch, "The Shepherd's Tent: Education and Enthusiasm in the Great Awakening," *American Quarterly* 30 (1978): 177–98; Harry S. Stout and Peter Onuf, "James Davenport and the Great Awakening in New Lon-

don," *Journal of American History* 70 (1983–84): 556–78. For an excellent treatment of Croswell and his importance to the radical Awakening, see Leigh Eric Schmidt, " 'A Second and Glorious Reformation': The New Light Extremism of Andrew Croswell," *William and Mary Quarterly* (3d ser.) 43 (1986): 214–44.

58. *Eccl. Recs. N.Y.*, IV, 2926, 2798–99; V, 3519; *Whitefield's Journals*, 413.

59. *Eccl. Recs. N.Y.*, IV, 3076; Douglas Jacobsen, "Johann Bernhard Van Dieren: Protestant Preacher at Hackensack, New Jersey, 1724–40," *New Jersey History* 100 (1982): 15–29, quotation on 18.

60. *Eccl. Recs. N.Y.*, IV, 2967; V, 3714. On parallel changes in New England, see Harry S. Stout, "Religion, Communications, and the Ideological Origins of the American Revolution," *William and Mary Quarterly* (3d ser.) 34 (1977): 519–41; idem, *The New England Soul: Preaching and Religious Culture in Colonial New England* (New York, 1986). Stout argues that the Awakening introduced a popular rhetoric that contrasted with established, more formalized modes of discourse.

61. *Mühlenberg's Journals*, I, 324–25.

62. *Eccl. Recs. N.Y.*, IV, 3124, 3126; V, 3455, 3661. Van Sinderen conducted the "funeral" in the spring of 1756; Antonius Curtenius died on October 19, 1756 (V, 3661, 3677–78).

63. *Mühlenberg's Journals*, I, 327.

64. *Eccl. Recs. N.Y.*, V, 3243.

65. Ibid., V, 3354.

66. *Doc. Hist. N.-Y.*, III, 193–94.

67. The preponderance of Anglicans had opposed the revival. See Gerald J. Goodwin, "The Anglican Reaction to the Great Awakening," *Historical Magazine of the Protestant Episcopal Church* 35 (1966): 343–71.

68. *Eccl. Recs. N.Y.*, IV, 2757.

69. Quoted in Edward Midwinter, "The Society for the Propagation of the Gospel and the Church in the American Colonies," *Historical Magazine of the Protestant Episcopal Church* 4 (1935): 73–4.

70. *Eccl. Recs. N.Y.*, IV, 2867, 2876, 2766, 2678–80.

71. Ibid., V, 3714.

72. Ibid., V, 3721.

73. *Documents Relative to the Colonial History of the State of New-York*, 15 vols., ed. by E. B. O'Callaghan (Albany, 1856–87), VII, 347.

74. *Eccl. Recs. N.Y.*, IV, 2822.

75. Ibid., V, 3499, 3680.

76. *Whitefield's Journals*, 343. The next year, Whitefield wrote: "I care not for any sect or party of men" (p. 412).

77. See *Lutheran Church in N.Y. and N.J.*, 16–17, 141. Mühlenberg relates the following story about his preaching at the Dutch church at Hacken-

sack: "One awakened Reformed man had ridden three miles from his home to the church and after the service, absorbed in sweet thoughts, walked all the way home before it finally occurred to him that he had left his horse standing near the church." *Mühlenberg's Journals,* I, 299.

78. On the Awakening as an Americanizing influence among the Dutch, see J. J. Mol, *The Breaking of Traditions: Theological Convictions in Colonial American* (Berkeley, Calif., 1968), chap. 2.

79. Theodorus Frielinghuysen [*sic*], *Wars and Rumors of Wars, Heavens Decree over the World: A Sermon Preached in the Camp of the New-England Forces* (New York, 1755).

80. Humphrey, *From King's College to Columbia,* chap. 4.

CHAPTER 7

1. *Ecclesiastical Records: State of New York,* 7 vols., ed. by Edward T. Corwin, (Albany, 1901–16), IV, 3037–38. This was, at least, Du Bois's last *official* correspondence with the Classis.

2. Ibid., V, 3459.

3. "Rev. Dr. Laidlie," *Christian Intelligencer* 27 (February 26, 1857): 137; cf. Alexander J. Wall, "The Controversy in the Dutch Church in New York Concerning Preaching in English, 1754–1768," *New-York Historical Society Quarterly* 12 (1928): 39–58. On the decline of Dutch political influence in New York City, see Bruce M. Wilkenfeld, "The New York City Common Council, 1689–1900," *New York History* 52 (1971): 249–73. As recently as 1744, Dr. Alexander Hamilton had written: "The government is under English law, but the chief places are possessed by Dutchmen, they composing the best part of the House of Assembly." *Gentleman's Progress: The Itinerarium of Dr. Alexander Hamilton, 1744,* ed. by Carl Bridenbaugh (Chapel Hill, N.C., 1948), 88.

4. *Eccl. Recs. N.Y.,* VI, 3935–6.

5. Ibid., VI, 3854.

6. Laidlie's call, which included a reference to "the decay of our Dutch language in this English colony," appears in ibid., VI, 3878–80. The hiring of an English minister did, however, meet with some opposition from church members; see their remonstrance to the Classis and the court case they initiated (VI, 3880–81, 3985–88). On the circumstances surrounding Laidlie's call and the transition from Dutch to English in the New York Dutch church, see Charles E. Corwin, "The Introduction of the English Language into the Services of the Collegiate Dutch Church of New York City," *Journal of the Presbyterian Historical Society* 10 (1919–20): 175–88; Nancy Krassner, "The Dutch-English Language Controversy," *De Halve Maen* 59 (November 1985): 1–3, 20; 59 (March 1986): 9–11, 21. De Ronde's reference to his

translation appears in *Eccl. Recs. N.Y.*, VI, 3904; regarding his facility in English, see VI, 4016.

7. *The Psalms of David, with the Ten Commandments, Creed, Lord's Prayer, &c. in Metre. Also the Catechism, Confession of Faith, Liturgy, &c. Translated from the Dutch* (New York, 1767), [iii]. The New York consistory had authorized this translation on July 5, 1763, just days before they approved Laidlie's call as minister. *Eccl. Recs. N.Y.*, VI, 3862.

8. *Eccl. Recs. N.Y.*, VI, 3898, 3912, 3946.

9. Ibid., VI, 4254–55, 4016, 4019, 4105–6, 4136. On the decline of the Dutch language in colonial New York, see Charles Theodor Gehring, "The Dutch Language in Colonial New York: An Investigation of a Language in Decline and Its Relationship to Social Change" (Ph.D. diss., Indiana University, 1973).

10. *Eccl. Rec. N.Y.*, VI, 3952, 3909–10. Mary Cooper's diary, written on Long Island from 1768–1773, contains several references to New Light meetings; see *The Diary of Mary Cooper: Life on a Long Island Farm, 1768–1773*, ed. by Field Horne (Oyster Bay, N.Y., 1981).

11. *Eccl. Recs. N.Y.*, VI, 3904, 4007, 4159; Lambertus De Ronde, *The True Spiritual Religion; or, Delightful Servide of the Lord . . .* (New York, 1767). As late as 1771, the New York consistory worried about the incursion of Methodism and Arminianism. *Eccl. Recs. N.Y.*, VI, 4200.

12. *Eccl. Recs. N.Y.*, VI, 4005; "Notes for a Sermon by John H. Livingston, Preached at New Church, New York, December 30, 1770," ms. in George Croghan Papers, New York Public Library

13. A version of this treatise appears in *Eccl. Recs. N.Y.*, V, 3762–92.

14. Ibid., VI, 3846–51, 3862. Both the Classis of Amsterdam and the Synod of North Holland specifically disapproved of an American classis and an American academy (VI, 3850). On April 11, 1763, the Classis wrote: "You will understand how much we disapprove of [Leydt's book], and how pleased we are with the opinions of the brethren who call themselves the Conferentie, and who are determined to remain subordinate to the Classis of Amsterdam" (VI, 3868–69).

15. Ibid., VI, 3865.

16. Ibid., VI, 3875–77.

17. Ibid., VI, 3883–86, 3981–82, 3961. Upon his return, Hardenbergh refused to discuss his mission with the Conferentie ministers; see VI, 3903.

18. Ibid., VI, 3925–28, 3936.

19. Ibid., VI, 3927, 3944.

20. Ibid., VI, 3945, 4021, 3950.

21. Ibid., VI, 4005; *Journals of Capt. John Montresor, 1757–1778*, New-York Historical Society, *Collections*, Publications Fund Series, XIV (New York, 1881), 350.

22. *Eccl. Recs. N.Y.*, VI, 3974, 3993.

23. Ibid., VI, 3944.

24. Ibid., VI, 4014, 3949.

25. Ibid., VI, 3994, 4121, 4124.

26. Ibid., VI, 4160.

27. Ibid., VI, 4210–18, 4229, 4242–48.

28. Adrian C. Leiby asserted the connection between Coetus-Whig and Conferentie-Tory among the Jersey Dutch in *The United Churches of Hackensack and Schraalenburgh, New Jersey, 1686–1822* (River Edge, N.J., 1976), chap. 6.

29. Sources for determining these affiliations are Edward T. Corwin, *A Manual of the Reformed Church in America, 1628–1902*, 4th ed. (New York, 1902); Leiby, *United Churches*, chap. 6; *Eccl. Recs. N.Y.;* James Tanis, "The Dutch Reformed Church and the American Revolution,"*De Halve Maen* 52 (Summer 1977): 1–2, 15; 52 (Fall 1977): 1–2, 12–13, 19.

30. Corwin, *Manual of the Reformed Church*, s.v. "Hardenbergh, Jacob Rutsen," s.v. "Livingston, John H.," s.v. "Laidlie, Archibald"; *Eccl. Recs. N.Y.*, VI, 4303; Leiby, *United Churches*, 158, 164; Tanis, "Dutch Reformed Church," 19. John Henry Goetschius, the pietist pastor of Long Island and Hackensack, had died in 1774, but his son John Mauritius was appointed major in the Bergen, New Jersey, militia in 1776. Leiby, *United Churches*, 152.

31. John Wolfe Lydekker, "The Rev. Gerrit (Gerard) Lydekker, 1729–1794," *Historical Magazine of the Protestant Episcopal Church* 13 (1944): 303–14, quotation on 308; cf. *Eccl. Recs. N.Y.*, VI, 4305. Although his evidence is rather fragmentary, Richard W. Pointer believes that the Revolution in New York had a minimal effect on religious life "Religious Life in New York during the Revolutionary War," *New York History* 66 (1985): 357–73.

32. *Eccl. Recs. N.Y.*, VI, 4295; Alice P. Kenney, "The Albany Dutch: Loyalists and Patriots," *New York History* 42 (1961): 331–50; idem, *Stubborn for Liberty: The Dutch in New York* (Syracuse, N.Y., 1975). Edward Countryman writes: "Perhaps the most thoroughly loyalist area in all America was the region surrounding New York City: the counties of Queens, Kings, and Richmond." "Consolidating Power in Revolutionary America: The Case of New York, 1775–1783," *Journal of Interdisciplinary History* 6 (1976): 650. The Dutch certainly contributed to that configuration.

33. This is the conclusion of Leiby, *United Churches*, chap. 6; cf. John W. Beardslee III, "The Dutch Reformed Church and the Revolution," *Journal of Presbyterian History* 54 (1976): 165–81; George De Vries, Jr., "The Dutch in the American Revolution: Reflections and Observations," *Fides et Historia* 10 (1977): 43–57.

34. *Eccl. Recs. N.Y.*, VI, 4321, 4324. When Amsterdam refused in subsequent correspondence to acknowledge this change, the new Synod wrote and

asked to be addressed as such (VI, 4346). In 1789, the Synod dropped "New York and New Jersey" from its title and replaced it with "North America."

35. Ibid., VI, 4345, 4348; cf. VI, 4332.

36. Ms. (no. 9544) at New York State Library, Albany, fol. 1. Just twenty years earlier, William Livingston had written to David Colden about "the prevalence of the Dutch language" in Albany. *The Letters and Papers of Cadwallader Colden*, Vol. IX, New-York Historical Society, *Collections*, Publication Fund Series, LXVIII (New York, 1937), 184.

37. *Eccl. Recs. N.Y.*, VI, 4333 35. Johannes Rubel of Long Island was also turned out of office. The New York church ousted Ritzema and De Ronde despite elaborate assurances in 1763, at the hiring of Archibald Laidlie, that there would be no more than one English minister and at least two Dutch ministers at New York; see VI, 3961.

38. William Strickland, *Journal of a Tour in the United States of America, 1794–1795*, ed. by J. E. Strickland, New-York Historical Society, *Collections*, Publication Fund Series, LXXXIII (New York, 1971), 63, 98, 102.

39. Jon Butler, *The Huguenots in America: A Refugee People in New World Society* (Cambridge, Mass., 1983), esp. 199–215.

40. Suzanne B. Geissler, "A Step on the Swedish Lutheran Road to Anglicanism," *Historical Magazine of the Protestant Episcopal Church* 54 (1985): 39–49, quotation on 39; Donald Einar Bjarnson, "Swedish-Finnish Settlements in New Jersey in the Seventeenth Century," *Swedish Pioneer Historical Quarterly* 27 (1976): 239–40.

41. John B. Frantz, "The Awakening of Religion among the German Settlers in the Middle Colonies," *William and Mary Quarterly* (3d ser.) 33 (1976): 266–88.

42. For an excellent study of the Scots and their ability to retain their particularity in the New World environment, see Ned. C. Landsman, *Scotland and Its First American Colony, 1683–1765* (Princeton, N.J., 1985); idem, "Revivalism and Nativism in the Middle Colonies: The Great Awakening and the Scots Community in East New Jersey," *American Quarterly* 34 (1982): 149–64. Marilyn J. Westerkamp points out the communal emphasis of Scottish revivalism in *Triumph of the Laity: Scots-Irish Piety and the Great Awakening, 1625–1760* (New York, 1988). Regarding the Huguenots, see Butler, *Huguenots in America*, 212–15. David Steven Cohen has shown that the immigrants to New Netherland were geographically and ethnically diverse; see "How Dutch Were the Dutch of New Netherland?" *New York History* 62 (1981): 43–60.

43. Strickland, *Journal of a Tour*, N.-Y. Hist. Soc., *Colls.*, Publication Fund Series, LXXXIII, (New York, 1971), 102–3.

BIBLIOGRAPHY

Manuscript Sources

Brooklyn Historical Society, Brooklyn, N.Y. Manuscript Collection.
Collegiate Church, New York. Record Books.
Franklin D. Roosevelt Presidential Library, Hyde Park, N.Y. Livingston Family Papers.
Holland Society of New York, New York. Dutch Church Records.
James A. Kelly Institute, St. Francis College, Brooklyn, N.Y. Bergen Papers.
_____. Long Island Town Records.
Lambeth Palace, London. Fulham Papers (microfilm).
New-York Historical Society, New York. Frederick Ashton DePeyster Manuscripts.
New York Public Library, New York. Emmet Collection.
_____. George Chalmers Papers.
_____. George Croghan Papers.
_____. Livingston Papers.
New York State Archives, Albany, N.Y. Manuscript Collection.
Presbyterian Historical Society, Philadelphia. Minutes of the Philadelphia Presbytery.
Society for the Propagation of the Gospel, London. Letterbook Series A, 1702–37 (microfilm).
_____. Letterbook Series B, 1701–86 (microfilm).
_____. Letterbook Series C (microfilm).
_____. Journals, 1701–1870 (microfilm).

Published Primary Sources

"Abstracts of Wills," 27 vols. New-York Historical Society, *Collections,* Publication Fund Series, XXV–XLI. New York, 1892–1909.
Adams, George Burton, and H. Morse Stephens, eds. *Select Documents of English Constitutional History.* New York, 1929.
Andrews, Charles M., ed. *Narratives of the Insurrections, 1675–1690.* New York, 1915.
Andrews, Wayne, ed. "A Glance at New York in 1697: The Travel Diary of Dr. Benjamin Bullivant." *New-York Historical Society Quarterly* 40 (1956): 55–73.
Augustine. *The City of God,* 2 vols. Trans. by John Healy. London, 1945.

Bergen, Teunis G. *Register in Alphabetical Order, of the Early Settlers of Kings County, Long Island, N.Y., from Its First Settlement by Europeans to 1700.* New York, 1881.

Bray, Thomas. *Rev. Thomas Bray: His Life and Selected Works relating to Maryland.* Ed. by Bernard C. Steiner. Maryland Historical Society Fund Publication No. 37. Baltimore, 1901.

Burnaby, Andrew. *Travels through the Middle Settlements in North America, in the Years 1759 and 1760; with Observations upon the State of the Colonies.* New York, 1904.

Bushman, Richard L., ed. *The Great Awakening: Documents on the Great Revival of Religion, 1740–1745.* New York, 1970.

Calendar of Council Minutes. New York State Library, *History Bulletin*, 6. Albany, 1902.

Calendar of State Papers, Colonial Series: America and West Indies, 44 vols. Ed. by W. N. Sainsbury, J. W. Fortescue, and Cecil Headlam. London, 1860–1969.

Calvin, [John]. *Institutes of the Christian Religion,* 2 vols. Ed. by John T. McNeill. Trans. by Ford Lewis Battles. Philadelphia, 1960.

[Chorley, E. Clowes]. "The Seal of the S.P.G." *Historical Magazine of the Protestant Episcopal Church* 12 (1943): 253.

Christoph, Peter R., and Florence A. Christoph, eds. *New York Historical Manuscripts: English: Books of General Entries of the Colony of New York, 1664–1673,* 3 vols. Baltimore, 1982.

Christoph, Peter, Kenneth Scott, and Kenn Strycker-Rodda, eds. *New York Historical Manuscripts: Dutch: Kingston Papers,* 2 vols. Trans. by Dingman Vensteeg. Baltimore, 1976.

The Colonial Laws of New York: From the Year 1664 to the Revolution, 5 vols. Albany, 1894–96.

Colonial Records: General Entires, 1664–65. New York State Library, *History Bulletin*, 2. Albany, 1899.

Cooper, Mary. *The Diary of Mary Cooper: Life on a Long Island Farm, 1768–1773.* Ed. by Field Horne. Oyster Bay, N.Y., 1981.

Corwin, Edward T., ed. *Ecclesiastical Records: State of New York,* 7 vols. Albany, 1901–16.

Cushing, John D., comp. *The Earliest Printed Laws of New Jersey, 1703–1722.* Wilmington, Del., 1978.

Danckaerts, Jasper. *Journal of Jasper Danckaerts, 1679–1680.* Ed. by Bartlett Burleigh James and J. Franklin Jameson. New York, 1913.

De Ronde, Lambertus. *A System: Containing the Principles of the Christian Religion, Suitable to the Heidelberg Catechism; by Plain Questions and Answers.* New York, 1763.

———. *The True Spiritual Religion; or, Delightful Service of the Lord . . .* New York, 1767.

"Documents Relating to the Administration of Leisler." New-York Historical Society, *Collections*, Publication Fund Series, I. New York, 1868.

Early Records of the City and County of Albany and Colony of Rensselaerswyck, 4 vols. Albany, 1869–1919. Vol. 3 Ed. by A. J. F. van Laer. Trans. by Jonathan Pearson. New York State Library, *History Bulletin* 10. Albany, 1918.

Edwards, Jonathan. *The Great Awakening*. Ed. by C. C. Goen. *The Works of Jonathan Edwards*, 4. New Haven, Conn., 1972.

Fernow, Berthold, ed. *The Records of New Amsterdam from 1653–1674 Anno Dominie*, 7 vols. New York, 1897.

Frelinghuysen, Theodorus Jacobus. *Sermons by Theodorus Jacobus Frelinghuysen*. Trans. by William Demarest. New York, 1856.

Frielinghuysen [sic], Theodorus. *Wars and Rumors of Wars, Heavens Decree over the World: A Sermon Preached in the Camp of the New-England Forces*. New York, 1755.

"Garrett Abeel's Records." *Year Book of the Holland Society of New York*. New York, 1916.

Goetschius, Joh. Hend. *De Onbekende God* . . . New York, 1743.

Haims, Lynn. "Wills of Two Early New York Poets: Henricus Selyns and Richard Steer." *New York Genealogical and Biographical Record* 108 (1977): 1–10.

Hall, Michael G., Lawrence H. Leder, and Michael G. Kammen, eds. *The Glorious Revolution in America: Documents on the Colonial Crisis of 1689*. Chapel Hill, N.C., 1964.

Hamilton, Alexander. *Gentleman's Progress: The Itinerarium of Dr. Alexander Hamilton, 1744*. Ed. by Carl Bridenbaugh. Chapel Hill, N.C., 1948.

Hawks, Francis L., ed. "The Memorial of Col. Morris concerning the State of Religion in the Jerseys." *New Jersey Historical Society Proceedings* 4 (1849–50): 110–21.

Helfferich, William U. "The Journal of Rev. Johann Heinrich Helfferich." *Pennsylvania Folklife* 28 (1979): 17–24.

Hoes, Roswell Randall, comp. *Baptismal and Marriage Registers of the Old Dutch Church of Kingston, Ulster County, New York*. New York, 1891.

Honeyman, A. Van Doren. "An Early DeReimer Dutch Bible." *New Jersey Historical Society Proceedings* (n.s.) 12 (1927): 451–55.

Hooker, Richard. *Of the Laws of Ecclesiastical Polity: An Abridged Edition*. Ed. by. A. S. McGrade and Brian Vickers. New York, 1975.

Jameson, J. Franklin, ed. *Narratives of New Netherland: 1609–1664*. New York, 1909.

Kalm, Peter. *The America of 1750: Peter Kalm's Travels in North America*, rev. ed., 2 vols. Ed. by Adolph B. Benson. New York, 1937.

Keith, George. " 'An Account of the State of the Church in North America, by Mr. George Keith and Others.' " *Historical Magazine of the Protestant Episcopal Church* 20 (1951): 363–71.

Leder, Lawrence H. " '. . . Like Madmen through the Streets': The New York City Riot of June 1690." *New-York Historical Society Quarterly* 39 (1955): 405–15.

———. "Records of the Trials of Jacob Leisler and His Associates." *New-York Historical Society Quarterly* 36 (1952): 431–57.

Letters and Papers of Cadwallader Colden, 7 vols. New-York Historical Society, *Collections,* Publication Fund Series, L–LVI. New York, 1918–23.

"Letters respecting New Jersey in 1681." *New Jersey Historical Society Proceedings* (n.s.) 15 (1930): 517–34.

Livingston, William. *The Independent Reflector; or, Weekly Essays on Sundry Important Subjects More Particulary Adapted to the Province of New-York.* Ed. by Milton M. Klein. Cambridge, Mass. 1963.

Loux, Joseph Anthony, Jr., trans. and ed. *Boel's "Complaint" against Frelinghuysen.* Rensselaer, N.Y., 1979.

Lutheran Church in New York and New Jersey, 1722–1760: Lutheran Records in the Ministerial Archives of the Staatsarchiv, Hamburg, Germany. Trans. by Simon Hart and Harry J. Kreider. New York, 1962.

The Lutheran Church in New York, 1649–1672: Records in the Lutheran Church Archives at Amsterdam, Holland. Trans. by Arnold J. F. van Laer. New York, 1946.

McQueen, David. "Kings County, N.Y., Wills." *New York Genealogical and Biographical Record* 47 (1916): 161–70, 227–32.

Mather, Cotton. *Magnalia Christi Americana, Books I and II.* Ed. by Kenneth B. Murdock with Elizabeth W. Miller. Cambridge, Mass., 1977.

Miller, John. *New York Considered and Improved, 1695.* Ed. by Victor Hugo Paltsits. Cleveland, 1903.

Minutes of the Executive Council of the Province of New York: Administration of Francis Lovelace, 1668–1673, 2 vols. Albany, 1910.

"Miscellaneous Documents." New-York Historical Society, *Collections,* Publication Fund Series, XLVI. New York, 1914.

Montresor, John. *Journals of Capt. John Montresor, 1757–1778.* New-York Historical Society, *Collections,* Publication Fund Series, XIV. New York, 1881.

Mühlenberg, Henry Melchior. *The Journals of Henry Melchior Mühlenberg,* 3 vols. Trans. by Theodore G. Tappert and John W. Doberstein. Philadelphia, 1942–53.

Munsell, Joel, ed. *The Annals of Albany,* 10 vols. Albany, 1849–59.

Murphy, Henry C. *Anthology of New Netherland; or, Translations from the Early Dutch Poets of New York with Memoirs of Their Lives.* New York, 1865.

Myers, Albert Cook, ed. *Narratives of Early Pennsylvania, West New Jersey, and Delaware, 1630–1707.* New York, 1912.

"New York in 1692." New-York Historical Society, *Collections*, 2d Series, II. New York, 1849.

New-York Weekly Journal, November 26, 1739.

O'Callaghan, E. B., ed. *Documentary History of the State of New-York*, 4 vols. Albany, 1850–51.

_____. *Documents Relative to the Colonial History of the State of New-York*, 15 vols. Albany, 1856–87.

_____. *Journal of the Legislative Council of the Colony of New York: Began the 9th Day of April, 1691, and Ended the 27 of September, 1743*. Albany, 1861.

Oppenheim, Samuel, ed. *Dutch Records of Kingston, Ulster County, New York (Esopus, Wildwyck, Swanenburgh, Kingston), 1658–1684, with Some Later Dates*. Cooperstown, N.Y., 1912.

Osgood, Herbert L., ed. *Minutes of the Common Council of the City of New York, 1675–1776*, 8 vols. New York, 1905.

Pearson, Jonathan, ed. *Early Records of the City and Colony of Rensselaerswyck*. Albany, 1869.

Perry, William Stevens, ed. *Historical Collections relating to the American Colonial Church*, 5 vols. Hartford, Conn., 1878; reprint ed. New York, 1969.

A Platform of Church Discipline Gathered out of the Word of God: and Agreed Upon by the Elders: and Messengers of the Churches Assembled in the Synod at Cambridge in New England. Cambridge, Mass., 1649.

The Psalms of David, with the Ten Commandements, Creed, Lord's Prayer, &c. in Metre. Also the Catechism, Confession of Faith, Liturgy, &c. Translated from the Dutch. New York, 1767.

"Records of the Harlingen Reformed Dutch Church, Montgomery Township, Somerset County." *Genealogical Magazine of New Jersey* 15 (1940): 25–30.

"Records of the Reformed Dutch Church in the City of New York—Church Members' List." *New York Genealogical and Biographical Record* 9 (1878): 38–35, 72–79, 140–47, 161–58; 59 (1928): 69–76, 158–65, 259–66, 372–79; 60 (1929): 71–78, 158–63.

"Rev. Dr. Laidlie." *Christian Intelligencer* 27 (February 26, 1857): 137.

Reynolds, Cuyler, comp. *Albany Chronicles: A History of the City Arranged Chronologically, from the Earliest Settlement to the Present Time*. Albany, 1907.

Romig, Edgar Franklin. " 'The English and Low-Dutch School-master.' " *New-York Historical Society Quarterly* 43 (1959): 149–59.

Scott, Kenneth. "Contributors to Building of a Dutch Church in New York City, 1688." *De Halve Maen* 55 (Spring 1980): 10–12.

_____. "Jacob Leisler's Fifty Militiamen," *New York Genealogical and Biographical Record* 94 (1963): 65–72.

Selyns, Henricus. *Records of Dominie Henricus Selyns of New York, 1686–7*. Holland Societey of New York, *Collections*, 5. New York, 1916.

Sheridan, Eugene R. "Daniel Coxe and the Restoration of Proprietary Government in East Jersey, 1690—A Letter." *New Jersey History* 92 (1974): 103–9.

Stillwell, John E., ed. *Historical and Genealogical Miscellany: Early Settlers of New Jersey and Their Descendants,* 5 vols. New York, 1903–32.

Strickland, William. *Journal of a Tour in the United States of America, 1794–1795.* Ed. by J. E. Strickland. New-York Historical Society, *Collections, Publication Fund Series,* LXXXIII. New York, 1971.

"Tax Lists of the City of New York, December 1, 1695–July 15, 1699," 2 vols. New-York Historical Society, *Collections, Publication Fund Series,* XLIII–XLIV. New York, 1910–11.

Taylor, Benjamin C. *Annals of the Classis of Bergen of the Reformed Dutch Church, and the Churches under Its Care.* New York, 1857.

Tennent, Gilbert. *The Danger of an Unconverted Ministry.* Philadelphia, 1740.

Valentine, D. T. *Manual of the Corporation of the City of New York.* New York, 1858.

Van der Linde, A. P. G., ed. *Old First Dutch Reformed Church of Brooklyn, New York: First Book of Records, 1660–1752.* Baltimore, 1983.

Van Laer. A. J. F., ed. *Correspondence of Jeremias Van Rensselaer, 1651–1674.* Albany, 1932.

——. *Correspondence of Maria Van Rensselaer, 1669–1689.* Albany, 1935.

——. *Minutes of the Court of Albany, Rensselaerswyck and Schenectady, 1668–1685,* 3 vols. Albany, 1926–32.

Whitefield, George. *George Whitefield's Journals (1737–1741).* London, 1905; reprint ed. Gainsville, Fla., 1969.

Whitehead, William A., ed. *Archieves of the State of New Jersey: Documents relating to the Colonial History of the State of New Jersey,* 1st Series, 42 vols. Newark, 1880–1949.

"The Winthrop Papers." Massachusetts Historical Society, *Collections* (6th ser.) 3. Boston, 1889.

Wolley, Charles. *A Two Years' Journal in New York and Part of Its Territories in America.* Ed. by Edward Gaylord Bourne. Cleveland, 1902.

Books

Archdeacon, Thomas J. *New York City, 1664–1710: Conquest and Change.* Ithaca, N.Y., 1976.

Biemer, Linda Briggs. *Women and Property in Colonial New York: The Transition from Dutch to English Law, 1643–1727.* Ann Arbor, Mich., 1983.

Birch, John J. *The Pioneering Church of the Mohawk Valley.* Schenectady, N.Y., 1955.

Bonomi, Patricia U. *A Factious People: Politics and Society in Colonial New York.* New York, 1971.

_____. *Under the Cope of Heaven: Religion, Society, and Politics in Colonial America.* New York, 1986.

Bridenbaugh, Carl. *Cities in the Wilderness: The First Century of Urban Life in America, 1625–1742.* New York, 1938.

Brodhead, John Romeyn. *History of the State of New York,* 2 vols. New York, 1853–71.

Butler, Jon. *The Huguenots in America: A Refugee People in New World Society.* Cambridge, Mass., 1983.

Cassedy, James H. *Demography and Early America: Beginnings of the Statistical Mind, 1600–1800.* Cambridge, Mass., 1969.

Coalter, Milton J, Jr. *Gilbert Tennent, Son of Thunder: A Case Study of Continental Pietism's Impact on the First Great Awakening in the Middle Colonies.* Westport, Conn., 1986.

Corwin, Edward T. *A Manual of the Reformed Church in America, 1628–1902,* 4th ed. New York, 1902.

Craven, Wesley Frank. *The English Colonization of North America.* Princeton, N.J., 1964.

Dallimore, Arnold A. *George Whitefield: The Life and Times of the Great Evangelist of the Eighteenth-Century Revival,* 2 vols. Westchester, Ill., 1979.

Davidson, Elizabeth. *The Establishment of the English Church in Continental American Colonies.* Durham, N.C., 1936.

De Jong, Gerald F. *The Dutch in America, 1609–1974.* Boston, 1975.

_____. *The Dutch Reformed Church in the American Colonies.* Grand Rapids, Mich., 1978.

Dix, Morgan, and Charles Thorley Bridgeman. *A History of the Parish of Trinity Church in the City of New York,* 6 vols. New York, 1901–62.

Douglas, Mary. *Natural Symbols: Explorations in Cosmology.* New York, 1970.

Duffy, John. *A History of Public Health in New York City 1625–1866.* New York, 1968.

Dwight, Sereno E. *The Life of President Edwards.* New York, 1830.

Edelman, Hendrik. *Dutch-American Bibliography, 1693–1794.* Nieuwkoop, Netherlands, 1974.

Eekhof, A. *Jonas Michaelius: Founder of the Church in New Netherland.* Leiden, 1926.

Fox, Dixon Ryan. *Yankees and Yorkers.* New York, 1940.

Frelinghuysen, Peter H. B., Jr. *Theodorus Jacobus Frelinghuysen.* Princeton, N.J., 1938.

Goebel, Julius, Jr., and T. Raymond Naughton. *Law Enforcement in Colonial New York: A Study in Criminal Procedure, 1664–1776.* New York, 1944.

Good, James I. *History of the Reformed Church in the United States, 1725–1792.* Reading, Pa., 1899.

Greenberg, Douglas. *Crime and Law Enforcement in the Colony of New York, 1691–1776.* Ithaca, N.Y., 1976.

Greene, Evarts B., and Virginia D. Harrington. *American Population before the Federal Census of 1790.* New York, 1932.

Hageman, Howard G. *Two Centuries Plus: The Story of New Brunswick Seminary.* Grand Rapids, Mich., 1984.

Henry, Stuart C. *George Whitefield: Wayfaring Witness.* New York, 1957.

Hinke, William J. *Ministers of the German Reformed Congregations in Pennsylvania and Other Colonies in the Eighteenth Century.* Ed. by George W. Richards. Lancaster, Pa., 1951.

Holifield, E. Brooks. *The Covenant Sealed: The Development of Puritan Sacramental Theology in Old and New England, 1570–1720.* New Haven, Conn., 1974.

Humphrey, David C. *From King's College to Columbia, 1746–1800.* New York, 1976.

Jamison, Wallace N. *Religion in New Jersey: A Brief History.* Princeton, N.J., 1964.

Johnson, Herbert Alan. *Essays on New York Colonial Legal History.* Westport, Conn., 1981.

Judd, Jacob, and Irwin H. Polishook, eds. *Aspects of Early New York Society and Politics.* Tarrytown, N.Y., 1974.

Kammen, Michael. *Colonial New York—A History.* New York, 1975.

Kemp, William Webb. *The Support of Schools in Colonial New York by the Society for the Propagation of the Gospel in Foreign Parts.* New York, 1969.

Kenney, Alice P. *The Gansevoorts of Albany: Dutch Patricians in the Upper Hudson Valley.* Syracuse, N.Y., 1969.

———. *Stubborn for Liberty: The Dutch in New York.* Syracuse, N.Y., 1975.

Kessler, Henry H., and Eugene Rachlis. *Peter Stuyvesant and His New York.* New York, 1959.

Kilpatrick, William Heard. *The Dutch Schools of New Netherland and Colonial New York.* U.S.Bureau of Education Bulletin No. 12. Washington, D.C., 1912.

Knittle, Walter Allen. *The Early Eighteenth Century Palatine Emigration: A British Government Redemptioner Project to Manufacture Naval Stores.* Philadelphia, 1936.

Kross, Jessica. *The Evolution of an American Town: Newtown, New York, 1642–1775.* Philadelphia, 1983.

Leder, Lawrence H. *Robert Livingston, 1654–1728, and the Politics of Colonial New York.* Chapel Hill, N.C., 1961.

Leiby, Adrian C. *The Early Dutch and Swedish Settlers of New Jersey.* Princeton, N.J., 1964.

_____. *The Revolutionary War in the Hackensack Valley: The Jersey Dutch on Neutral Ground.* New Brunswick, N.J., 1962.

_____. *The United Churches of Hackensack and Schraalenburgh, New Jersey, 1686–1822.* River Edge, N.J., 1976.

Levitt, James H. *For Want of Trade: Shipping and the New Jersey Ports, 1680–1783.* New Jersey Historical Society, *Collections* 17. Newark, 1981.

Lovejoy, David S. *The Glorious Revolution in America.* New York, 1972.

McCusker, John J. *Money and Exchange in Europe and America, 1600–1775.* Chapel Hill, N.C., 1978.

Maxson, Charles Hartshorn. *The Great Awakening in the Middle Colonies.* Chicago, 1920.

Memorial of St. Mark's Church in the Bowery. New York, 1899.

Messler, Abraham. *Forty Years at Raritan: Eight Memorial Sermons, with Notes for a History of the Reformed Churches in Somerset County, N.J.* New York, 1873.

Mol, J. J. *The Breaking of Traditions: Theological Convictions in Colonial America.* Berkeley, Calif., 1968.

Morgan, Edmund S. *Visible Saints: The History of a Puritan Idea.* New York, 1963.

Niebuhr, H. Richard. *The Social Sources of Denominationalism.* Hamden, Conn., 1929.

Nobbs, Douglas. *Theocracy and Toleration: A Study of the Disputes in Dutch Calvinism from 1600 to 1650.* Cambridge, Eng., 1938.

O'Callaghan, E. B. *History of New Netherland; or, New York under the Dutch,* 2 vols. New York, 1846–48.

Price, J. L. *Culture and Society in the Dutch Republic during the 17th Century.* London, 1974.

Reich, Jerome R. *Leisler's Rebellion: A Study of Democracy in New York, 1664–1720.* Chicago, 1953.

Rink, Oliver A. *Holland on the Hudson: An Economic and Social History of Dutch New York.* Ithaca, N.Y., 1986.

Ritchie, Robert C. *The Duke's Province: A Study of New York Politics and Society, 1664–1691.* Chapel Hill, N.C., 1971.

Schama, Simon. *The Embarrassment of Riches: An Interpretation of Dutch Culture in the Golden Age.* Berkeley and Los Angeles, 1988.

Sheridan, Eugene R. *Lewis Morris, 1671–1746: A Study in Early American Politics.* Syracuse, N.Y., 1981.

Shipton, Clifford K. *New England Life in the 18th Century: Representative Biographies from "Sibley's Harvard Graduates."* Cambridge, Mass., 1963.

Smith, William, Jr. *The History of the Province of New-York,* 2 vols. Ed. by Michael Kammen. Cambridge, Mass., 1972.

Stiles, Henry R. *A History of the City of Brooklyn,* 3 vols. Brooklyn, N.Y., 1867–70.

Still, Bayard. *Mirror for Gotham: New York as Seen by Contemporaries from the Dutch Days to the Present.* New York, 1956.

Stoeffler, F. Ernest. *The Rise of Evangelical Pietism.* Leiden, 1965.

Strong, Thomas M. *The History of the Town of Flatbush, in Kings County, Long Island.* New York, 1842.

Stout, Harry S. *The New England Soul: Preaching and Religious Culture in Colonial New England.* New York, 1986.

Sweet, William Warren. *Religion in Colonial America.* New York, 1942.

Tanis, James. *Dutch Calvinistic Pietism in the Middle Colonies: A Study in the Life and Theology of Theodorus Jacobus Frelinghuysen.* The Hague, 1967.

Taylor, Benjamin C. *Annals of the Classis of Bergen, of the Reformed Dutch Church, and the Churches under Its Care: Including, the Civil History of the Ancient Township of Bergen in New Jersey,* 3d ed. New York, 1857.

Turner, Victor W. *The Ritual Process: Structure and Anti-Structure.* Chicago, 1969.

Valentine, David T. *History of the City of New York.* New York, 1853.

Van Rensselaer, Mrs. Schuyler [Mariana Griswold]. *History of the City of New York in the Seventeenth Century,* 2 vols. New York, 1909.

Wabeke, Bertus Henry. *Dutch Emigration to North America, 1624–1860: A Short History.* Booklets of the Netherlands Information Bureau No. 10. New York, 1944.

Wacker, Peter O. *Land and People: A Cultural Geography of Preindustrial New Jersey: Origins and Settlement Patterns.* New Brunswick, N.J., 1975.

Weber, Max. *Max Weber: The Interpretation of Social Reality.* Ed. by J. E. T. Eldridge. New York, 1975.

Wertenbacker, Thomas Jefferson. *The Founding of American Civilization: The Middle Colonies.* New York, 1938.

Westerkamp, Marilyn J. *Triumph of the Laity: Scots-Irish Piety and the Great Awakening, 1625–1760.* New York, 1988.

White, Philip L. *The Beekmans of New York in Politics and Commerce, 1647–1877.* New York, 1856.

Wilson, Bryan R., ed. *Patterns of Sectarianism: Organisation and Ideology in Social and Religious Movements.* London, 1967.

Wilson, Charles. *Profit and Power: A Study of England and the Dutch Wars.* London, 1957.

Woolverton, John Frederick. *Colonial Anglicanism in North America.* Detroit, 1984.

ARTICLES

Albion, Robert Greenhalgh. "New Jersey and the Port of New York." *New Jersey Historical Society Proceedings* 58 (1940): 84–92.

Allbee, Burton H. "Ancient Dutch Architecture." *Bergen County Historical Society Papers and Proceedings* 5–6 (1908–10): 19–22.

Amerman, Richard H. "Dutch Life in Pre-Revolutionary Bergen County." *New Jersey Historical Society Proceedings* 76 (1958): 161–81.

Archdeacon, Thomas. " 'Distinguished for Nation Sake': The Age of Leisler in New York City." In *Colonial America: Essays in Politics and Social Development,* 2d ed. Ed. by Stanley N. Katz. Boston, 1976.

Bachman, Van Cleaf, Alice P. Kenney, and Lawrence G. Van Loon. " 'Het Poelmeisie': An Introduction to the Hudson Valley Dutch Dialect." *New York History* 61 (1980): 161–85.

Balmer, Randall H. "The Social Roots of Dutch Pietism in the Middle Colonies." *Church History* 53 (1984): 187–99.

Beardslee, John W. III. "The Dutch Reformed Church and the American Revolution." *Journal of Presbyterian History* 54 (1976): 165–81.

Bergen, James J. "The 'Rebellion' at Raritan in 1723." *Somerset County Historical Quarterly* 3 (1914): 173–84, 241–49.

Bjarnson, Donald Einar. "Swedish-Finnish Settlement in New Jersey in the Seventeenth Century." *Swedish Pioneer Historical Quarterly* 27 (1976): 238–46.

Blackburn, Roderic H. "Dutch Material Culture: Architecture." *De Halve Maen* 57 (Fall 1982): 1–5.

––––––. "Dutch Material Culture: Silversmiths." *De Halve Maen* 55 (Fall 1980): 5–11.

Bonomi, Patricia U., and Peter R. Eisenstadt. "Church Adherence in the Eighteenth-Century British American Colonies." *William and Mary Quarterly* (3d ser.) 39 (1982): 245–86.

Breen, Quirinus. "Dominie Everardus Bogardus." *Church History* 2 (1933): 78–90.

Brenner, Robert. "The Social Basis of English Commercial Expansion, 1550–1650." *Journal of Economic History* 32 (1972): 361–84.

Broshar, Helen. "The First Push Westward of the Albany Traders." *Mississippi Valley Historical Review* 7 (1920–21): 228–41.

Bultmann, William A. "The S.P.G. and the French Huguenots in Colonial America." *Historical Magazine of the Protestant Episcopal Church* 20 (1951): 156–72.

Burnham, Koert. "Godfrey Dellius: An Historical Obituary by a Protagonist." *De Halve Maen* 54 (Summer 1979): 4–6, 14–15.

Burr, Nelson R. "The Episcopal Church and the Dutch in Colonial New York and New Jersey—1664–1784." *Historical Magazine of the Protestant Episcopal Church* 19 (1950): 90–111.

––––––. "New Jersey: An Anglican Venture in Religious Freedom." *Historical Magazine of the Protestant Episcopal Church* 34 (1965): 3–34.

––––––. "The Religious History of New Jersey before 1702." *New Jersey Historical Society Proceedings* 56 (1938): 169–90, 243–66.

Chorley, E. Clowes. "The Beginnings of the Church in the Province of New York." *Historical Magazine of the Protestant Episcopal Church* 13 (1944): 15–19.

Cody, Edward J. "The Growth of Toleration and Church-State Relations in New Jersey, 1689–1763: From Holy Men to Holy War." In *Economic and Social History of Colonial New Jersey.* Ed. by William C. Wright. Trenton, N.J., 1974.

Cohen, David Steven. "How Dutch Were the Dutch of New Netherland?" *New York History* 62 (1981): 43–60.

Cohen, Ronald D. "The New England Colonies and the Dutch Recapture of New York, 1673–1674." *New-York Historical Society Quarterly* 56 (1972): 54–78.

Cohen, Sheldon S. "Elias Neau, Instructor to New York's Slaves." *New-York Historical Society Quarterly* 55 (1971): 7–27.

Corwin, Charles E. "The First Dutch Minister in America." *Journal of the Presbyterian Historical Society* 12 (1925): 144–51.

———. "The Introduction of the English Language into the Services of the Collegiate Dutch Church of New York City." *Journal of the Presbyterian Historical Society* 10 (1919–20): 175–88.

Corwin, Edward T. "The Character and Development of the Reformed Church in the Colonial Period." In *Centennial Discourses: A Series of Sermons Delivered in the Year 1876 by the Order of the General Synod of the Reformed (Dutch) Church in America,* 2d ed. New York, 1877. 41–66.

———. "The Ecclesiastical Condition of New York at the Opening of the Eighteenth Century." *American Society of Church History Papers* (2d ser.) 3 (1912): 79–115.

Countryman, Edward. "Consolidating Power in Revolutionary America: The Case of New York, 1775–1783." *Journal of Interdisciplinary History* 6 (1976): 645–77.

Cranmer, William Stockton. "The Famous Frelinghuysen Controvery." *Somerset County Historical Quarterly* 5 (1916): 81–89.

Davisson, William I., and Lawrence J. Bradley. "New York Maritime Trade: Ship Voyage Patterns, 1715–1765." *New-York Historical Society Quarterly* 55 (1971): 309–17.

De Jong, Gerald F. "Dominie Johannes Megapolensis: Minister to New Netherland." *New-York Historical Society Quarterly* 52 (1968): 39–45.

———. "The Education and Training of Dutch Ministers." In *Education in New Netherland and the Middle Colonies: Papers of the 7th Rensselaerswyck Seminar of the New Netherland Project.* Ed. by Charles T. Gehring and Nancy Anne McClure Zeller. Albany, 1985.

———. "The Formative Years of the Dutch Reformed Church on Long Island." *Journal of Long Island History* 8 (1968): 1–16; 9 (1969): 1–20.

———. "The Ziekentroosters or Comforters of the Sick in New Netherland." *New-York Historical Society Quarterly* 54 (1970): 339–59.

De Vries, George, Jr. "The Dutch in the American Revolution: Reflections and Observations." *Fides et Historia* 10 (1979): 43–57.

De Vries, Jan. "On the Modernity of the Dutch Republic." *Journal of Economic History* 33 (1973): 191–202.

Duffy, Eamon. "*Correspondence Fraternelle*; The SPCK, the SPG, and the Churches of Switzerland in the War of the Spanish Succession." In *Reform and Reformation: England and the Continent c1500–c1750*. Ed. by Derek Baker. Oxford, Eng., 1979.

Duncan, Robert Wm., Jr. "A Study of the Ministry of John Talbot in New Jersey, 1702–1727: On 'Great Ripeness,' Much Dedication, and Regrettable Failure." *Historical Magazine of the Protestant Episcopal Church* 42 (1973): 233–56.

Ehrlich, Jessica Kross. " 'To Hear and Try All Causes Betwixt Man and Man': The Town Court of Newtown, 1659–1690." *New York History* 59 (1978): 277–305.

Ely, Warren S. "Dutch Settlement in Bucks County." *Bucks County Historical Society Papers* 5 (1926): 1–13.

Frantz, John B. "The Awakening of Religion among the German Settlers in the Middle Colonies." *William and Mary Quarterly* (3d ser.) 33 (1976): 266–88.

Friis, Herman R. "A Series of Population Maps of the Colonies of the United States, 1625–1790." *Geographical Review* 30 (1940): 463–70.

Gabert, Glen. "The New York Tobacco Trade, 1716–1742." *Essex Institute Historical Collections* 105 (1969): 103–27.

Geissler, Suzanne B. "A Step on the Swedish Lutheran Road to Anglicanism." *Historical Magazine of the Protestant Episcopal Church* 54 (1985): 39–49.

Gerlach, Larry R. " 'Quaker' Politics in Eighteenth-Century New Jersey: A Documentary Account." *Journal of the Rutgers University Library* 34 (1970): 1–12.

Goodfriend, Joyce D. "The Social Dimensions of Congregational Life in Colonial New York City, 1664–1730." Paper given at the Organization of American Historians Annual Convention, New York, April 1986.

Goodwin, Gerald J. "The Anglican Reaction to the Great Awakening." *Historical Magazine of the Protestant Episcopal Church* 35 (1966): 343–71.

Hageman, Howard G. "The Dutch Battle for Higher Education in the Middle Colonies." In *Education in New Netherland and the Middle Colonies: Papers of the 7th Rensselaerswyck Seminar of the New Netherland Project*. Ed. by Charles T. Gehring and Nancy Anne McClure Zeller. Albany, 1985.

———. "Henricus Selyns." In *Cultural Mosaic of New Netherland*. Rensselaersville, N.Y., 1972.

———. "William Bertholf: Pioneer Dominie of New Jersey." *Reformed Review* 29 (1976): 73–80.

Hansen, Marcus L. "The Minor Stocks in the American Population of 1790." *American Historical Association Proceedings* (1932): 360–397.

Harmelink, Herman III. "Another Look at Frelinghuysen and His 'Awakening,' " *Church History* 37 (1968): 423–38.

Henshaw, R. Townsend. "The New York Ministry Act of 1693." *Historical Magazine of the Protestant Episcopal Church* 2 (1933): 199–204.

Hewitt, John H. "New York's Black Episcopalians: In the Beginning, 1704–1722." *Afro-Americans in New York Life and History* 3 (1979): 9–22.

Hinke, William J. Introduction to "Church Record of Neshaminy and Bensalam, Bucks County, 1710–1738." *Journal of the Presbyterian Historical Society* 1 (1901–2): 111–18.

──────. "Rev. Paulus Van Vlecq." *Bucks County Historical Society Papers* 4 (1917): 688–702.

Hoffman, William J. "The Ancestry of Rev. Gualtherus du Bois and Two Generations of His Descendants." *New York Genealogical and Biographical Record* 82 (1951): 134–39.

Howard, Ronald W. "Apprenticeship and Economic Education in New Netherland and Seventeenth-century New York." In *Education in New Netherland and the Middle Colonies: Papers of the 7th Rensselaerswyck Seminar of the New Netherland Project.* Ed. by Charles T. Gehring and Nancy Anne McClure Zeller. Albany, 1985. 17–33.

Jacobsen, Douglas. "Johann Bernhard van Dieren: Peasant Preacher at Hackensack, New Jersey, 1724–40." *New Jersey History* 100 (1982): 15–29.

James, Bartlett Burleigh. "The Labadist Colony in Maryland." *American Society of Church History Papers* 9 (1897): 149–60.

Johnson, Herbert Alan. "English Statutes in Colonial New York." *New York History* 58 (1977): 277–96.

──────. "The Prerogative Court of New York, 1686–1776." *American Journal of Legal History* 17 (1973): 95–144.

Judd, Jacob. "Frederick Philipse and the Madagascar Trade." *New-York Historical Society Quarterly* 55 (1971): 354–74.

Kenney, Alice P. "The Albany Dutch: Loyalists and Patriots." *New York History* 42 (1961): 331–50.

──────. "Religious Artifacts of the Dutch Colonial Period." *De Halve Maen* 53 (Winter 1977–78): 1–2, 16, 19, 14.

Kierner, Cynthia A. "A Concept Rejected: New York's Anglican 'Establishment,' 1693–1715." *Essays in History* 26 (1982): 71–100.

Kingdon, Robert M. "Why Did the Huguenot Refugees in the American Colonies Become Episcopalian?" *Historical Magazine of the Protestant Episcopal Church* 49 (1980): 317–35.

Klein, Milton M. "Church, State, and Education: Testing the Issue in Colonial New York." *New York History* 45 (1964): 291–303.

_____. "The Cultural Tyros of Colonial New York." *South Atlantic Quarterly* 66 (1967): 218–32.

_____. "New York in the American Colonies: A New Look." *New York History* 53 (1972): 132–56.

Klingberg, Frank J. "The S.P.G. Program for Negroes in Colonial New York." *Historical Magazine of the Protestant Episcopal Church* 8 (1939): 306–71.

Krassner, Nancy. "The Dutch-English Language Controversy." *De Halve Maen* 59 (November 1985): 1–3, 20; 59 (March 1986): 9–11, 21.

Kupp, Jan. "Aspects of New York–Dutch Trade under the English, 1670–1674." *New-York Historical Society Quarterly* 58 (1974): 139–47.

Landsman, Ned C. "Revivalism and Nativism in the Middle Colonies: The Great Awakening and the Scots Community in East New Jersey." *American Quarterly* 34 (1982): 149–64.

"Law in Colonial New York: The Legal System of 1691." *Harvard Law Review* 80 (1967): 1757–72.

Leder, Lawrence H. "Captain Kidd and the Leisler Rebellion." *New-York Historical Society Quarterly* 38 (1954): 48–53.

_____. "The Politics of Upheaval in New York, 1689–1709." *New-York Historical Society Quarterly* 44 (1960): 413–27.

_____. "Robert Hunter's *Androboros*." *Bulletin of the New York Public Library* 68 (1964): 153–50.

_____. "The Unorthodox Dominie: Nicholas Van Rensselaer." *New York History* 35 (1954): 166–76.

Levermore, Charles H. "The Whigs of Colonial New York." *American Historical Review* 1 (1895–96): 238–50.

Lewis, Charles Smith. "George Keith, the Missionary." *New Jersey Historical Society Proceedings* (n.s.) 13 (1928): 38–45.

Lodge, Martin E. "The Crisis of the Churches in the Middle Colonies." *Pennsylvania Magazine of History and Biography* 95 (1971): 195–220.

Lovejoy, David S. "Equality and Empire: The New York Charter of Libertyes, 1683." *William and Mary Quarterly* (3d ser.) 21 (1964): 493–515.

Lydekker, John Wolfe. "The Rev. Gerrit (Gerard) Lydekker, 1729–1794." *Historical Magazine of the Protestant Episcopal Church* 13 (1944): 303–14.

Maar, Charles. "Causes of the Dutch Migrations Into and Out of New Jersey." *Somerset County Historical Quarterly* 7 (1918): 168–71.

McCormick, Charles H. "Governor Sloughter's Delay and Leisler's Rebellion, 1689–1691." *New-York Historical Society Quarterly* 62 (1978): 238–52.

McCreary, John R. "Governors, Politicians, and Sources of Instability in the Colonies: New Jersey as a Test Case." *Journal of the Alabama Academy of Science* 42 (1971): 215–27.

McCulloch, Samuel Clyde. "The Foundation and Early Work of the Society for the Propagation of the Gospel in Foreign Parts." *Huntington Library Quarterly* (1944–45), 241–58.

McKinley, Albert E. "The English and Dutch Towns of New Netherland." *American Historical Review* 6 (1900–1): 1–18.

―――. "The Transition from Dutch to English Rule in New York." *American Historical Review* 6 (1900–1): 693–724.

McMahon, Reginald. "The Achter Col Colony on the Hackensack." *New Jersey History* 89 (1971): 221–40.

Mason, Bernard. "Aspects of the New York Revolt of 1689." *New York History* 30 (1949): 165–80.

Melick, Harry C. W. "The Fordham 'Ryott' of July 16, 1688." *New-York Historical Society Quarterly* 36 (1952): 210–20.

Merwick, Donna. "Becoming English: Anglo-Dutch Conflict in the 1670s in Albany, New York." *New York History* 62 (1981): 389–414.

Midwinter, Edward. "The Society for the Propagation of the Gospel and the Church in the American Colonies." *Historical Magazine of the Protestant Episcopal Church* 4 (1935): 67–115.

Moore, Charles B. "English and Dutch Intermarriages." *New York Genealogical and Biographical Record* 3 (1872): 153–65; 4 (1873): 13–20, 127–39.

Murrin, John M. "English Rights as Ethnic Aggression: The English Conquest, the Charter of Liberties of 1683, and Leisler's Rebellion in New York." In *Authority and Resistance in Early New York.* Ed. by William Pencak and Conrad Edick Wright. New York, 1988. 56–94.

Narrett, David E. "Preparation for Death and Provision for the Living: Notes on New York Wills (1665–1760)." *New York History* 57 (1976): 417–37.

Naughton, T. Raymond. "Criminal Law in Colonial New York." *New York History* 14 (1933): 235–40.

Nettles, Curtis P. "The Economic Relations of Boston, Philadelphia, and New York, 1680–1715." *Journal of Economic and Business History* 3 (1931): 185–215.

―――. "England's Trade with New England and New York, 1685–1720." *Colonial Society of Massachusetts Publications* 28 (1935): 322–50.

O'Connor, Thomas F. "A Jesuit School in Seventeenth Century New York." *Mid-America* (n.s.) 3 (1932): 265–68.

―――. "Religious Toleration in New York, 1664–1700." *New York History* 17 (1936): 391–410.

Olson, Alison Gilbert. "Governor Robert Hunter and the Anglican Church in New York." In *Statesmen, Scholars and Merchants: Essays in Eighteenth-Century History Presented to Dame Lucy Sutherland.* Ed. by Anne Whiteman, J. S. Bromley, and P. G. M. Dickson. Oxford, Eng., 1973. 44–64.

Osterhaven, M. Eugene. "The Experiential Theology of Early Dutch Calvinism." *Reformed Review* 27 (1974): 180–89.

Overton, Jacqueline. "The Quakers on Long Island." *New York History* 21 (1940): 151–61.

Painter, Borden W. "The Vestry in the Middle Colonies." *Historical Magazine of the Protestant Episcopal Church* 47 (1978): 5–36.

Penny, Sherry, and Roberta Willenkin. "Dutch Women in Colonial Albany: Liberation and Retreat." *De Halve Maen* 52 (Spring 1977): 9–10, 14–15; (Summer 1977): 7–8, 15.

Pierce, Arthur D. "A Governor in Skirts." *New Jersey Historical Society Proceedings* 83 (1965): 1–9.

Pointer, Richard W. "Religious Life in New York during the Revolutionary War." *New York History* 66 (1985): 357–73.

Prime, Samuel Irenaeus. "Early Ministers of Long Island." *Journal of the Presbyterian Historical Society* 23 (1945): 180–94.

Prince, J. Dyneley. "The Jersey Dutch Dialect." *Dialect Notes* 3 (1910): 459–84.

Prince, John D. "Netherland Settlers in New Jersey." *New Jersey Historical Society Proceedings* (3d ser.) 9 (1914): 1–7.

Prozesky, Martin H. "The Emergence of Dutch Pietism." *Journal of Ecclesiastical History* 28 (1977): 29–37.

Pryde, George S. "The Scots in East New Jersey." *New Jersey Historical Society Proceedings* (n.s.) 15 (1930): 1–39.

_____. "Scottish Colonization in the Colony of New York." *New York History* 16 (1925): 138–57.

Purvis, Thomas L. "The European Origins of New Jersey's Eighteenth-Century Population." *New Jersey History* 100 (1982): 15–31.

Rainbolt, John C. "A 'Great and Usefull Designe': Bellomont's Proposal for New York, 1698–1701." *New-York Historical Society Quarterly* 53 (1969): 336–51.

Rink, Oliver A. "The People of New Netherland: Notes on Non-English Immigration to New York in the Seventeenth Century." *New York History* 62 (1981): 5–42.

Ritchie, Robert C. "The Duke of York's Commission of Revenue." *New-York Historical Society Quarterly* 58 (1974): 177–87.

_____. "London Merchants, the New York Market, and the Recall of Sir Edmund Andros." *New York History* 57 (1976): 5–29.

Rubincam, Milton. "The Formative Years of Lord Cornbury, the First Royal Governor of New York and New Jersey." *New York Genealogical and Biographical Register* 71 (1940): 106–16.

Runcie, John D. "The Problem of Anglo-American Politics in Bellomont's New York." *William and Mary Quarterly* (3d ser.) 26 (1969): 191–217.

Scanlon, James Edward. "British Intrigue and the Governorship of Robert Hunter." *New-York Historical Society Quarterly* 57 (1973): 199–211.

Schenck, Garret C. "Early Settlement and Settlers of Pompton, Pequannoc and Pompton Plains." *New Jersey Historical Society Proceedings* (n.s.) 4 (1919): 44–87.

Schmidt, Hubert G. "Germans in Colonial New Jersey." *American-German Review* 24 (June–July 1958): 4–9.

Schmidt, Leigh Eric. " 'A Second and Glorious Reformation': The New Light Extremism of Andrew Croswell." *William and Mary Quarterly* (3d ser.) 43 (1986): 214–44.

Schrag, F. J. "Theodorus Jacobus Frelinghuysen: The Father of American Pietism." *Church History* 14 (1945): 201–16.

Scott, W. W. "Dutch Buildings, Customs, Habits, etc." *Americana* 16 (1922): 368–79.

Seybolt, Robert Francis. "The S.P.G. Myth: A Note on Education in Colonial New York." *Journal of Educational Research* 13 (January–May 1926): 129–37.

Spencer, Charles Worthen. "The Cornbury Legend." *New York State Historical Association Proceedings* 13 (1914): 309–20.

Stern, Steve J. "Knickerbockers Who Asserted and Insisted: The Dutch Interest in New York Politics, 1664–1691." *New-York Historical Society Quarterly* 58 (1974): 113–38.

Stout, Harry S. "Religion, Communications, and the Ideological Origins of the American Revolution." *William and Mary Quarterly* (3d ser.) 34 (1977): 519–41.

Stout, Harry S. and Peter Onuf. "James Davenport and the Great Awakening in New London." *Journal of American History* 70 (1983–84): 556–78.

Tanis, James. "The Dutch Reformed Church and the American Revolution." *De Halve Maen* 52 (Summer 1977): 1–2, 15; 52 (Fall 1977), 1–2, 12–13, 19.

———. "Reformed Pietism in Colonial America." In *Continental Pietism and Early American Christianity.* Ed. by F. Ernest Stoeffler. Grand Rapids, Mich., 1976. 34–73.

Tucker, William L. "New Jersey—Her People." *New Jersey Historical Society Proceedings* 57 (1939): 172–77.

Turner, Gordon. "Church-State Relationships in Early New Jersey." *New Jersey Historical Society Proceedings* 69 (1951): 212–23.

Vermeule, Cornelius C. "Influence of the Netherlandish People in New Jersey." *Genealogical Magazine of New Jersey* 4 (1928): 49–56.

Wacker, Peter O. "The Dutch Culture Area in the Northeast, 1609–1800." *New Jersey History* 104 (1986): 1–21.

———. "Dutch Material Culture in New Jersey." *Journal of Popular Culture* 11 (1977–78): 948–58.

Wagman, Morton. "The Rise of Pieter Claessen Wyckoff: Social Mobility on the Colonial Frontier." *New York History* 53 (1972): 5–24.

Wall, Alexander J. "The Controversy in the Dutch Church in New York concerning Preaching in English, 1754–1768." *New-York Historical Society Quarterly* 12 (1938): 39–58.

Waller, G. M. "New York's Role in Queen Anne's War, 1702–1713." *New York History* 33 (1952): 40–53.

Warch, Richard. "The Shepherd's Tent: Education and Enthusiasm in the Great Awakening." *American Quarterly* 30 (1978): 177–98.

Weaver, Glenn. "John Frederick Haeger: S.P.G. Missionary to the Palatines." *Historical Magazine of the Protestant Episcopal Church* 27 (1958): 112–25.

Weis, Frederick Lewis. "The Colonial Clergy of the Middle Colonies: New York, New Jersey, and Pennsylvania, 1628–1776." *Proceedings of the American Antiquarian Society* 66 (1956): 167–351.

Wilkenfeld, Bruce M. "The New York City Common Council, 1689–1900." *New York History* 52 (1971): 249–73.

[Wyer, James I., Jr.]. "Report of the Director, 1909." *New York State Library Annual Report* 92 (1909): 3–71.

Dissertations (Ph.D.)

Gehring, Charles Theodor. "The Dutch Language in Colonial New York: An Investigation of a Language in Decline and Its Relationship to Social Change." Indiana University, 1973.

Goodfriend, Joyce Diane. " 'Too Great a Mixture of Nations': The Development of New York City Society in the Seventeenth Century." University of California at Los Angeles, 1975.

Hinshalwood, Sophia Gruys. "The Dutch Culture Area of the Mid-Hudson Valley." Rutgers University, 1981.

Howard, Ronald William. "Education and Ethnicity in Colonial New York, 1664–1763: A Study in the Transmission of Culture in Early America." University of Tennessee, 1978.

Jordan, Jean Paul. "The Anglican Establishment in Colonial New York, 1693–1783." Columbia University, 1971.

Lodge, Martin Ellsworth. "The Great Awakening in the Middle Colonies." University of California at Berkeley, 1964.

Luidens, John Pershing. "The Americanization of the Dutch Reformed Church." University of Oklahoma, 1969.

McAnear, Beverly. "Politics in Provincial New York, 1689–1761." Stanford University, 1935.

McCormick, Charles H. "Leisler's Rebellion." American University, 1971.

McLaughlin, William John. "Dutch Rural New York: Community, Economy, and Family in Colonial Flatbush." Columbia University, 1981.

Murrin, John M. "Anglicizing an American Colony: The Transformation of Provincial Massachusetts." Yale University, 1966.

Narrett, David E. "Patterns of Inheritance in Colonial New York City, 1664–1775." Cornell University, 1981.

INDEX

Academy, Dutch, 129–31, 146. *See also*
King's College; Queen's College
Acquackanonck. *See* Passaic
Aertsen, Reynier, 78
Act of Toleration, 89
Albany, 4, 8, 9, 11, 15, 16–17, 19, 21,
33, 40, 48, 49, 70, 80, 88, 89, 96, 97,
102, 111, 128, 133, 139
court at, 12, 18, 19
Dutch church in, 17–19, 43, 73–74, 89,
99, 102
Albany County (New York), 57, 58, 61,
80, 87
Albion, Robert Greenhalgh, 62 *n*
Allbee, Burton H., 61 *n*
American Revolution, ix, 87, 149–52,
153, 155, 156
American Weekly Mercury, 123
Amerman, Jan, 78
Amerman, Richard H., 61 *n*
Ames, William, 108
Amsterdam, vii, viii, 3, 10, 22, 25, 38,
50, 61, 66, 68, 74, 75, 85, 89, 93, 94,
103, 105, 109, 113, 115, 120, 122–
23, 125–26, 128, 134, 137, 138, 141,
143, 145, 146, 148, 149, 152
Classis of, vii, 4, 11, 12, 16–18, 22–25,
28, 38, 40, 47, 54, 59, 66, 68, 69, 71,
73–75, 78, 81, 85, 89, 90, 92, 93, 95,
96–97, 103, 105, 106, 108, 113, 115,
116, 119, 124, 125, 126, 127–28,
130, 131–32, 137, 144, 145–46, 147–
48, 149, 151, 152
Amwell (New Jersey), 124
Anabaptism, 51, 102, 135, 145
Andrews, William, 102
Andros, Edmund (governor), 9, 15, 16–
17, 18–19, 22, 26, 30, 82, 89
Anglicanism, viii, ix, 52, 53, 55, 69, 82,

87, 90–91, 102, 131, 136, 156. *See
also* Church of England
Anglicanization, 85–88, 91, 100
Anglicans, viii, 17, 18, 20, 30, 53, 54, 55,
60, 69, 79, 80–81, 83, 87, 90, 100,
118–19, 131, 136, 139, 144, 148, 154
Anglicization, viii, 9, 29, 30, 37, 38, 47,
48, 49, 68, 72–73, 81, 83, 84, 86–88,
89, 97, 98, 100–101, 118–19, 139,
140, 141, 154–56
Anglicized Dutch, politics of, ix
Anglicizers, 9
Anglo-Dutch tensions, 9, 13, 16, 32, 155
Anne (queen of England), 81, 82, 86, 90,
96
anticlericalism, 45, 64, 65, 67, 154. *See
also* Salary disputes
Anti-Coetus party. *See* Conferentie
Anti-Leislerians, 34, 36, 40–41, 44, 46,
47, 48, 54, 58, 70, 86, 99, 105
Antirevivalists, ix, 124, 126, 130, 134, 145
Antonides, Vincentius (dominie), 76–78,
80, 89, 90, 91, 92–95, 111, 134
Antwerp, 73
Archdeacon, Thomas J., 25 *n*, 31 *n*, 36 *n*,
37 *n*, 49 *n*, 71 *n*
Arnold, Jonathan, 136
Arondeus, Johannes (dominie), 126, 135
Arminianism, 145. *See also* Arminius,
Jacobus
Arminius, Jacobus, 51
Articles of Capitulation (1664), 4, 6, 9,
89, 101, 148
Articles of the Synod of Dort, 152
Artisans. *See* Dutch lower class
Augustine, 20 *n*

Bachman, Van Cleaf, 61 *n*
Balmer, Randall H., 133 *n*

Scandinavians, vii, x. *See also* Finns;
 Swedes
Scanlon, James Edward, 91 *n*
Schaats, Gideon (dominie), 11, 12, 13,
 17, 18
Schama, Simon, 10 *n*
Schenck, Garret C., 59 *n*, 61 *n*
Schenectady (New York), 67, 70, 75, 80,
 102, 106
 Dutch church in, 67, 74
Schmidt, Hubert G., 64 *n*
Schmidt, Leigh Eric, 134 *n*
Schools
 Anglican, ix, 80, 87–88, 89, 117–19,
 155
 Dutch, viii, 29, 72–73, 86, 89, 97, 118–
 19, 143
 English. *See* Schools, Anglican
Schraalenburgh (New Jersey), 151
Schrag, F. J., 108 *n*
Schuurman, Jacobus, 109, 112–13
Schuyler, John, 102
Schuyler, Peter, 102
Scotland, 120
Scots, 64, 155
Scott, Kenneth, 8 *n*, 31 *n*, 101 *n*
Scott, W. W., 61 *n*
Seabury, Samuel, 145
Sebring, Daniel, 111, 114
Secker, Thomas (archbishop of Canter-
 bury), 137
Second River (New Jersey), 136
Sectarianism, 51–52, 102–8, 149, 156
Sects. *See* Sectarianism
Selyns, Henricus (dominie), 4, 8, 24, 28–
 29, 30, 33, 35, 38–39, 40, 42, 43, 44,
 46, 47, 50, 51–52, 54, 55, 64, 65, 66,
 67, 68, 69, 71, 74, 85, 104–5, 129
Seminary. *See* Academy, Dutch
Seybolt, Robert Francis, 88 *n*
Shepherd's Tent, 133, 134
Sheridan, Eugene R., 58 *n*, 62 *n*
Shipton, Clifford K., 80 *n*
Short Refutation of Leydt's Book, A,
 145–46
Simons, Menno, 51
Six Mile Run (New Jersey), 119

Slaves, vii, 87
Sloughter, Henry (governor), 40, 41, 43,
 52, 59
Sluis (the Netherlands), 23, 66
 Classis of, 66
Smak, Antje, 110
Smith, William, Jr., 4 *n*, 14 *n*, 21 *n*
Society for the Propagation of the Gos-
 pel, viii, 26, 48–49, 78–81, 82, 84,
 85–88, 90, 95, 96, 102, 117, 122, 155
Society Hill (Philadelphia), 121
Society of Jesus, 32. *See also* Jesuits
Somerset County (New Jersey), 63
Spencer, Charles Worthen, 82 *n*
Spinoza, Benedict, 51
Staats, Abraham, 102
Staats, Samuel, 37
Stamp Act, 147, 148
Staten Island, 13, 65, 79, 88, 111
 Dutch church on, 64, 68, 70
Steenwyck, Cornelius, 8, 9, 68
Stern, Steve J., 30 *n*
Stiles, Henry R., 94 *n*
Still, Bayard, 56 *n*
Stockholm, 65
Stoeffler, F. Ernst, 22 *n*, 108 *n*
Stone Arabia (New York), Dutch church
 in, 132
Stout, Harry S., 134 *n*
Strasbourg, 7
Strickland, William, 153, 156
Strong, Thomas M., 94 *n*
Stuyvesant, Pieter, 3, 5, 6, 25, 88, 99,
 100, 101, 155
Stuyvesant's Chapel, 71
Suffolk County (New York), 58
Suriname, 128
Swedes, vii, 134, 154
Swedish Lutheran Church, 65, 154
Sweet, William Warren, 56 *n*
Switzerland, 123

Talbot, John, 62, 82
Tanis, James, 22 *n*, 109 *n*, 112 *n*, 113 *n*,
 114 *n*, 120 *n*, 150 *n*, 151 *n*
Tappan (New York), 134, 146
 Dutch church in, 67, 141

Tarrytown (New York), Dutch church in, 67
Taxes, 12, 25, 32, 34, 38, 53, 56, 62, 69, 83, 84, 87
Taylor, Benjamin C., ix *n*, 66 *n*, 124 *n*
Tennent, Gilbert, 119, 120, 121, 124, 127, 129, 133, 134, 138, 139
Tennent, William, 121
Tesschenmaeker, Petrus (dominie), 22–25, 26, 67, 71
Test Act, 52
Teunissen, Jan, 110
Tollstadius, Lars, 65, 154
Tory, 95, 150–52
Treaty of Westminster, 15, 38
Trenton (New Jersey), 61
Trinity (Episcopal) Church, 54–55, 72, 80, 83, 86, 87, 102, 123, 151
True Liberty the Way to Peace, 145–46
True Spiritual Religion, The, 145
Tucker, William L., 61 *n*, 64 *n*
Turner, Gordon, 83 *n*

Ulster County (New York), 57, 58, 61, 63
United Provinces, 61, 155. *See also* Dutch Republic; Holland; Netherlands, the
Unknown God, The, 124, 126, 127
Urquhart, William, 83
Utrecht (the Netherlands), 22
University of, 108, 129

Valentine, David T., 4 *n*, 8 *n*
Van Cortlandt, Maria, 101
Van Cortlandt, Stephanus, 19, 21, 31, 34, 105
Vanderlinde, Benjamin (dominie), 125
Van Dieren, Johann Bernhard, 134
Van Duyn, Cornelis, 78
Van Lodensteyn, Jodocus, 108
Van Loon, Lawrence G., 61 *n*
Van Niewenhuysen, Wilhelmus (dominie), 17, 18, 20, 21, 22
Van Rensselaer, Jeremias, 16
Van Rensselaer, Killian, 59, 102

Van Rensselaer, Mariana Griswold, 4 *n*, 14 *n*, 19 *n*
Van Rensselaer, Nicholas (dominie), 16–22, 25, 26, 27, 34, 73, 76, 82, 120
Van Rensselaer, Richard, 16
Van Rensselaer affair. *See* Van Rensselaer, Nicholas
Van Rensselaer family, 9
Van Ruyven, Cornelius, 8, 27
Van Santvoord, Cornelius (dominie), 111
Van Sinderen, Ulpianus (dominie), 126, 135, 150, 153
Van Wagenen, Gerrit, 118
Van Zuuren, Casparus (dominie), 96, 105
Varick, Rudolphus (dominie), 9, 30, 33, 36, 39, 40, 42, 43, 47, 48, 50, 64, 65–66, 67
Vas, Petrus, 111
Verbryck, Samuel (dominie), 146–47
Vermeule, Cornelius C., 61 *n*, 63 *n*
Verrazano, Giovanni da, vii
Vesey, William, 54, 54, 80, 83
Victoria (queen of England), 90
Voetians, 108
Voetius, Gysbertus, 108
voluntarism, 11, 68, 138
Vroom, Hendrick, 111, 114

Wabeke, Bertus Harry, 61 *n*
Wacker, Peter O., 56 *n*, 61 *n*
Wagman, Morton, 10 *n*
Walcheren, Classis of, 23
Wales, 20
prince of, 32–33
Wall, Alexander J., 143 *n*
Waller, G. M., 58 *n*
Walloons, vii, 3
Warch, Richard, 134 *n*
Weaver, Glenn, 79 *n*
Weber, Max, 104 *n*
Weiser, Conrad, 134
Wertenbacker, Thomas Jefferson, 68 *n*
Westchester County (New York), 57, 58, 84, 88
Westerkamp, Marilyn J., 155 *n*